IS IT YOU?

OR IS IT SPIRIT?

JEAN KELFORD

Note for Librarians: a cataloguing record for this book that includes Dewey Decimal Classification and US Library of Congress numbers is available from the Library and Archives of Canada. The complete cataloguing record can be obtained from their online database at:
www.collectionscanada.ca/amicus/index-e.html
ISBN 1-4120-5519-9

Printed in Victoria, BC, Canada

 Printed on paper with minimum 30% recycled fibre. Trafford's print shop runs on "green energy" from solar, wind and other environmentally-friendly power sources.

TRAFFORD   *Offices in Canada, USA, Ireland and UK*

This book was published *on-demand* in cooperation with Trafford Publishing. On-demand publishing is a unique process and service of making a book available for retail sale to the public taking advantage of on-demand manufacturing and Internet marketing. On-demand publishing includes promotions, retail sales, manufacturing, order fulfilment, accounting and collecting royalties on behalf of the author.

Book sales for North America and international:
Trafford Publishing, 6E–2333 Government St.,
Victoria, BC v8t 4p4 CANADA
phone 250 383 6864 (toll-free 1 888 232 4444)
fax 250 383 6804; email to orders@trafford.com

Book sales in Europe:
Trafford Publishing (uk) Ltd., Enterprise House, Wistaston Road Business Centre,
Wistaston Road, Crewe, Cheshire cw2 7rp UNITED KINGDOM
phone 01270 251 396 (local rate 0845 230 9601)
facsimile 01270 254 983; orders.uk@trafford.com
Order online at:
trafford.com/05-0417

10   9   8   7   6   5   4   3   2

In memory of my very special sister:

Christine Jordan. (nee Chew.)

and close friends:

Charles and Shirley.

Jean Kelford - foreword

I first met Jenny at my local Spiritualist Church in Merionnydd. Although I have not known her long I am totally impressed by her dedication, sincerity and commitment to our movement.

God knows it is hard enough in this day and age to find people who have a Christian faith let alone the drive and vitality to 'spread the word' without coming across as fanatical as I believe that can have a detrimental affect on the whole religious base. Zealots are one thing but a quiet faith that manifests through everyday deeds and actions is far more powerful and impressive. Empty vessels make the most noise.

Without spoiling your reading of this book, I will let Jenny tell her own story but certainly in my opinion in a movement full of people who just want 'a reading' but are prepared to accept the 'divine' side of Christian Spiritualism it is wonderful that you have the chance to be in touch with a lady whose psychic power comes from the heart and whose focus is to give proof and evidence that there is life after death and isn't in it for the wrong reasons.

Russell Grant - www.russellgrant.com

CONTENTS.

First of all my everlasting gratitude, thanks and dedication comes to my Guardian Angel, Guides and helpers in the Spirit World, for their closeness, help and continuing patience in working with and through me to convey the fact that there is no death.

I would like to express my gratitude and thanks to Mike once again and to my good friend Chris Beech, without whom this book would not have been possible for some time to come.

I would like to pay special tribute, and give thanks to Russell Grant, Doug Beaumont, and Phil McKnight for all their help and encouragement. To Simone for her input and friendship to David Crichton for his work on the cover and pictures in my book and last but by no means least to Chris Beech for all her help, work, friendship, and encouragement during the writing of this book.

I would also like to thank Andy Holmes, Chris Beech, Hazel Ashford, Laureece Curly, Sue Bragg and Tess and Glen Salt for their inspiration and friendship during my recent trying times. Writing a book of this nature requires true Spiritual inspiration, which they have all in turn given to me. Thank you all. They are all truly Spiritual people and I am lucky to consider them as my closest friends.

My children, mum, brothers, sisters, grandchildren, nephews, nieces and friends are all part of who I am and being a Medium is about who you are, so special thanks comes to you all.

Last but definitely not least, my everlasting gratitude and thanks to all those people whom I have worked with and who have inspired me. This is anyone that I have been lucky enough to give communication from Spirit to and to the Spirit World themselves for choosing to make the effort to not only communicate their messages to loved ones through me but most of the time, to do this clearly.

Introduction.

When I wrote my first book entitled Oblivious but True, I in no way thought that it would sell as well as it did and is still doing. This was and is very encouraging. I also did not expect people to be so excited in anticipation for book two. I am really grateful to all my readers and hope that this book will also become a source of inspiration to them. After hearing that the only complaint about my first book was that people wanted there to be more of it, I decided to accomplish this in this book that you are about to read.

A closeness of Spirit Guardian Angels answers the question, 'Why do pregnant ladies glow?' This can also give reason to the fact that my parents always said that I had an over active imagination, or friends sometimes thought that I was a 'strange girl' when in fact I am and always have been a very ordinary person, and proud of it too.

As a child, my innocence allowed Spirit to connect more closely with me. This being so, partially because I was never afraid of the dark or things that go bump in the night!! I rarely saw the bad in anyone, which of course meant that I was more likely to talk to and listen to any person that happened along and wanted to communicate with me at any given time. Spirit frequently took advantage of this and this in turn allowed me plenty of practise with Spirit linking.

You will find many different topics in this book which are naturally either directly or indirectly to do with the Spirit World and the fact that there is no such thing as death. These include some of my childhood and adult adventures of getting to know Spirit and the fact that they are real and really do exist. There are also true stories of ghost activity, with explanations of how each individual case was handled, thus allowing the lost Spirit to return home to the Spirit World. I talk about various sittings telling how Spirit chose to come through to prove to their loved ones that they are genuinely still around and NOT DEAD but alive and well in the Spirit World.

There are development exercises to help with developing your own gifts and abilities to link with those on the Spirit side of life. A whole chapter has been dedicated to dreams and their interpretations, therefore divulging what they mean to the person read on to find out many of the exciting but sometimes spooky occurrences that have taken place during my lifetime of living with visitors from the other side.

Just as a taster of how Spirit work, I thought it would be good at this point to tell you something that has recently happened. My daughter, Toni, came to visit me Wednesday morning, 8th June 2005, after her pre-natal check at the hospital where they had told her that if she had not given birth by Friday, 17th June 2005, they would induce labour.

I explained this to my friend Chris that evening and she replied "Oh no they cannot do that!" When I asked her why this was, she explained that as I was looking forward to being present at the baby's birth and at that time was teaching a class on a Friday evening, it would be better if Spirit could help by letting the baby arrive on Thursday morning which would allow me time to be present at the birth and also teach the Friday classes. The following morning, Thursday 9th June 2005, I was travelling through Central London on my way to a hospital appointment when Toni telephoned me at approximately 8.40 am to say "Mum I am in labour and on the way to the hospital, can you come?" I explained where I was and said that it would take me 3 or 4 hours to get back but I would be there as soon as possible.

My grandson, Thomas, was born at 9.50 am and needless to say I was not present for the birth. As you can see Chris' request to the Spirit World for a Thursday birth was adhered to. Unfortunately she forgot to mention that she meant Thursday week, therefore I was away in London on the Thursday of the birth. The moral of this story is, if you ask Spirit for anything try to be specific because they will take you at your word and try to help exactly as you have asked.

Chapter One.

Childhood Beginnings, Working With Spirit.

I felt that it was appropriate to start this book with some details of ways in which the Spirit World link close to babies, both on their conception into the womb and also on there arrival into this world.

Whilst, inside our mother's womb, which is after all where our life as we know it begins. It is believed that we hear all that is going on in close proximity to our mother in the 'outside world,' whilst we are cosy within the womb. As someone who has worked closely with Spirit for many years, I realise that this ability extends to babies being aware of the closeness of Spirit, even before their birth. I also feel that this is the reason why children tend to see, hear, and, or sense Spirit. They are aware because they recall the connection before their birth. Unfortunately if the gift is not embellished and encouraged into full use then it becomes rusty and can therefore be forgotten. Just like any other talent or memory it is stored away into the eves at the back of our mind.

Those in the Spirit World work, in curious ways at times, in order to get their point across. Here are some of the examples of how they do this where babies are concerned:-

When my granddaughter Georgina was born six weeks prematurely just under two years ago, a midwife at the hospital commented that the baby recognised my voice? She felt this because every time I spoke the baby would open her eyes and look towards the part of the room where I was standing. This struck us as very interesting because of the fact that during the whole time that her mum, my daughter Toni was pregnant, every time I saw her I used to rub her tummy and say: "Hello sweetheart. Is nanny's little darling okay in there? Are Spirit looking after you for me?"

Unfortunately, before Georgina was born, my daughter Toni had lost two babies to the Spirit World over recent times. A few days after losing her first child, baby George, She was sitting in our home, talking to my husband and I, when she looked up at a baby scan, which is in our glass cabinet. She declared: "Look mum, there is a light shining onto that scan picture like a spotlight."

As I turned, the light disappeared, which amazed us all. Later that day, I noticed that a photograph of a special little girl called Gemma, 'who is the daughter of some friends of ours' had disappeared from its place on our sideboard. This little girl is the same child that is shown on the scan in the glass cabinet. Gemma's parents were unfortunate enough to loose a child before Gemma was born. After which they had undergone a lot of treatment, in order to try to conceive another baby. By showing this light shining onto the scan picture, Spirit were trying to reassure Toni that she would one day hold her own baby in her arms. By highlighting the scan picture they were saying that it looked impossible for baby Gemma to be born yet she was born, therefore the same thing would happen for Toni.

To explain further: one day, when Gemma's parents, Lisa and Roy had arrived at a workshop, which I was conducting, Lisa was crying. I immediately said to her: "This is about babies isn't it?" She nodded 'yes,' and proceeded to tell me that she had been told that she would never be able to give birth to a baby, so she should either have IVF or adopt a child. Without hesitation, I told her that they were wrong and she would have a baby. She instantly responded with: "No they are sure."

It was at this point that I called my husband Mike over to confirm my version of events, which he did. Lisa and Roy still doubted, and understandably so, but I retorted that: "If you do not either give birth to a baby, or are heavily pregnant by this time next year, then I will retire as a Medium." Their immediate response was: "Are you that sure?" and of course I was. They knew that my work with and love for communicating with the Spirit World meant that I would need to feel very certain of what I was saying to make a promise like that. Because anyone who knows me well knows that I would never break a promise if at all possible. Needless to say, 'because of the fact that I am still a Medium and did not retire,' they did have a child and gave birth to baby Gemma the following year; she was nine pounds, eleven ounces, and perfect in every way.

As soon as Gemma was old enough to walk, she would go to a bookcase in her parent's home and take a book off the shelf. The book she always chose was a paperback book called, 'A host of voices' by Doris Stokes. Because Doris works with me quite often, we thought it was very appropriate and Lisa and Roy gave us a photograph of Gemma holding Doris' book. It was this picture that had disappeared. On the Thursday, the day after the photograph had disappeared; I asked Lisa and Roy if there was an anniversary around the day before, because this could explain why the photograph had vanished? They answered that they could not think of anything and we left it at that. However, after class that evening Lisa telephoned me to say that they had remembered that the day before was the anniversary of losing their first baby. I said that, this was obviously what they had been trying to tell us. My husband Mike and I then went into the kitchen so that we could take our medication, and Mike could make a drink to take to bed with us. When he returned to the lounge, he called: "Jean, come here quickly."

When I did just that, he pointed out to me that the photograph was back in its original place, we were both amazed. You see Spirit had made their point, which was that Lisa, and Roy's first baby was okay and being looked after in the Spirit World. So you see even unborn babies are protected by the Spirit World even though this would be a difficult fact to prove.

I definitely cannot remember being in the womb myself, however, I do know that I personally do not recall a time when Spirit were not making their presence known in my life. There are many different ideas and explanations for things that occur in our world, but this is especially so with things which connect our world to the Spirit side of life. Your Guardian Angel is a person who is assigned to take care of you throughout the whole of your earthly life. They are by your side, or at least not far away, at all times, from the moment of your conception.

People will often say that a pregnant lady glows. However, my memories of being pregnant, with all three of my children, is one of feeling too bulky to move, feeling nauseous, and tired most of the time, in fact far from glowing. Yet people often told me that I was doing just that! I now realise that a logical explanation for this is one that my Guardian Angel 'who I will refer to as Mr R,' gave me.

From a very young age, in fact as soon as I was able to go to the bathroom alone I have been aware of seeing this man on the stairs. He is always there to reassure and protect me from harm. As time went by I would grow to know this man very well, in fact it is mainly because of him that I am a medium today. He is my Guardian Angel: my main Guide from the Spirit World. As this book progresses, I will be referring to him from time to time, probably as Mr R. He is a gentleman from Russia, standing almost seven feet tall, and wearing a top hat. His name I am told is Izeakial Ramminskicorsicoff and he is my Guardian Angel or main Guide. This means that he is around whenever I need help or direction, he has not lived on the earth for hundreds of years now and therefore has a lot of knowledge and experience in linking the two worlds together, which is very important for a Medium such as myself. Whenever he is around everyone feels really cold. Even people, 'whom are not aware of Spirit generally,' can feel the cold atmosphere which is part of him as I will explain later.

Mr R's explanation to me was that as soon as a baby is conceived, the child's Guardian Angel moves in close to protect her, or him. Because the baby is obviously at this point inside the mother's womb, it becomes necessary for this Guardian Angel to come in close to the child's mother. Remembering that the mother's Guardian Angel will also move in closer to look after and protect her, then this means that during the duration of her pregnancy, she has two Guardian Angels close by. For those of us who are fortunate enough to be able to see Spirit as I do, I am sure we would all agree that Spirit visitors have a definite radiance about them? A beautiful light which reaches out from the Spirits and stretches all around the people connected to them who are still in their earthly life. Therefore, it makes sense that, if a person has two Spirit Guardian Angels close by them, as when a lady is pregnant, they are going to glow.

If a mother is having twins or triplets, etc, then there is a Guardian Angel close by for each child being carried and because there is only the same amount of space, for them to be in, they huddle in close together to take a share in protecting each child together. I believe that this is why children from multiple births have a closeness to each other that is not seen so often in usual brothers and sisters. It is a closeness that is often linked to Psychic powers and awareness, which is so because of this close connection of and to, the children's Guardian Angels in the Spirit World, which is after all connected to psychic awareness.

For myself, Jean Kelford, the Medium, it was nine am, on the morning of Friday, August 22nd 1952, when I put in my first appearance into this world. My mother says that she will always remember that the country was still on rations after the second-world-war, and once a month they received extra sugar. I was born on the day that the extra sugar arrived. I was not aware of this fact until just recently, yet I have always had a strong interest in sugar, and used to get books from the library on the cultivation of sugar cane.

My mum would sit at the large wooden table in our dining room, where there would be a tray of tea things and often a little spilt sugar. She used to crack the sugar granules with her nail, which always fascinated me. Strangely enough I do not have a particularly sweet tooth in fact I do not drink sugary drinks at all.

My point is that we are psychically drawn to certain things in life for many reasons. In this case sugar had a direct link to my birth, making it the re-entry into this world of my Guardian Angel, who would guard and protect me throughout my life.

I joke with mum that I was sweetness itself and that this was the real reason for my affinity, but I am sure you would agree that the first explanation is more likely?

My mum would often laugh as she reminisced about things I did as a child. Remembering my fear of water as a baby always made her laugh. When it was bath time and whoever was giving me my bath, had lifted me into the water, I would immediately stare at the water, lift one leg out and start to cry. My parents said that it was quite comical, watching me stand on one leg, but they could never understand the reason why I did this?

When my son, Dean was born, we often laughed because he had inherited the same trait, and would stand on one leg, crying and staring at the water. Then much later on my granddaughter, Leah, would do the same thing. This was an amazingly funny coincidence, or so we thought at first.

That is, until one day, whilst giving an address, from the rostrum in Glasgow, Scotland. My Guide explained that, quite often, young children who are very psychically aware begin to use the energy from water to make strong links with the Spirit World, without even knowing that they are doing it. Because of this, when they look into the water, they see many Spirit faces staring back at them, which of cause serves to frighten them. This is the reason why children who are very psychic, 'and have the ability to see Spirit' such as myself, retract one leg out of the water whilst starting to cry.

It is a natural response, to put one leg down first, which is of course, what the child does. Then they see the faces staring up at them out of the water and retract the other leg up into the air. Fortunately, as the child grows older, seeing these faces becomes normal, and therefore water has the opposite effect. It is then that parents of a child, who is extremely psychic, need to watch their child with water because they become drawn to it, and subsequently do not see the danger that can and often does come from children playing in water.

This true story about myself and other members of my family, whom have developed their psychic gift more and more around water, makes me think about stories going back in our history, where people who could link to the Spirit World were considered to be witches. Most of those poor unfortunate people, did not even know why, or how they knew the things they knew. Let alone practised Witchcraft. Yet these knowing people 'who were mainly women' would be dunked into the river on a dunking stool, to see if they would drown. If, however, they did not, this proved them to be a Witch and they were then burnt to death, to get rid of their evil Spirits.

Sadly, it would be more likely to work the opposite way round. People like myself who are lucky enough to be very psychic, are fascinated by water, yet they have a very definite fear whenever, they are in a place where there is a lot of water concerned. This is because they become distracted by the Spirit World who, take every opportunity presented to them to use the extra energy produced by the water to communicate with 'the would-be Medium.' This distraction makes the water more dangerous and they become aware of this factor.

Mediums are, therefore, more likely to drown quickly if in a situation where it is possible to drown. This is purely because their attentions are elsewhere and not on staying alive in the water. So you see those people who did survive being dunked, were put to death by fire for the wrong reason. Although 'not Witches' the ones who were drowned quickly, were most probably the psychic ones who had gained their reputation of being a Witch because of this gift.

I was the third child and third daughter. My parents would go on to have nine children, five of whom were girls and four boys. I realise now that they all could be Mediums. However, growing up in a busy family, with a hectic life, I was not aware that some of the people with whom I regularly conversed, were actually dead and that I was talking with the Spirit World.

As I indicated before I cannot claim to remember the day I was born, but I say without hesitation that I was aware of the Spirit World from the very beginning of my life in this one. I was so sure of this that I grew up believing that everyone shared my awareness and knowledge of those people with whom I held conversations daily. This of course, included the animal kingdom.

If asked to reminisce about my childhood, again I would have quite a mixture of stories that most would think are unusual. My first memory, which I can now relate to the Spirit World, happened when I was four. My sister Chris, whom sadly passed to Spirit as this book was being written, was affectionately known to my dad as 'Crispo' she is thirteen months older than me.(Please note that I do not refer to her in the past tense because I know that she is still very much here.)

As children, we did most things together, which I was and am very proud of, however, this one time I would have preferred not to join her, because you see she had fallen ill with pneumonia, having suffered with a bad chest all her life, and had been taken into hospital, I missed her sorely until, unfortunately, I too came down with pneumonia and joined her in hospital.

I clearly remember being carried down the hospital corridor by the ambulance man. All I could see were people in beds with red blankets over them. Although red was the standard colour for hospital blankets in those days, they scared me and made me cry. Suddenly, a lady in a uniform with a large hat came up behind us; she stroked my hair and said, gently: "Do not cry Jean, I am here with you."

I was not sure why, but I was fascinated by the realisation of why I knew that I was safe with this woman. I was put in the bed next to my sister's, which made me feel better instantly. We always laughed a lot when we were together and this time was no exception.

Although she had been more poorly than I, she went home first because she had gone into hospital a few days earlier. I was upset because I wanted to go home too, or of course for Chris to stay.

The lady in the funny hat appeared again and tried to comfort me, to which I replied that I would be all right if only Chris could stay one more day. Strangely enough, the ambulance which was due to collect her did not turn up, which meant that Chris had to undress again and stay until the next day. Selfish as it may seem, I was really pleased!

This lady was to appear many times throughout my life, and she still does. It turns out that she was a nurse many years ago she looks after me and all those connected close to me whenever we are worried or unwell. My children came to know her very well, since all three are lucky enough to see the Spirit World just as I do.

They all have memories of seeing her walking up and down in their bedrooms, whenever they were unwell as children. With this in mind, I often wonder whether she deliberately delayed that ambulance in order to help me, after all, my sister did not mind being there as long as I was there too.

Children are innocent which makes it easier for Spirits to get in touch with them. Sceptics might say that this is because children are gullible. It is an understandable conclusion when you consider my own incomprehension of the people I was in touch with as a child. However, on the other hand, perhaps it is just that children have not yet learned to blinker themselves like adults. After all, their education in life can only come from the people around them.

Whilst growing up as a member of a large family with four sisters and four brothers, (two of whom are now in the Spirit world). I remember listening with great interest to my parents' Spiritual experiences. But I was never afraid in fact I have always found it hard to understand people's fear of the dark. Personally, I have always known I was safe.

If Chris was not around, I would happily chat and play with a little girl called Amy without giving a moment's thought to where she lived: or where she came from. Call it gullibility or innocence, but any way you look at it, it is acceptance! I accepted these other people as part of my life and my already large family. And I loved them as much too!

I am telling you all this because I would like my more sceptical readers to give me the benefit of the doubt, and to believe me when I say that Spirits really do exist. The rest of you have already taken the first step, which is accepting the possibility that we live on and come back to communicate with our loved ones: it means you are curious: it means you are open-minded.

Chapter Two.

Innocence And Invisible Friends.

Coming out of hospital at the age of four, is always a strange experience, but for me, it was exceptionally odd because being in the Hospital where I was nursed better from pneumonia, made me more aware of those people who spoke to me constantly from the other side. This was because I had commented to people about the large hat that was worn by one of the nurses, only to be told by other children in hospital that I was mad, there was no one there.

Young children are usually very blunt and say things exactly as they are which is what they were doing because they genuinely could not see the nurse with the big hat like I could. Before this, I had only spoken about these things to my family particularly Chris, my sister, who had at first been in hospital with me, but had now been discharged. Yet here I was, suddenly alone amongst people whom I had only known for a few days. This had served to make me think, about whom this lady (and others like her) who conversed with me, really were.

Strange as it may seem, most of my early memories include the Spirit World in some way. Although many members of my immediate family are afraid of the dark, I never shared their fear. This is because, as far back as I can remember, there has been the man close by (I mentioned him earlier), whom I know very well and trust implicitly. That man is Mr R my Guardian Angel.

Not long after going home from hospital at that tender age of four, my parents left me at home with a baby-sitter whilst they took my two older sisters swimming, and to visit friends. Although, I am sure that my parents never realised this. I was really scared at being left behind without them and asked why they did not take me swimming too? They replied that I was not old enough and that one day I would be able to go, but at that moment the water would be too strong for me.

After they had left home for their trip, I at first settled down underneath the big dining room table to play with my dolls. This was a place where I could converse with these people whom to my confusion, were apparently unknown by those around me. I therefore often resorted to playing there whenever I was left to play on my own.

This time, however, within minutes, I heard a voice say: 'Let's go and play outside.' Looking up to see the familiar face of a young girl called Amy, whom I had seen on several occasions so recognised her but did not really know at that point who she was.

She was in fact another companion from my infant years, who used to talk with me often, mostly about things that did not make sense at the time, or which it did not seem possible that she could know. She was and is, a very nice young lady but, to my surprise, almost everyone else was oblivious to her presence. She asked me not to tell anyone that we played and talked together so I did not tell a soul, apart from dropping the occasional hint to Chris.

This was unusual. I normally told her everything and vice versa. Of course, now that we are grown-up, I realise that she probably knew anyway.

I looked up, smiled and at once, without hesitation, asked the sitter if I could go out to play and he said yes, lifting me down the three concrete steps, which led to the back yard outside Passing my toys out to me, he went back indoors. The voice, which as I indicated in the previous sentence, had emanated from a little girl called Amy who, I now realise, was in fact dead and resided in the Spirit World and who you will read about more fully in the next chapter.

Yet whilst we played happily, I never for one moment stopped to ask whom she was and where she had come from. However, I did tend to follow her lead. After a while she got up and disappeared up the entry at the side of our house. I hesitated for a moment, before following her.

Up our entry, there were three doors, which at the time looked huge to me. There was also a gate at the end of the entryway with a huge bolt half way up, and another at the top, which was there to stop people getting in, and indeed myself and my sisters getting out.

The first door, I knew was my father's shed where he kept all his tools. Because on occasions he had shown me what was in there and asked me not to touch them as they could be sharp and cut me. At those times, when he took me into the shed I used to see a man turning a handle at the side of the workbench. Although I did not know it then, this man was dead too and it was the handle of my father's vice that he was turning.

Amy said do not look at him or he will put you into the vice's teeth and turn the handle. I at this point would pull away, but my father would laugh and say: "You are okay if I am here Bean."

He said this, obviously thinking that I was afraid of the sharp tools, and not realising what I was really trying to back away from. It was to be many years later when events happened involving this man turning the vice. I will come back to this further on in the book.

The second door along in the entry, opened out into a very dark place full of coal and spiders, 'The Coalhouse'. Once again I will return to the happenings in the coalhouse later in my story.

Finally, we came to the third door, which I had never seen open! Amy reached up to the latch, which she could only just reach, and pushed with all her might so that the door could slide ajar. I gasped, as I looked inside to see a toilet with a wooden seat and a long chain hanging from a black box near to the ceiling. It was dark, and there were cobwebs everywhere, with spiders crawling about, but this was alright because fortunately I had never been afraid of either spiders or the dark come to that.

Amy reached up her thin spiny fingers as she stood on her tiptoes, trying to reach the chain, 'when my Russian Guide,' Mr R, appeared and pulled the chain for us.

I was standing just close enough to see the water cascade all around the toilet. I was also suddenly aware of the nurse with the large hat who told me that I should not play in the water. Mr R, then prodded me with his fingertips, and spoke quite loudly, making me jump. "My Child water itself is not dangerous. It is the way people use it that makes it become so. You can watch, but you should not touch, until you are old enough to understand. Then I will tell you. Now listen to the nurse."

At this he shooed me out of the toilet to play and closed the door. That was to be the end of my first visit with Spirit, to the outside toilet.

I was very uncertain of the man in the shed, because he had hard eyes, and a way of staring at you, which made him appear quite scary. However, I knew that my dad would not have let him harm me, therefore, that was okay.

I knew that I should never go into the coalhouse because it was so dirty. Yet that incident in the outside toilet had in fact intrigued me, and was to be, therefore, only the beginning.

From that day on, I became more and more aware of unusual things taking place. By this I mean incidents that were hard to explain, especially as I did not understand them myself yet.

People quite often describe Ghost activity, as: 'Things that go bump in the night'. After reading about my lifetime's experiences, living amongst those from the Spirit World, however, I am sure that you will agree that this is definitely not a good description of my lifetime alongside frequent Spirit activities. Yes, sometimes things do go bump in the night, as I will explain later. But there are all manner of things that take place, when you come to live in the same house as someone like myself.

That is a person who is born to be a Medium and has therefore been blessed with a large amount of psychic energy, which in turn allows those in the Spirit World to make their presence known. I am I now realise: 'A Medium' with the ability to attract all kinds of phenomena, connected with those dead people who reside on the other side of life.

This book will tell you many of these events, which have served to change, 'not only my life' but the lives of those who have lived with me, around me, or indeed stayed at my home for a visit.

Sometimes it is hard as a child, to understand our fears and worries and where they come from. I have always been the type of person who would take notice of things happening around me and the incident with the water in our outside toilet was to have many effects on me over the years.

Many of the funny and unusual things that people remember about me as a child, 'although unknown to myself and the people around me at the time', were in fact linked to my ability to link with those people who are in the Spirit World. That is, those friends, relatives, and strangers, who wanted to communicate with their loved ones here.

As a child, there were a lot of things that were created by, 'those from the Spirit World linking with me' that I neither, realised nor understood. For instance, whenever I went upstairs to use the bathroom, I would come into contact with my Guide, Mr R. However, I never fully understood why he never entered the bathroom with me. One day I reopened the bathroom door to ask him why he did not come in. His simple reply was: "I did not realise that you wanted me to. If you do, then I will".

For my part, I felt much safer when he was around, even from an early age. This was because he has been with me as far back as I can remember.

As soon as he entered the bathroom and I was seated on the toilet, the room became full of a smoke like substance, as it often did when he was in close proximity.

I now realise that this substance was ectoplasm, but at the time I just took it for granted as being part of Mr R.

I would then become aware of several people, who seemed to be talking to me rather quickly, and the need to cough, which I put down to the steam irritating my throat, but now realise that it was these people 'who were visiting from the Spirit World' vibrating my voice box, to make the sounds which are necessary for them to talk, and for me to hear.

This is called Clairaudience, which literally means Clear Hearing, and this is how Spirit produces the sound. They use their energy to vibrate the Medium's voice box, and sometimes, if Spirit move too close, then this vibration makes the Medium cough or have the desire to cough.

It took me many years to understand that the Spirit World find it easy to link close to water, due to the increased energy levels produced whilst water is around. 'This is because the more energy that the Spirit World, have available to them, the more they are able to communicate messages to people here.'

However, from that day on, I was always more capable of receiving these messages clearly, whilst in the bathroom. To this day, close friends know and laugh at the fact that I always talk to Spirit on my visits to the bathroom.

Sometimes during the summer my parents used to take us out to Harleston for the day. We would take a picnic and our fishing nets to try to catch some tiddlers in the narrow stream. It was whilst sitting on the bank of the river that I became aware of a lot of people who had joined us. Although I enjoyed these days out, I became a bit bored because there were too many people around for us to play.

My sister Chris and I started to discuss the different shapes that we could see taking place in the water. At first they were just shapes and swirls under the current of the water, but then I became aware of a little girl, she suddenly appeared out of the stream, throwing her arms about and fighting for breath, before joining us at the waters edge. I smiled at her, not sure what to think, and she smiled back, saying: "Hello Jean." I of course was amazed to see that it was Amy and said so. She smiled once more, but did not reply. After which she spent most of the afternoon in our company, and I came to the decision that I liked her.

Amy resides in the Spirit World and for her part was, and 'is' a much happier person, now that she is in the Spirit World. She was to spend a lot of time playing with me and generally being in my company as I grew up. For this reason it makes me very sad when I hear people laughing at children who have: 'Invisible Friends'. Because I am sure that in most cases these invisible friends are people from the Spirit World, there to guide and protect the child. I can also assure you that there is nothing invisible about them.

Recently, 'during my recovery period, after a period of extreme poor health,' whilst I was speaking to my son Dean on the telephone, he said that he would like to ask me something, if I was well enough to answer. I naturally said that I was and he proceeded to say: "Over the last two or three weeks, his daughter had started to kiss people on both cheeks whenever she greeted them. Nobody that we know does this so we wondered where she had got it from? So one day when she did it I asked her why she kissed people on both cheeks like that. Do you know what she said mum?"

26

Before I could respond, he went on: "She said that Emily does it to her when she is in bed, before she goes to sleep."

I asked him whether he knew anyone called Emily that visited their home. To which he said 'no.' He went on: "I told my mate Ian about it, because you were too ill to ask, and he said that lots of young children have an 'imaginary friend', and they are usually about the same age as themselves, so I should ask her how old Emily is, next time she mentions her?"

I at this point was already smiling to myself because I knew that it was a Spirit visitor, but I asked if he had found out anyway. He replied: "Yes, the next time she did it, I said: "Darling, how old is Emily? Do you know what she said mum? She said she is fifty-six."

'Well, the reason that this came across as strange, was not only the fact that this was a little old for a so called "imaginary friend". But his daughter could only count to ten and she always quoted a number between one and ten if anyone asked her anything to do with numbers'.

Dean went on: "I went cold, and asked her if she was frightened of this person, but she said no she liked her and thought that she was a nice lady. She will not hurt her, will she mum?"

I was laughing at this point, because he sounded horrified, and I assured him that Emily was only looking after her and that she would keep his daughter out of trouble, and wake them up if she was in any danger in the night. I also thought that maybe she was about to be poorly, but I kept this to myself because he was already uncertain without me adding to it.

His response to this was: "Mum, do not get me wrong, I am not saying that I think you are off your rocker! But, for me the jury is still out. I am not sure if I believe in life after death."

We both laughed at this and I assured him that I was not offended, and that he needed to make up his own mind, in his own time. In fact I am very proud of the fact that he is finding things out for himself and not just believing that they are true, just because I am his mother, and I say so.

He went on to say that after seeing me work with Spirit at my home Church, which is the Sutton Coldfield Spiritualist Church, he realised that I could link very well and he was impressed.

He told me that when he also took into consideration the fact that I had always been honest and straight forward in my approach towards him and everyone else, he had already started to think that maybe there was something in my strong belief that the Spirit World did exist.

I believe that these things were happening to his daughter, not just for her benefit, but also to plant some more seeds on his pathway to the belief in life after death.

I could not help but laugh, when I visited my son and his family the following Sunday. This was because Dean explained to me, that before this incident had occurred, he would get out of bed to see to his children, if they cried out in the night. However, he now sent his partner instead, because he was afraid of meeting up with Emily.

Can I just add that this is a very normal and natural fear to those who do not understand the workings of the Spirit World.

As for my granddaughter, she is extremely happy knowing Emily and frequently talks to, and about, her 'IMAGINARY!' sister Emily.

Dean is becoming less spooked by the fact that she talks about and to, a sister that she has not got, and is also getting closer to believing in a Spirit World whose existence help people to move forward with love.

Sadly she was quite poorly starting a few days after first mentioning the existence of her new found sister Emily. She was suffering from a viral infection, which was hard to get rid of. However, with much love and the aid of the doctor and Spirit World she started to recover after three weeks of being poorly.

I should point out that Spirit had nothing to do with her becoming poorly they just made their presence more clear at that point in time, so as to aid her recovery.

Because Amy had drowned, she needed to imply that the water had something to do with her passing. However, if she had gone into explicit details of her death, when I was just a little girl, it may have put me off totally? She therefore showed that she had been drowning without showing the full story. Unfortunately, however, it can also have the opposite effect on some people.

Some children become quite afraid of the people who visit them from the Spirit side of life, because they show them the way that they passed to Spirit, which can appear quite scary when you do not understand what they are doing.

From early in my childhood, my two fears have been to die of either drowning, or in a fire. This fear has always been very real to me and some people would say that I am experiencing past life events, which create these fears. I know however, that the truth is that because one of my Guides called Amy died in an extreme way to do with both fire and drowning, she has made me aware of these feelings, therefore, now I have a natural fear of these things.

This for me explains a lot of the things and experiences that make people feel that they are reliving past life experiences. When a Guide describes their way of life to the person that they are here to guide, then they frequently do so by using subliminal messages.

Because a subliminal message simply places something that is similar to a thought into the recipient's head, or a feeling in their heart, then it is easy for this to be misinterpreted as being something that has really happened in that person's own life instead.

In fact, when a Guardian Angel, Guide, or helper, from the Spirit World moves close and portrays a story that has happened in their own lifetime, to themselves, it can feel very real, just like it has happened to us.

Whilst talking to me, Amy would go to great lengths to explain how she had died because of a fire, which made her drown. Of course this did not make any sense at all, until you hear the whole story. Having been badly burnt when a fire broke out in the barn like shack her family called home, Amy received virtually no treatment because her family could not afford it there being no National Health Service in those days.

Both her parents died within eighteen months of each other in separate incidents whilst Amy was very young, her father in an accident at the sawmill where he worked when she was four years old and her mother whilst giving birth to Amy's brother Charles two years earlier.

Amy was adopted by Jack and Mary Randell, not because they liked children, they evidently did not but in order to use her as unpaid domestic labour. Worse still, Mary called Amy by her second name, Sarah, claiming that she preferred it. Mary knew that the name reminded Amy of her mother and was upsetting to her but used it regardless as a way of making Amy toe the line and do as she was told. I, however, shall use her proper name throughout this book.

Amy's father Fred Burke, had been an amiable enough man but not very clever and he had his meagre means which were not enough to provide for his children after his death.

Amy's arms, right leg and torso were severely scarred by the fire. These should have been treated continuously and above all kept dry if they were to heal well. Unfortunately, her washing duties meant that the wounds were almost constantly wet and never had a chance to heal. It was this that led to her fate.

Made to wash the family's clothes in a giant barrel of water in the back yard, she would clamber up onto a concrete boulder to reach far enough into the tub. One day she dropped the soap into the tub and, afraid to tell Mary, she stretched down in an effort to reach it. Over-reaching herself, her scarred flesh being to stiff to manoeuvre easily, toppled into the barrel. Her rigid limbs could not find purchase on the barrel; she struggled, panicked and, tragically, drowned.

It was not until many years later that I realised why Amy had asked me to keep her visits secret. It was because not everyone can see her, hear her or even sense her presence.

One of Amy's jobs in the Spirit World is to exchange fear, vulnerability, and loneliness, for peace, laughter, and love. Having realised this, I asked why I became extremely cold whenever she was around. It did not after all seem to fit with the notions of peace, laughter and love!

She laughed, saying: "It is only because I have been in the Spirit World for many years, and that means we come in on a cold vibration. This is because the longer we are in the Spirit World, the more plains of existence we progress, through – therefore we have further to travel to reach you. Because we occupy the same space as you, but on a much faster Wavelength, the speed with which we join you brings about a frisson of cold air. Feeling this cold from the Spirit World means excessive love! Coming from Spirit to the person they are contacting. You see, I am not really still a little girl. The age at which you see me is my age when I passed to the Spirit World. Although I am now grown-up, I prefer to be a little girl so I am allowed to be just that. I should explain that once you have passed over from your world to mine, time is no longer of importance. The most important thing is love. It is after all, the vibration of love that allows us to cross over from where we now reside to the existence we once knew as life."

It was at this point that my curiosity really got the better of me. Questions were popping into my head at a great rate of knots. I answered: "Alright if you say it is the vibration of love that allows us to communicate with one another, I believe you. But what is this vibration of love?"

At that moment Amy disappeared. That was not unusual for her; in fact I had become used to her sudden departures without knowing why they happened. This time, though, I was caught by surprise but before I had time to reflect, I was overwhelmed by a feeling of perfect peace; a feeling so real that I could almost touch it; a silence you could almost hear. There in front of me stood someone else I had become to know well.

It was Mr R, as I explained before he was always around when I needed direction or guidance as I surely did right then! He put his right hand in front of his face, arm outstretched, palm towards me in a 'stop' gesture. "Wait, slow down my child and I will explain." he said. Having known him all my life I knew not to be impatient. He would answer my, as yet, unvoiced questions in his own time. Lowering his hand, he half-smiled and said: "The answer you are waiting for is a simple one. The word love is a word with which everyone is familiar. We all love someone or something at some time during our lives, even if it is ourselves. Do you understand?"

After listening to what he had to say, although moments before I had, had lots of things to say, I suddenly could not think of one. So I was silent. He continued as though there had been no interruption: "The word love is spelt

L, O, V, E."

The meanings of those four letters are: 'Light Of Vibration Eternity.' Do you understand my child?"

I cannot put into words how I felt at that moment but I can say that I now know what love means. You may find it strange that I talk to this most unusual man who spoke so differently from the way we now accept as the norm. What you need to bear in mind, though, is the fact that he has been around for as long as I can remember, sitting on the stairs whilst I sleep.

I usually have a chat with him if I go to the bathroom during the night. This has been part of my life wherever I have lived, so it is completely natural to me. Often, after I have been in bed for about ten minutes I hear his footsteps crossing the landing outside my bedroom door. Then the door handle goes down and the door opens suddenly. This would be quite scary stuff for those who do not understand the Spirit World, but not for me. As I have said before, it is completely natural to me.

Throughout my childhood the fact that these people were dead escaped me, probably a good thing too because it might have made me afraid of the unknown like so many others.

In my experience, people are not really afraid of the Spirit World as such, more of the unknown factor we call 'dying'. Death, after all, is a word like any other until you add to it the knowledge that we all die- which, naturally leads to the question on most peoples-lips, which is: "What is death?" And the next question: "What happens to us when we die?" Or: "Where do we go when we die?"

Of course, all this is for the people curious enough to accept that there really is something else. It is sometimes easier to dismiss the unknown than to accept that there might be something without being sure what it is?

I cannot tell you why as a child I did not suspect the reality of things, but I can say how proud and pleased I am that this knowledge came to me naturally, for my own guidance and to help many others along the way.

If you are curious and open-minded, you have taken the first step towards knowing that the Spirit World exists and that its inhabitants can and do communicate with the living.

I would like to ask readers to bear in mind that which has made them decide to read this book. For some it may be purely be the fact that they know me and are naturally interested in reading what I have to say. For others, it will be a keen interest in anything to do with the Spirit World; a thirst for knowledge about a subject that is surrounded with so much controversy and is therefore fascinating.

There will be many reasons for reading this book but I put it to you that since you are reading it, you are curious. So you have taken the first step. The next is to read on with an open mind!

One of the other surprising things that occurred, between myself, and the Spirit World, from a very early age, was that I would hide my head under the bedclothes at night, trying hard to make sure that no light whatsoever came in. There were two reasons for this. The first was that I could never sleep when a light was on. I needed to be in complete darkness.

The second however, was because I used to occupy my time talking to various people from the Spirit World before going to sleep at night.

I soon found out, that it was much easier to see these people when it is dark. I should, however, point out that the only reason for this is because when the ectoplasm first builds up, it is extremely faint and therefore difficult to see clearly when the lights are on. Whereas, whilst the lights are switched off, the room is dark, therefore the white ectoplasm, contrasts against the blackness of the dark atmosphere.

This is purely because white shows up more clearly on a black background and vice versa. This is also the reason why it is easier to see Spirit using a red light-bulb. Because a red light tends to have the affect of altering the way we use our eyes. It encourages us to use the infrared part of our vision just as we do whilst looking at an Aura, therefore stimulating our third eye.

Whilst under the bedclothes, I was fascinated by the swirls of smoke, which turned into faces as I watched. Some were too close making their images too big to see, and some were too far away and therefore tiny in comparison to the real thing. This gave them a distorted appearance, which could be a bit perturbing to a child who did not understand the logic of what was occurring? I do feel that, at first, this factor of linking to the Spirit World, feels a bit daunting to all who experience it. However, I was never afraid by any of this, just fascinated, and of course at times confused.

Young children tend to believe what adults tell them, and I was no exception to this unspoken rule. For me however, it was slightly more confusing because a lot of the Spirit people that took this opportunity to speak to me, were in fact adults. There were occasions when the adults from the Spirit World told me things that contradicted what my parents were saying. This was usually when they were telling me things for the future, like when I was told that my auntie Margaret, 'who was a close family friend' would visit the next afternoon.

I happily relayed this message to my mum, because I loved it when auntie Margaret came because she was such a happy lady and always made me laugh. My mum, however, would insist that she was not coming and of course I would argue the point, until I finally accepted defeat. That afternoon, however, auntie Margaret turned up, and my mum was amazed!

Things like this happened frequently and I became accustomed to it as did my family, but I never fully understood why people doubted me. And, I suppose, they never fully understood how I knew the information that I was telling them. I did not understand that they could not see, hear, or sense, these very real people around me, 'who, were actually in the Spirit World.' If only I had known that I was communicating with the 'dead'? What a difference it could have made!

For me going to school was a happy experience. I loved school and particularly enjoyed being in the infants because it was time for me. If that sounds strange, bear in mind that you do not get any time alone in a large family like mine, everyone has to do their bit.

The extensive family has many good points, for instance, you learn how to do housework, look after babies and young children, cook, wash up and do the shopping at quite a young age, which is all good preparation for adult life. You also learn to share your possessions and your time.

But sometimes it would be nice to have some peace and quiet: a bit of space in which to do your own thing. Even whilst doing your homework you had to learn to put up with the constant noise and the constant interruptions. Mind you, this does teach you to concentrate on more than one thing at a time, sometimes even listening to and responding to two conversations at the same time!

When it comes to communicating with the Spirit World this helps a lot because it involves listening and answering simultaneously. Sometimes you also have to listen to the person for whom the message is intended while other Spirit people are vying for your attention, which is quite a feat of concentration.

So you see my up-bringing has been a great help. Generally, people are not aware that television, radio, and computers prevent us making full use of our senses. Actually, when I was young I did not watch much television. Admittedly we did not have one until I was older. But even when we acquired one I would always be told to make a cup of tea as the programme was about to start. By the time I had made tea for everyone, the programme would be halfway through so that it was hard to get interested. Instead, I would settle down on the floor behind my dad's armchair and chat with Amy.

I quickly learnt that I did not need to speak out loud for her to hear me and we conversed in silence so that I would not get shouted at for making a noise. Even if the programme was not well under way by the time I had made tea, there were never any seats left. But behind my dad's chair stood the family's organ and its cushioned foot-peddles served as my pillows as I lay on the floor.

If we were in the back room I would sit under the large wooden kitchen table out of the way in the hope that someone else would get collared for whatever job was at hand and I could get on with my homework.

Junior school was a different story because that is when I began to be bullied. This was partly because I came from a large family and my clothes were usually my sisters' or my mum's friends' daughters' hand me downs. It was also partly because I was too gentle to retaliate and also very shy, which made me an easy target.

Bullies tend to go for shy people because they know they will meet little resistance. I did have a group of close friends who would stand up for me and I am sure they would be surprised to see me these days happily addressing large congregations in my work as a Medium!

Once I was in bed at night I could converse with the people of whom everyone else seemed oblivious. I had to sleep with the lights on because my two older sisters, with whom I shared a room, were afraid of the dark. But I would put my head under the blankets to block out every bit of light before speaking to Mr R.

Our talks were very informative and since my family did not know the source of my new-found knowledge, they thought I had dreamt it or simply made it up. This always puzzled me. I just could not understand why they could not see the people I could see.

What did dad mean when he would say that I had an over-active imagination? This is how I got into the habit of talking to my Guides for at least ten minutes every night before going to sleep and for another ten minutes on waking each morning. I would recommend this to anyone who wants to get used to communicating with the Spirit World. Sometimes they show you very detailed information about all sorts of things, which can be a bit scary until you get used to it. Mostly, though, it is fascinating.

Chapter Three.

Discovering The Voices In The Coalhouse.

From that first day, after I had taken a look into the outside toilet, I was always aware of the middle door up our entry, which was the coalhouse.

A few weeks later, I was outside with my dad when he decided to clean out the coalhouse. The coalman delivered sacks of coal to our house once a fortnight, on a Wednesday and they were tipped on top of the coal pile, which was mainly slack by the time the delivery was due.

It was a Tuesday and the coalman was due the next day, therefore there was more, slack than coal making it the perfect time, for cleaning out the coalhouse. I found watching my father clearing it out extremely interesting that day, but at that time, I personally did not have to do it myself, for at least a couple more years.

I stood by the bottom concrete doorstep watching as my dad lifted out the two wooden planks, which were slotted in, just inside the coalhouse door, to stop the coal from tipping out into the entry, as soon as the door was opened.

Out it slid, like a landslide of sand from a sandpit, after a child has been playing in it. A large cloud of black dust rose into the air, making my father cough. I just giggled because I thought the sight of my dad with a blackened face was extremely funny. He, however, did not seem too impressed.

After a comment containing strong language, 'my father often swore' using words that I could not possibly repeat in a book of a Spiritual nature. He resumed work by picking up the spade that he had propped up by the wall before opening the coalhouse door.

He dug the spade hard into the slack and coal-dust, throwing it from the shovel into a strange object, made of wire mesh, surrounded by a wooden rim. This conjured up another huge cloud of black dust, and as I watched, I could suddenly see a pair of dark staring eyes glaring out of the dust, from the back of the coalhouse. A voice whispered: "Shhhh." I looked towards my father, who had not appeared to notice the eyes or the voice. I stammered: "D-dad." He replied without stopping what he was doing: "Not now Bean. Be quiet there's a good girl." I looked with amazement towards the back of the dark dusty orifice, which was the inside of the second door.

Amy had appeared and was jumping up and down excitedly beside me. I decided that it was time to move away and play, because I was a little uncertain of why my dad did not take any notice of the person who was watching him work, but even more unsure of the reason why the man lived in the dark room with the black sand. I stepped forward towards where my dad was working, to get a closer look, and accidentally stepped onto the object that he was throwing the dust into, tipping it over, and spraying coal-dust everywhere. My father shouted: "You stupid girl. Now you have tipped the riddle up, and made a mess everywhere, why don't you clear off and pester your mum for a change? Go on get into the house."

I was upset and ran to the steps to do as I was told and go into the house, when suddenly my father had second thoughts about his order, coming over and lifting me into the air, placing me down next to where he had stood the object back on the ground. It was probably at the sight of me struggling to clamber up the concrete back steps, which were far too high for my little legs, and even at that tender age, I was too proud, or scared, or both, to ask my already angry dad for his help.

I was always a bit of a daddy's girl, so could usually get back onto his good side very quickly. He smiled down at me, appearing to be almost a giant to me, from my small height.

"Come on Bean, you can help your old dad." This cheered me up straight away, but I tried very hard not to take too much notice of the man inside the coalhouse as I helped, 'or maybe hindered' my father with the job in hand.

I have always been a person to ask lots of questions, which is a good trait for a would-be Medium. I was therefore confused and curious to know why this strange object was called a riddle. At that moment in time, my dad looked down at me to see me wriggling about on the spot. He smiled, asking: "Do you need to go to the toilet Bean?" I was surprised at his question and assured him that I did not. He looked a little shocked and asked: "Well why are you wriggling about like that?" I stood still and pointed across the yard to where Amy was doing exactly the same thing. My father's face contorted into a strange expression, as he pointed out that he could not see anything.

I quickly said that Amy was doing it too because I had asked her why the object that my dad was using was called a riddle and she had replied that it was called this because they wriggled it about to sift out all the dust that was not wanted.

Being me, I had enquired what she meant by this, and she had started to wriggle about to show me what a 'wriggle' was. Telling me to copy her and do it too, which of course I did. My father laughed, saying once again as he turned to get back to his work: "Oh Bean, you do have an overactive imagination." I was left once again wondering what he meant when he said this to me. It was after all something that he said to me on frequent occasions.

Time flies by extremely quickly, and I had reached the age of eight years old before I knew it, and was breaking up from school for the six weeks summer holidays. In actual fact, as children we always had seven weeks holiday, much to my disappointment.

This was because my father worked at a car factory, and had his fortnight's annual holidays from work, the week before the schools broke up, and the first week of the school holidays. This was the time that all car factories had their annual holidays as a matter of course. Because of this he always kept us at home for the extra week in case my parents wanted to go out anywhere so that, us children going to school would not interfere with any plans they may decide to make. I always liked school, so would have preferred the shorter holiday, but would not have dared answer my father back, therefore, an extra week it was.

Saturday was always a day when it was probably a good idea, to be seen and not heard where my father was concerned. If he was likely to be in a bad mood, then this always seemed to be the day. It was the first morning of our break from school and my dad seemed agitated from the moment he got up. Before he left home to go out with our mum to get the weekly shopping, then go to the public house for a drink, he told us that we were big enough to do some extra chores and that he wanted us to clean the coalhouse out before he came home, because the coalman would not be calling until autumn returned.

As we clambered down the three concrete steps into the backyard, I was remembering the time all those years before when I had seen the dark glaring eyes staring at me through the dust. Chris caught my attention at that moment as she gave me a gentle push towards the shed where the spades were kept, and we fell about giggling as we often did when we were together, which was a lot.

Once armed with a spade and a shovel from the shed, I opened the coalhouse door peering into the darkness. At the back there were a few car wheels and an old pram, which had been put in there for storage.

We discussed it and decided to climb over the slack and coal, and remove these articles first. I clambered over the boards that blocked the doorway and grabbed Chris' hand pulling her in after me. We were both sitting in a heap on top of the black lumpy surface that was now the floor, laughing when I heard: "Shhhh". We looked at one another, and scrambled quickly to our feet. It was at this point that I realised that Chris may have heard it too. She was out of the coalhouse, quicker than I, because I was on the bottom of the pile, having pulled her in on top of me. She asked me to pass the articles out to her from the back of the dark hole I was sitting in. That was, therefore to be the order that we cleared the rubble from the back of the coalhouse.

I realise that a lot of you will start to wonder why, I allowed myself to be the one who stayed inside to pass things out whilst Chris was standing safely on the outside ready to run should anything happen. However, the answer is a simple one. Not only was Chris uncertain of the dark, but she suffered from arachnophobia as well. Spiders were something that she even had nightmares about regularly but as I have said before I, on the other hand have never been afraid of spiders, or the dark come to that.

The coalhouse was not only very dark, but there were spider webs everywhere, and we all know that where there are spider webs, there are spiders. For me, however, there was another problem. I had always harboured a thought that the person with the staring eyes was kept locked in there, and if this was so, what had he done? It then struck my realisation that the person was indeed a man. However, I was not certain how I knew this.

I reached out towards the old pram and someone lifted it towards me causing a cloud of dust to rise so that it was impossible to see who was in the coalhouse with me. I started to cough as my throat tickled with irritation, and a voice clearly sounded out with the words: "Be careful Jeannie". I asked Chris what she had said to me, and a puzzled expression came back, as she explained that she had not said anything.

This was not the first time that I had asked someone, what they had said, when in fact the voices had come from elsewhere. It was also by no means the last time that this would happen. To this day I still do it. In fact I drive Mike crazy when I keep asking him what he has said. Yet he has not spoken a word.

I also noticed that on these occasions, the voices seemed to call me Jeannie, and not Jean. From an early age, I had hated to be called Jeannie because of this. I was uncertain of why the owners of those voices, always stood back in hiding, whilst using an elongated form of my name to beckon me. However, as an adult and a Medium, I am not quite so bothered by this title.

The reason is things are different now. I now know that on these occasions, the voices are coming from people in the Spirit World. I am also, now very capable of knowing where and from whom these voices are coming, even at times when I am not able to see the person that they belong to. This being so because I am in greater control of my senses than I was as a child.

This is because those voices are very different that come from the shadows in your heart, because the signs to look for are different. Yes the shadows are there and your heartbeat has speeded up, and the fluttering sensation is also there because of these shadows, which have been created due to the fact that Spirit have stepped up close within your Auric field. But you will also feel an irritation and a fluttering sensation in your throat area, due to the fact that Spirit are vibrating your voice-box in order to make the sound that becomes their own voice. Therefore, instead of there, only being shadows in your heart, there is a feeling of a heartbeat inside your throat created by those very shadows being within your heart.

I pushed the pram out towards my sister, and she tugged at it until she was sitting on the side of one of the back door steps with the pram balanced in her lap, and black sooty clouds of smoke-like substance all around her. As the dust settled, Chris and I burst into laughter, as we looked at each other's faces to see that they were both black as soot.

Laughter filled the building and I was suddenly aware of voices coming from behind me, although I was uncertain of what they were saying because they all seemed to be talking at once. I turned to look, but found that I could not see anything apart from clouds of dust, and what appeared like a bright light shining through the middle of these clouds.

At that point Chris called out and caught my attention, as she was ready for me to pass the next object out to her. We then got on with the job at hand, stopping from time to time to get over our fits of laughter, which as I have said before was a fairly common occurrence whenever we were together.

By the time our father came home, all the rubble was outside, and we were shovelling the slack into the riddle, to sift the dust into the bags. As we did this, we left the lumps of coal behind to put into another bag, to save in readiness for winter when once again there would be need to light the coal fire.

We were wriggling about, and laughing at one another as we did so, just like Amy and I had done some years earlier. We thought that he would be pleased by our progress, however, he was angry because the back yard was in a state and so were we, and the job was not yet finished, even though we had started it five hours earlier. He for his part thought that we had been messing about, instead of getting on with the job at hand.

As I got older, I was given the job of lighting the coal-fire at the weekends. 'This was a job, which I hated.' I was also responsible for fetching the coal from the coalhouse, amongst other things. To start with, I used to try to fill the coal bucket before it became dark because I could always see shadows moving about in the reflection made by the torch, against the dark and the dust clouds, but was uncertain of their origins.

For some reason, I have never been afraid of ghosts, or things that go bump in the night. However, I have always been a person who likes to know where they stand. I am like that to this day. Yet those eyes, and voices, with shadows that seemed to swirl in the dark and the dust, were an unknown quantity to me at those times.

One evening, I had been sidetracked with other things and had not fetched the coal in on time, before darkness loomed upon us. I was told to go out to collect the evening's fuel, even though I tried hard to object, saying that it was too dark outside, and I would not be able to see.

My father said that I had a torch, and if I was quick and did not mess about, it would not take long. He also told me that the coalhouse was only just outside and no one could get me because the back gate was locked, and anyway if I screamed he would hear me and come to my rescue.

This was because he assumed that my fear was of the darkness of night and all that it brings to 'an overactive imagination'. In truth though, my fear was more straight- forward than that. Since an incident with a rat in our shed, I had been afraid of rats getting into places where they should not be, by gnawing their way through the doors that were there to block them out.

This may seem like an irrational way of thinking, coming from someone who happily watches ghosts walking through doors etc, without batting an eyelid, but you have to be aware that I had already been given a safe haven, from troubles by those very people who appear and disappear without any warning, through doors, and walls etc.

Spirits were always there, whenever I was afraid, or uncertain and alone. Whereas a rat had attacked our rabbit by chewing his way slyly through the door, and wooden boards that had been put there to protect him, and should therefore have kept the rat out. This occurred one Sunday morning when Chris and I had gone out to the shed to open up and to feed and water the rabbit, and although we did not realise it we were in for a shock. As we walked towards the shed, we could hear scuffling noises and a squealing sound. I was, to say the least a little concerned at this thinking that the noises had something to do with the man in the shed.

We slowly opened the door, and to our horror saw the rabbit under the bench. The once pure white rabbit was now bright red, due to the fact that he was covered in blood. Grabbing the rabbit we quickly ran indoors to show our mum, but not before I noticed the vice handle spinning like mad, and the man waving his other arm about.

Our mother was feeding the baby, and suggested that we leave the rabbit with her and go back outside to check the shed. This was an extremely scary experience but we did as we were told and went back out, armed with a broom each. We both peeped inside the shed, looking back at each other as we did so! We decided to enter because there was nothing untoward to be seen, forgetting the fact that I could see the man with the vice. Therefore, we both stepped over the boards that blocked the bottom of the doorway, and stared around carefully in the darkness. After a few moments, we decided that it would be a good idea to move the crate in the dark corner of the room. As we were about to step forward, I clearly heard the words: "Be careful". After discussion we decided that it would be best to push the crate out of the way, using the brooms. Therefore, stepping forward, keeping one eye on the man by the vice, I pushed the crate with the broom and all at once, the vice fell off the corner of the bench and I saw the longest tail of a rat that I was ever likely to see. The experience was made worse by the fact that neither of us had ever been that close to a rat before. We both screamed, as I shouted: "Quick, it's a rat."

We turned tail and ran back up the three concrete steps into the house. After which we refused to return to the shed until our father came home and could go in with us.

It was always, with great interest that I pondered on the fact that through the many years, when I had seen the man turning the vice in my father's shed. He had never spoken any words at all, until he said those two little words: "Be careful".

It was these very words that had made me hesitate, before pushing the crate, and therefore making me more alert. This along with the vice falling to the floor at the right moment, had probably stopped one of us from being bitten by the rat.

My father put the vice away after that day, and I was always a little confused, that the man had also disappeared as well. Although this was so, I was always on the lookout for his return whenever I had occasion to go into the shed. Yes the rabbit had survived that attack, but it was not long afterwards that the rabbit developed a lump in his neck where he had been bitten by the rat. And as a consequence he had died.

Just after the incident with the rat, and the rabbit, our father told us to be careful and watch ourselves because the rat was probably nesting nearby and that if he was cornered he would spring for our throat and bite into it and cling on to our flesh. We should therefore be careful not to trap it if we saw it.

Since then I had got it into my head that the rat lived in the coalhouse and that the eyes that I had seen all those times, belonged to the rat. I therefore, felt that he was just waiting to pounce if I should corner him whilst getting the coal. I never once thought about the fact that I had also heard my name being called at those times whilst I saw the eyes staring back at me, and rats cannot talk can they?

I made my way down the steps having a quick glance around the yard, by shining the light of the torch about, and then stopped for a moment taking a deep breath before lifting the latch that held the coalhouse door tightly shut. The door slid open squeaking as it did so. I shone the beam of the torch inside. Firstly at the front just behind where the door had been closed, then towards the back of the dark shed type building.

Because the coal had not yet been disturbed, there were no clouds of dust to hinder my view more than the fact that it was dark. Straining my eyes against the darkness, I looked towards the back of the outhouse, trying hard to see both sides at the same time.

I saw the now familiar eyes staring back at me, which gave me a start, making me jump, dropping the torch as I did so. I bent quickly reaching my hand down into the darkness to try and retrieve the torch, which was no longer giving light. All at once, I heard: "Jeannie, be careful". I straightened up immediately, and at the same time heard a scuffling sound, followed by the voice again. However this time it said: "Pick up your shovel". On hearing this, I looked to my right on the ground where I had placed my bucket, in which was the shovel.

I nervously bent and picked it up. As I leaned towards the coal heap with my shovel at the ready to dig out some coal, I looked once more towards the back both eyes scanning in different directions.

It was then that I saw the man that used to turn the vice in my father's shed. As I watched with uncertainty, the shovel fell heavily out of my hand as if some strange force had grabbed it out of my grasp. It landed with a clank followed by a dull thud, and suddenly the beam of the torch relit shining in the direction where the shovel had fallen. I gasped with fright, turned tail and ran into the house, calling for help from my father. He sighed as he put his evening paper down at the side of him and tilted his head to look at me over the top of his glasses. This was something that he did regularly. He said in a flat voice: "Where is the coal?" He asked this question, unperturbed by the fact that I had ran into the house screaming. He was, you see, a man who thought that children should be seen but not heard and a lot of the time, like this one, he was invariably wrong. I was panting away ten to the dozen, as I managed to cry out the words: "There is a dead rat in the coalhouse!"

He sighed once more, and I could not help but think what my grandmother, his mother, would say to that. If we sighed she would retort in a loud, high shrill voice: "Do not sigh child. Sighing is a sign of bad breeding". I was wondering what she would think of her son sighing, and wandered if his breeding was bad. However, before I could take that line of thought any further, my father called: "Come on then Bean, let us have a look at this rat you have found. It will be a piece of old wood I expect".

I found myself almost running behind him to keep up with his long strides. As I reached the bottom step my father had picked up the deserted torch from the coalhouse floor, and was now extending his arm out straight, where he was holding a dead rat by the tail between his index finger, and thumb.

The shovel had sliced into the dazed rat as it started to recover from being hit on the head by the falling torch. At that moment I looked into the darkness of the coalhouse to see the man smiling back at me, and winking his eye.

I had never seen him smile before and this warmed me to him. From that day on I was less uncertain of the man in the outhouses up our entry. He had after all saved me from the rat therefore he could not be all that bad, could he? It was to be many years before I would realise why this man looked after me that day, or in deed why he showed up on numerous occasions during the course of my life.

Whilst looking to the back of the coalhouse on that evening, I had inadvertently used both eyes separately when I tried to see both sides of the back of that outhouse at the same time. This stimulated my third eye and allowed me to see that man more clearly, whereas in the past I had just been looking straight at his eyes, so had not seen him clearly.

When I was nine, my uncle died. He had spent some time in a wheelchair, having suffered from shell shock since the war, although I feel that the family were never quite sure what, was really the matter with him. It was my first experience of someone close to me dying. I cried although I had not known him very well. Perhaps it was the awareness of death that upset me? However, just before my tenth birthday my grandmother on my dad's side passed away. This time though, I could not cry, and felt bad about it for a long time because I had known her really well. Having given this a great deal of thought I feel sure that my lack of tears was because I was afraid of her. My grandmother was very strong minded and strict and, when in her company, you did not dare move a muscle without her permission.

Actually it was while visiting her that I learnt to astral travel. She would go to the kitchen, leaving us sitting in the parlour, as she did so she would tell us not to move because she had eyes in the back of her head and she would see us if we did.

Because she always seemed to know everything, even when she was not looking, we completely believed her. I used to say the same thing to my own children as they grew up. I would tell them off and they would ask, "How did you know that...? You had your back to us". To which I would reply that I had eyes in the back of my head. The truth was that I used to come out of my body to see what they were up to!

I now realise that perhaps my grandmother was doing the same thing. Mind you, her manner was so sharp that we would never dare to look for the eyes in the back of her head, like my children did in mine, we just took her word for it. Moving around in her presence was out of the question but I found that I could slip out of my body and go into the kitchen without her knowing I had even moved. My sisters never caught on because we were not allowed to talk, so they could hardly notice my absence.

My paternal grandmother was High Church of England by religion and would often say that she did not believe in life after death. However, one evening she suddenly screamed and my dad and his brother ran downstairs to find her by the front parlour door. She told them she had just seen a man go into the room and described him in great detail. As the men were about to investigate, she stopped them, telling them to fetch the poker from the other room for protection. This they did then entered the room, only to find it empty! There were locks on the windows and no other doors, no possible escape route. When told there was no one there, grandmother said she must have imagined the whole thing. This seemed unlikely given that she had described the man so clearly. Having said that she did not believe in the Spirit World, she obviously was not about to consider that as a possible explanation!

As I have already indicated, by the age of ten, I was quite grown up, and already baby-sitting my two younger brothers, yet I was naïve in some ways, and still not aware of the fact that I could talk to dead people and hear their reply. However, my sisters, brothers, friends and myself would go into my father's shed on many occasions to borrow his tools. This was the reason why he kept his best tools in a toolbox in his bedroom.

We were always careful when moving things about in there because of the fact that our father did not like us using his tools, or in fact going into his shed. Whenever we did enter the shed, I was always aware of the vice being turned, by the stern looking man whom the others seemed to ignore. This of course puzzled me, but I decided that if the others did not mention him then nor would I.

It was always dark in there because there was no light and only a small window, which at that time, the bench was in front of. The small amount of sunlight that shone through the window seemed to miss the corner of the bench where the man was standing scowling and turning the vice. I often wandered if this was the reason why my family and friends had not mentioned him? I thought that maybe they could not see him in the dark.

This I thought was a reasonable assumption because as I have said before, I knew that they were afraid of the dark and I was not. This could easily explain why they did not look into the darkness and why they would avoid looking in the direction of the vice. This solution seemed to work for a while, until one day my father decided to move the contents of the shed around, so that we could make a home in there for our pet rabbit, until he had time to make him a larger hutch.

Before this, whenever the shed door was opened, it was necessary to turn to the right where the bench was against the back wall below the window, with the vice attached to the front right hand corner of the bench. Now, however, the bench faced the door, and the light from the window shone directly onto the vice. Therefore, I had to rethink my idea about other people not noticing the man because of the dark. In the corner of the shed where the vice used to stand now stood a large wooden crate 'standing upended', which would be made into a hutch when time allowed. It had been at this time that the incident involving the rat mentioned earlier, had occurred.

We often played with our friend who lived a couple of doors away, and her father had let her use their shed as a playhouse. Because it was an identical shed to ours, I always felt a little uncertain about being in there after the incident with the rat in our shed. Yet we were to have many happy hours in that shed, using it as a clubhouse as young children do.

As children, the topic of conversation often turned to ghosts, and it was at these times, that for me, the shed would come alive. Yet when, one day our friend suggested that we have a go at the ouija board, to try and call up the dead. The man, whom I had not seen since the vice had been removed from my dad's work bench, appeared in front of me and simply said: "Be careful." This made me think back to the time when he had uttered these words before. It was to save my sister and myself from harm. I therefore, decided not to join in with my friends on that occasion, which I later found out as an adult, was a good decision because using this method of contacting the Spirit World, we never know who we are calling to join us.

There is a dark side to the Spirit World, and using ouija boards, without a trained Medium being present can sometimes mean that the Spirits, who join the participants using the board, are in fact bad Spirits. These are not easy to get rid of, once they have been summoned up.

Chapter Four.

Spirits' Peculiar Ways Of Letting Us Know That They Are There.

I can remember one incident when I was about ten years old. My auntie May had come to visit us and during her visit, I went upstairs to the toilet. Because I did not want to miss anything, I raced up the stairs, deciding as I did so that once in the bathroom I would come out of my body to see what was taking place downstairs.

Sitting on the toilet in such a way as to allow me to concentrate on the water below me, because I had already learnt by that tender age, that things like coming out of your body, or 'astral travelling', were easier to do whilst water was around. Although I have to admit that I did not know why this was so at that time during my life.

This meant that I needed to sit with my legs apart if I wanted to see the water below, but unfortunately I had not taken into account that I was only small, and suddenly without warning I slipped and found myself stuck fast in the toilet with only my head, arms and legs sticking out.

I obviously needed to scream for help and my family have laughed about the occasion when Jean fell down the toilet, for many years, since that day.

For me, however, the incident taught me a lot more than my family realised. It did not in fact quell my fascination with water it just made me more careful and aware when water was around, during times when I wanted to come out of my body. (You need to realise that I thought that all people came out of their body.) I also assumed that Mr R, or someone had explained to everybody about the strength of water.

This was to be only the beginning of my journey of exploration of Spirit working with the energy of water.

I have never forgotten another incident that occurred when I was still approximately about ten years old that made me aware of just how much my father loved me. Dad never left the house without two clean, starched, freshly ironed hankies, one for show and one for use. One lunchtime on the way home from school, I fell over and grazed my knees so badly that they bled. As I rounded the corner into our road, dad was coming towards me in the car, on his way to work for the afternoon shift. Seeing that I was upset, he stopped. There was no time to take me home without being late for work so he wrapped one of his handkerchiefs around each of my knees and went on to work without them. This proved to me one hundred percent how much he loved me.

It was at this time of life that I found myself thinking about love and death, although I still had no idea that I had been communicating with the dead for most of my life. Growing up was a confusing time for me. I spent a lot of time dressing up as various elderly people, which made my friends and family laugh. They just thought it was me being me, a bit of a comedian with a good sense of humour. Yet really I was trying in earnest to portray the various people who had spoken to me on any given day, or perhaps the previous night.

If only I had realised that the Spirit World were there helping. I am sure that if I had known then I would have understood who they were much sooner.

My brothers, Keith and Kenneth, who were five and seven years younger than me respectively, were very close. Whilst I babysat them for my mum and dad, I used to entertain them with magic tricks, with the help of my psychic powers. Of course it was not really magic at all but it kept them quiet for hours at a time. Keith would squeak with delight and shout, "Do it again Jean, show us some more magic! Tell her Ken!" It was wonderful to watch the pair of them getting so excited, even though I knew that I was not moving those marbles around by sleight of hand or the kind of magic they had in mind.

As children, Chris and I spent many happy hours looking out of the bedroom window in the evenings. We would stare up at the sky watching the clouds float by and taking turns to describe the shapes we saw and what they meant to us. It was during one of these discussions that Chris and I discussed whether we thought there was a heaven.

We came to the conclusion that if we were able to get messages from the clouds (that is where we thought they were coming from), then it was likely that there must be a heaven, which we assumed was above the clouds and the Angels were communicating with us from there.

Chris asked if I thought there were gates leading into heaven because earlier that day we had been watching the Remembrance Day processions on the television and pretending to place poppy wreathes like they had been doing, but using books instead of flowers and an armchair as the memorial stone.

Usually all wreathes that were being placed were circular shaped poppy wreathes but on that particular day some ladies had placed some flowers made up in the shape of the gates of heaven. These had been for their sons who had been killed in recent conflicts to show them the way home.

I said that I was sure there must be gates that led into heaven. To which Chris replied: "How will we know where to find them, if no one buys us a wreath of that shape?" Good logic when you are twelve!!! I told her that the one of us whom was still alive should buy some flowers in the shape of the gates of heaven to show the other the way through. Although she liked this idea she then enquired how the one who died last would find their way. I told her that that would be easy because the one who went first would meet the one that was left behind and show them the way home.

We made each other a promise that this is what we would do and unfortunately it has been necessary for me to keep my side of the promise first. I therefore know that when I pass to Spirit Chris will keep her side of the promise and be there to meet me.

Spirit Guides (I now know that is what Amy is), come in very handy when you need to know what the clouds are saying to you. I suppose I was an unusual child in a lot of ways. For example, my family remembers my wearing my duffel coat, hood and all, in the middle of the summer. Everyone else was saying how hot it was whilst I was very definitely cold. I now realise that this was due to the vibration of cold introduced into the atmosphere by those visitors from the Spirit side of life.

One day, Chris and I were playing at jumping across the brook on the way home from the shops. As I went to jump, I missed my footing and landed with my foot in the water. As I took off my shoe and sock, Chris laughed and said she would tell mum because we were not allowed to go near the brook.

I asked Mr R to make something happen to stop her telling mum. Immediately, Chris tried to kick a stone into the brook and her shoe flew off and splashed into the water! Needless to say, she did not tell mum after that (we have told her now, after reaching adulthood!)

Another time, one evening after school, Chris and I were on our way to the shops when we noticed a commotion over by the same brook at the bottom of our road. Crossing over, we found that a girl and a boy from our school were stuck in the mud where a kind of sinking sand had formed from sand dumped by builders from a nearby site. The fire brigade was called and soon the girl was freed. The boy, however, was still sinking in the mire and I could see that the firemen were getting very worried, so I asked Mr R for help. Suddenly, the firemen were able to pull the boy from the mud, leaving behind a single forlorn Wellington boot. I know that the sceptics will say this is mere coincidence, but the fact is that things like this have been happening around me all my life.

Still as a child of about ten years of age, I loved my maternal grandmother, but at times my siblings and I were a bit unsure of her. She was a person, who was very strong-minded and would give orders to us all, which we were expected to follow, and of course we did just that, most of the time.

One cold, winter's day, I was sitting by the fireside with my grandmother, when she started to poke the embers in the coal fire with the poker out of the grate. As I watched with great interest, she suddenly exclaimed: "Look at that lady in the flames of the fire, Jean". I, of course stared intensely into the flames as she went on to give me a description of the lady she could see. It was with great excitement that I said 'yes' I too could see the lady. My grandmother smiled and carried on with the job at hand. After a few moments thought, however, I asked her: "Nan, why can that lady stand in the flames of the fire and not get burnt?" She appeared to be a bit embarrassed by this. She placed the guard back by the fire, and standing up she answered in a sharp voice: "Do not ask silly questions child, she just does." I of course did not realise it at the time, but my grandmother did not know the answer to my question so therefore fobbed me of by becoming angry, because she knew that I would not dare to question her authority. I, for my part however, always remembered the lady in the flames and was always inquisitive to know how she could do it.

This also applied to the many people and animals, which I would see whilst staring into the embers of the fire after that occasion, because I did of course always look out for them from then on. It was, however, to be many years later before I would get the answer to my question, because it was one of the first questions that I asked of my Guides in the Spirit World as soon as I knew that I could ask them questions.

The Spirit World, link with us, by means of extending the normal uses of the parts of our body that always come naturally to us. For instance, we cannot see our third eye even though it exists, but we can see our two physical eyes. Therefore, they use one to help activate the other into use. In other words, it comes naturally to us to use our physical eyes to see what is around us. Although most of the time we only half use them, and do not use them to their full ability. Spirit work, however needs us to use them to that full ability, whereby, this in turn opens the third eye, which is needed to both see, and build up the ectoplasm required for seeing Spirit physically, and not psychically.

As is usual of things connected to Spirit, the answer was a simple one, and here it is. Most people will have looked at a fire or the sun at some point and noticed that they can see the heat waves looking a bit like the waves below.

∧∧
∧∧
∧∧

These are zigzag shaped waves close to the heat.

The reason for this is because as we look at something hot like a fire, or the sun, the heat is too much for our eyes and we naturally divert our eyes in a different direction away from the heat. We at these times, automatically look in two different directions, one with each eye to avoid either eye coming into contact with the heat. As we do this we are not using our eyes normally, but separately and this tends to stimulate the third eye, thereby, making it possible to see Spirit.

This is the reason why, if we stare into the fire for long enough, we can see people, or animals, like when my grandmother and I saw the lady in the flames on that afternoon back in my childhood. The lady did not burn because she was not in fact, in the flames as it appeared.

Everything in our world is made up of molecules, and can be broken down or dematerialised, so as not to be in the way, and as such these material items do not stop those in Spirit World from appearing anywhere. This is also the reason why they can and do, walk through walls and doors.

Sometimes, Spirit link through to us in class situations, and by doing this they get the opportunity to choose many different ways to show themselves.

I was about twelve when death came close again. One of my four close school friends used to bring her six year old sister with her when she came to play at our house. Sadly, the younger sister suffered from a hole in the heart and died suddenly. My friend was never quite the same again, it was as though all the fun had gone out of her. I was deeply affected, both on behalf of my friend and her sister, who had become a friend too. I found it hard to understand how someone just half my age could possibly die. From that day on I worried about dying, probably because I did not understand about death or dying, which is part of my reason for writing this book: to help people to understand that there is no death.

Around this time the Spirits grew much stronger in the way that they communicated with me. I remember quite clearly telling my mum about a gorilla that must have escaped from a local zoo. She laughed but to me it was very real and I was very careful on the way home from school in case it leapt out of the bushes at me. I now realise that we all have an animal Spirit with us for protection and that mine is a silver back gorilla of which I have no reason to be afraid. This was probably the only occasion on which I was a little unsure or afraid of them, and then only because I did not understand.

As a young girl, I shared a bedroom with my two older sisters, Pam and Chris, and of course many Spirit visitors. Our bedroom was a fairly large, square shaped room with an added alcove by the door. Just inside the entrance to our room there was a trapdoor on the ceiling, which led to the loft. There was also a fitted wardrobe adjacent to the door, on the same wall.

We all occupied our own three quarter divan bed, in that room. The four large panes, and two small panes that made up the window, faced the wardrobe, and our headboards were below the windows. My bed was situated so that I slept with my feet facing the wardrobe, with about four feet of space between the bottom of my bed and that wardrobe. There was also a space of approximately one foot between my bed and Chris' bed, and the same between my two sisters' beds.

Lying in bed at night, I would listen to the many noises that appeared to come from the wardrobe and the loft. I have to admit that although I was always more curious than scared, our house and particularly that bedroom were a bit spooky to say the least. I should point out that the rest of my family were also aware of these strange noises and spooky goings on, my mother and my grown up brothers are still aware of the strange noises and movements in that room, to this day, because they still live in my childhood home.

Some people who are reading this book will have already started to think that maybe these noises were natural noises like the central heating etc? However, these possibilities have been investigated many times over the years and I can assure you that Spirit have had a hand in most of these events. For one thing there was never any central heating in that house, either then, or now. This I know because as I say, my mum and brothers still reside in the house that I was born in.

As I lay on my bed, watching with great fascination, many people were coming and going in our bedroom. A man in dark clothes would go into, or out of the wardrobe. Although he never opened the doors, you would hear them rattling, and see them moving about. Sometimes, people, some of which were children would walk out into the space between the foot of my bed and the wardrobe, and show me scenes, some of which could be seen as a bit scary. All that they were in fact doing was trying to show me how they had lived, and subsequently died.

Periodically, our mum would insist that we tidy our bedroom, and clear out the wardrobe, as mums do. However, this was a job that we all tried to get out of, but when this failed, we would put off tidying the dreaded wardrobe, until the very last.

We rarely used the wardrobe for our clothes because obviously, we preferred not to enter it on a daily basis. Our clothes were therefore mainly in the chest of drawers or either, in my mum and dad's room or in the airing cupboard. Instead our toys and games were kept in that large double fitted wardrobe.

Needless to say, because my two sisters were unsure about the happenings in there, so wanted to get out quickly and because I was so inquisitive or nosy, whichever way you want to put it, so paid more attention to Spirit than I did to what I was doing, things were always just shoved onto the pile, without any of us checking where they had landed.

This led to it being much cluttered. Meaning, the job of tidying that wardrobe was a full afternoon's work. We, as children, laughed and giggled a lot, and we would make ghostly noises to one another as a joke. Unfortunately we would end up frightening ourselves with this Tom foolery.

I now realise that there were two reasons for this. Firstly, we were heightening our own awareness to the slightest sounds. Some of which, were not Spirit orientated. Secondly our laughter would raise the vibrations and I now realise that this would help Spirit to manifest themselves.

I feel sure, that if asked, my mum would have said that the reason for the cluttered wardrobe was because we were being lazy, but really it was because we were all a bit uncertain of that wardrobe, which seems to have a life all of its own.

Now, as an adult and a professional Medium, I realise, that the whole of my childhood family home is haunted. As I am sure, are many of the houses on that estate, because of the history of the land on which the estate was built. Ghosts after all, haunt spaces, and not the occupants of the building. Unfortunately the latter is the theory of most people, which obviously creates more fear.

The houses on that part of the estate had after all been built after a large stream had been drained and filled with hardcore, before they were built on the top. As I said in a previous chapter, the energy from water helps Spirit to manifest themselves, so haunting these houses was made easy for them by this factor. However, I have also grown to realise that the reason the bedroom was so alive with Spirit activity, was because of all the laughter and tears that have taken place in that room. We, three sisters spent a lot of happy times in that room and house.

Both of these emotions serve to raise the vibrations high enough to create more psychic energy, which in turn gives the energy needed for any Spirits that are present to be able to show themselves. I should also mention at this point, that due to the fact that there are psychic people on both my father's and my mother's side of the family, then all of their children have a large amount of psychic ability because psychic energy, like most other things is hereditary and therefore, passed on in the genes.

Because it is on both sides of our family, we were fortunate enough to get a double dose of psychic power. Sadly my brothers and sisters are all either uncertain or really scared of their psychic powers, although my sister Hazel is starting to develop her psychic gifts now. I know that she will make a very good Medium one day. I guess, from my point of view, I am the lucky one because I am not afraid of Spirit visitors, in fact to the contrary, I become more afraid if I think that it is too quiet and Spirit are not obviously about. I put it like this because even at times when we are not aware of their presence, Spirit, are still around us.

As the years went on, the door of the wardrobe developed a habit of opening on its own. It may have looked to some as though it was opening by itself because of a faulty latch, but my dad checked and rechecked the catch and it was not broken. Truthfully, those in the Spirit World were opening it to catch my sisters' attentions because they were not noticing these Spirit people as much as I was.

It could be a bit disconcerting, especially when it happened in the middle of the night, waking you from your sleep. Although it was probably worse for my sisters because they did not see these people like I did. They just heard the noises and saw the doors opening on their own. I should imagine this would be quite scary. I can only compare how they felt with the way I became scared when later in life I thought there was a burglar downstairs in my home whilst I was the only responsible adult around. This is because fear is usually based on any unknown factors that are portraying themselves.

One day our father got fed up of us moaning about being woken up at night so he suggested that we change the bedroom furniture around, placing one of our beds in front of the doors to stop them from opening in the night. He assured us that if there was a bed in front of the doors, then whatever, or whoever, was in there, could not get out. This explanation seemed reasonable to all of us, therefore it was agreed that this would be done. However, the next obvious problem was to decide whose bed would be used to block the doors. Everyone said that because my bed was by the wardrobe now, it was only fair that I should be the one to sleep there.

I had learnt a long time before, that it was no good arguing because I was the youngest person who shared the room and therefore, had the last say. Therefore it was agreed that my bed would go there with the foot of my bed facing the alcove, where the trapdoor to the loft, and door were situated. Chris' bed was alongside mine, with a two-foot gap between them, and Pam's bed stayed where it was originally, placing it at the foot of Chris' bed.

My first night sleeping in my new position in our bedroom was a little bit strange to say the least. At first I lay on my back with the covers up to my neck, just watching and listening.

I could hear loud laughter coming from inside the wardrobe at the right hand side of my bed, so turned my head to look. A boy's head popped out through the doors just above me, which startled me at first. It was at that point I heard a rattling noise coming from the trapdoor to the loft. I glanced across, in time to see the trapdoor lifting a few inches on the nearest side to me. I could clearly see two eyes sparkling back in my direction from the hatch.

I had become used to people walking through the wardrobe, and had decided that these people were probably ghosts, who were obviously not going to hurt me, because they had not done so far. I came to this opinion using the logic of an innocent child. However, those eyes, which I could see glaring back at me, looked real. It appeared to be a man and he was lifting the trapdoor, and not going through it like the others. This for some reason unnerved me. I dived under the bedclothes, blocking every gap so that he could not get me, or so I thought.

As I lay there, shivering, for a few moments wondering whether the person up the loft would come down to get me. I suddenly became aware of a gentle smoke like substance in front of my eyes.

Under the bedclothes with all the gaps blocked, it was totally dark. The light bulb in the room could not be seen through several layers of blankets. This meant that the smoke like substance, which was white in colour, could be seen easily against the black background.

This sight fascinated me, and as I watched, the substance turned into a face. At first this made me jump, but then I realised that the face was familiar. It was the face of Mr R, my Guardian Angel. My surprise turned to interest as I watched people emerging in front of my eyes, even though I was under the covers. From that day on, I always slept with my head under the blankets. Partly to hide from the person up the loft, and partly to block out the light, because I preferred it in the dark.

Over the next few weeks, I was to catch regular glimpses of the person up the loft, which I now knew was definitely a man. He only seemed to peep through the trapdoor, but he did make a lot of noise. In the quiet of night, you could hear noises like footsteps crossing the loft above the bedroom. Then there would be whistling sounds, like wind howling and the trapdoor would rattle, along with a rustling sound moving down the wall. It was always at this point that I would see the man staring down at me, unless of course I was tucked up in bed, with my head under the blankets.

One night, the trapdoor rattled far more than normal, therefore the three of us complained to mum and dad that we thought that there was someone up the loft. We did not like going to bed at night in case someone came down to get us whilst we were asleep.

My dad laughed, but said that he would sort it out if it was really scaring us. I went up to the bedroom with him, whilst he checked the loft, because I always liked to watch him work. He took his small wooden ladder, which was just tall enough for him to climb into the loft. I held the bottom of the ladder steady as he climbed up and removed the trapdoor, which was the cover to the hatch. He stuck his head through the hole for a moment or two, then climbing back down the ladder. Smiling at me he said: "There is nobody up there; I told you it was just the wind, didn't I? Wait there Bean, I will just fetch some tools, and I will lock the hatch down to stop it from rattling. "My father's pet name for me was Bean.

He disappeared into his bedroom, which was next to ours. As I stated before, he always kept his toolbox there so that we children did not play with his best tools and leave them out in the garden to go rusty or get stolen. As soon as he disappeared, I heard a rustling sound above me, so I looked up. Glaring down at me was the man I had seen so many times before, he was peeping at me from inside the loft.

At that moment my father returned, and the man disappeared back inside the loft. I hurriedly told my dad that I had seen him again. He sighed and once again climbed the ladder, sticking his head inside the hatch. After a moment or two he came back down a couple of the steps, remarking: "You are imagining things Bean, there is no-one up there I promise you."

He immediately pulled the cover of the hatch down into the bedroom, and set about screwing a hinge onto each side. After, which he re-climbed the ladder, putting the hatch cover back in place and screwing all the sides down tightly? He then gave the lid a good push upwards, to make sure that it was secure, before saying: "There. Nobody can come down from there now, can they? You girls are safe, but I promise you that it is only the wind."

I lay in bed that night thinking about the events of the day. The more I thought about it the more I worried. After all I had definitely seen that man up the loft, and I had not left the room so he could not have got out, yet my father swore there was nobody up there.

The only explanation that I could come up with was that my dad, whom I loved dearly, had just locked a man in the loft with no way to get out or no way of getting any food. Once again I was 'using a child's logic, I had added two and two together to make five!'

This problem was to worry me for a long time to come. Because the truth was, that the man up the loft was in fact in the Spirit World and as such could get out of that loft in the same way as the ghosts came out of the wardrobe, yet he did not appear to do that, so why not? Therefore, even later in life when I was able to understand the comings and goings of the Spirit World, the man up the loft, just did not make sense, even to me. It was to be many years before I would fully understand this factor.

My father would often enquire who was in the front bedroom on his return home from work. He did this because he had caught a glimpse of someone looking out of the window. Only to be assured by my mum, that there was no one upstairs. So you see, even my dad caught glimpses of the spooky goings on in our bedroom.

You may now be thinking that I am a bit weird because I was not afraid of the ghosts in the wardrobe yet I was very worried by the man being hungry up the loft. The fact is that I had been used to those Spirits floating through walls and doors from an early age, and they had never hurt me, therefore, I felt safe in their company. Whereas, in a child's logic, the man in the loft, hid away and peeped out at us and obviously could not come through walls etc because if he could, then he would come out through the ceiling, now that the hatch is locked down, yet he did not.

Over the next few weeks and months, I often thought about him, but as time went by, I began to realise that on occasions I could still hear movement up our loft, and I was old enough by then to know that he would have starved to death by now if he was a real man locked up there. As I stated before, many years later I got the answer to this particular puzzle.

Chapter Five.

Using Our Senses.

Again, when I was about twelve, I used to go shopping for my mum after school. I often got into trouble for taking a long time over it. Unknown to my mum I used to visit the old people's dwellings at the bottom of our road. I would help the senior citizens, then sit and talk with them, often gaining very interesting information which I would repeat to my family. They found this very amusing and were sometimes amazed at how I could possibly know all this- especially since it concerned people who were dead. I remember one old lady in particular who told me about herself and how she had died after suffering dropsy. I thought she said 'dropped knee' and asked what it was. To my puzzlement she chuckled away to herself and replied, "Dropped knee, is when your knees drop down towards your ankles so that, if you sit at the kerbside, you need to sit right back, allowing your feet to hang over the edge of the kerbstone. "

She showed me a picture of herself doing exactly that, sitting down at the kerbside, dangling her feet over the edge into the road and pulling her skirt up over her ankles onto her legs as she did so. To my eyes, her knees had dropped to her ankles. I spent quite a bit of time trying to imagine what that would be like, but because it was time for me to go home, the lady never had a chance to tell me she was joking. So of course I went home and told my mum all about the lady who suffered from dropped knee. She laughed, saying "Oh Jean, your dad's right, you have got an over-active imagination. You are funny!"

My family, as usual, put the whole thing down to 'another one of Jean's funny stories' designed to make them laugh, which of coarse they did. No matter how hard I tried I could not get them to understand that I really had met this lady, that she was real and not just a figment of my imagination.

This incident comes to mind whenever my pupils or people in general ask me why Spirits do not make themselves clearer. Can you imagine the frustration that the old lady must have felt when, try as she might, she could not get me to understand what she was talking about. This is one of the reasons why it is vitally important to train our forgotten senses by practising the exercises in this book. Mediums are people, they are fallible. So they make mistakes in transferring information from the Spirit World to people's loved ones in this world.

The English language is open to misinterpret as it is, without the added complication of trying to communicate using half-forgotten senses. I am sure you will have heard the saying: 'No sense, no feeling'. For example, when a friend is hit on the head by a ball and does not react, we would laughingly say, 'Look. No sense, no feeling!'

Yet the truth is that we do not actually feel things through these senses. This is easy to understand if we imagine our right hand to be completely without feeling and paralysed. Thus numbed, if we were blindfolded and then someone stuck a pin into our hand we would not feel the pinprick at all. However, if the blindfold was taken off, and we were pricked again we would not be one hundred per cent sure that we had not felt anything. Or at least we would flinch when the pin's point came close to our hand. This is because our senses come back into play.

Next time someone close to you is asleep, move your hand slowly towards the bottom of their foot as though you were about to tickle them. You will be surprised how many times they will move their foot as you near it. This is not because they are really awake as it might seem, but because when we are sleeping we have naturally altered our state of consciousness, thereby changing our vibration to a faster one. This is the same vibration or wavelength if you like, that we need to communicate with the after life because spirit live in the same space as us, but are usually undetectable since they exist on this faster vibration. This is why some who would not claim to be Mediums can still obtain information from the Spirit World it comes to them whilst they are sleeping.

Another phenomenon which people find hard to understand is the fact that we can hear silence. Understandable, really, since silence means without sound. But we can hear silence if we try. I am again talking about using your senses. Imagine turning up at some friend's house just as they were in the middle of an argument with their partner. Even if they pretended things were fine between them, most of us would be aware that something was wrong even if we could not say why. This is because we can sense awkwardness about them as they pass the silence between them.

Sound is the oscillation of the air at particular frequencies, which our ears interpret as sound without us consciously realising it.

If a room usually has noises in it and suddenly they are missing we would notice the difference straight away, even if we could not put our finger on exactly what had changed. It is the same with the arguing couple but how can that be if we cannot hear silence? I did say after all, that they were trying very hard to pretend everything was normal. It is because silence is a sound we can sense so it is possible to hear it.

I never did manage to erase the lady with 'dropped knees' from my mind and could not understand why people did not believe me. It was only as an adult, realising that I could communicate with the Spirits, that I actually asked them. That is when I finally found out that the lady was already a Spirit back then and that she had suffered from a condition called 'Dropsy' and had been joking about her knees all along!

This changed everything. I asked my mum whether she remembered the incident I was assured that she did. She had a good laugh when I told her the truth behind the story, and it made perfect sense to my family because I have always been naïve!

On my fourteenth birthday my father bought me a new bike. There was, however, a story attached to the bike. When I was about thirteen and a half, a really nice lady who lived a few doors away asked me if I wanted an old bike, which was on top of her shed. Of course I jumped at the chance and went round to fetch the cycle, whose brakes, she had warned, needed looking at. Chris and I had a look at the brakes but, I must admit, that even after our attention they still did not work properly. Anyway, as far as we were concerned that was what feet were for! However, one night whilst I was playing on my bike outside our house, my father arrived home early. And he was not pleased. But he could see how upset I was when he banned me from riding it, so he promised that if I did not ride it he would buy me a new one for my fourteenth birthday. I stopped riding the bike; dad put it on top of our shed and, true to his word, bought me a new one on my birthday.

My first day's riding was marred, however, by the fact that Chris did not have a bike of her own. After a brief discussion, we decided that if she rode the old one, dad might buy her a new one too. The plan did not work, although we had a lot of fun before dad took the old bike away from her. One day we decided to cycle to Sutton town centre, about two miles away. To get there we had to go down the very steep Reddicap Hill, which was fine until we reached the bottom and the fact that Chris had no brakes gained new importance.

The theory was that I would ride in front so that I could help her to slow down, not one of my better plans! I braked and slowed down, putting out my right arm to stop Chris as she went past. Chris rammed her feet down onto the road in a vain attempt to brake, but unfortunately she was going too fast and went careering past at great speed, sparks flying from her feet as she went. Suddenly I saw the nurse guide appear, stepping out to catch Chris' bike. Looking back, we are convinced that Chris only avoided being killed or badly injured by a miracle, Spirits to the rescue once again!

I should point out though, that had it been Chris' time to go to the Spirit side of life, the Spirits would not have been allowed to help. This has been proved to me by something that happened four years later to my brother Ken. On Whit Sunday the year before my brother's death, my mum, dad, brothers and sisters, my dad's friend and I went to the Lichfield Bower. For those who have never heard of this, it is an annual funfair held in the streets of Lichfield. At the time, my father owned a car but it was not big enough for all of us so some of us caught a bus, then a train and met the rest of them at the fair.

Heading home after a wonderful day, we caught the train to Sutton, and headed for the bus stop by the side of the Empress cinema which, sadly, is no more. By the bus stop was a four foot wall, on the other side of which was a stairwell leading to a door making the drop on the other side a good twenty feet. Ken and Keith were sitting on the wall, while I leaned against it. During a bout of horseplay atop the wall, Ken toppled backwards, falling head first over the other side. Luckily I saw this out of the corner of my eye, and with a reflex action caught him by the ankle as he dropped which broke his fall. Had his fall been unbroken he would have definitely died. This was June 1970. Just eight months later on February 26th, 1971 Kenneth died of an illness. So you see, the time has to be right for us to pass over to the Spirit World, and when that fall happened a few months before Ken's death, the time was not right.

Maybe it is time for you to start stretching your senses. If we ask most people how many senses they have they will probably say five, which of course are:

*Sight.

*Hearing.

*Smell.

*Taste.

*Touch.

They are forgetting the most important of all, and that is awareness of our aura. This is most important because with it we can be aware of many things around us, by which I mean both here and in the Spirit World. For those of you who do not know what an aura is, I will explain briefly.

We all have a magnetic energy field around our bodies this is what we mean by an aura. If you were sitting alone in a room and someone came up silently from behind, the chances are you would notice them coming before they actually touched you. This is because you would have sensed them. Your aura enables you to do this. As soon as someone touches this magnetic field, a minor shock takes place, like a little electrical surge. Sometimes we are not sure what has affected our aura, but simply know that something has, actually you can train yourself to be aware of why and how this happens.

Many years ago people had no televisions, radios or computers to occupy their time, phones with which to call up anyone, anywhere and any time they like. People had no choice but to make use of what was available to them, so they made much more use of their senses. As I mentioned earlier, I rarely watched television as a child. We did not have a phone either. I was brought up being told not to speak unless I was spoken to and, since my siblings and I would always do what our father told us, we learned very quickly how to say a lot with just a look. One glance could speak volumes!

In fact we were using our senses. Sight, being a sense we are all used to, can help if you take the time to look properly. But if you add to that a feeling we can all pick up on, like anger, it is a different story. If you were unfortunate enough to be deaf, just the sight of someone talking quickly and going red in the face would tell you that they were telling someone off. You would be sure of this even though you had not heard a thing. If that person were looking directly at you, you would know you were on the receiving end of a scolding. It is just common sense, yet people do not seem to realise that they can take it a step further. If you were to ask yourself, 'How does this make me feel?' You would immediately know the answer. You would feel angry, upset, belittled or all manors of other reactions, depending whether you knew why you were being told off and whether or not you felt you deserved it. You are probably wondering what all this has to do with the Spirit World or even auras, come to that. Well, I am coming to that.

I would like you to adapt part of your everyday life. I am not suggesting that you stop watching television or using the telephone or anything similarly hard to keep up. But I am going to ask you to follow a few simple steps for a few weeks. By then I feel that I will have piqued your natural interest and that you will want to carry on learning how to use your other senses.

I suggest that this moment is a new beginning for you. It is the start of real communication with yourself and others around you. Step one is to humour me by having an open mind and accepting a new beginning and being aware of that new beginning. I am asking you to try, for once, not to be oblivious to your own needs and your surroundings as most of us are.

Tomorrow morning, when you first wake up, I want you to take the time to ask: 'What is today going to be like?'

Many of you will raise the first stumbling block here by saying they do not have the time. Not true. I am one of the busiest people I know and suffer a great deal of pain along the way which slows me down in some activities and prevents me taking part in others. Yet I find the time for myself and for the Spirit World because it is important. It does help to make the suffering easier to cope with and to help other people along the way. You do not have to put any time aside, you could actually ask yourself this question whilst you are rushing around, getting ready for the day ahead. I do not expect you to know straight away what is about to happen because sometimes it is a very subtle feeling if you are not careful you could miss it.

If, for instance, you had a sudden sense of rushing around and you were doing just that at the time, it would be easy to mistake this new feeling for something more mundane when it is actually the answer to that question! That is the main reason for asking you to do this exercise. When people first begin to develop senses that have become dormant through lack of use they are often sure that nothing is happening.

In fact, a good friend of mine called Laureece, says that she is oblivious to the Spirit World, but the truth is that she has exceptional ability and understanding in this area. The trouble is that half the time she simply does not listen to what her senses are telling her.

The title of my first book came to me when she told me she was oblivious to the Spirit World and Mr R said: "That is a good title for your book: Oblivious But True".

I am asking you to learn to trust yourself. I promise, it is the most difficult thing I will ask you to do. Now, as you go about your life's business, I want you to pay more attention to the people with whom you come into contact. I am asking you to listen to what people are not saying. This may sound back to front but it does make a lot of sense once you understand it. For example, if you know someone very well, you begin to realise that they do not always mean exactly what they say, often because they do not want to bore you with their problems.

If someone asks me, 'How are you?' I quite often respond with, 'I am fine thank you.' My answer is my way of hiding the fact that things are not so good. On the other hand, if my reply is: 'Alright thank you' or 'Great, thank you.' Then things are going great in my part of the world. Good friends of mine such as Laureece now interpret the phrase, 'I am fine thanks' to mean precisely the opposite. They are, you see, listening to what I am not saying!

People who know me well know that I am very good at listening to what other people are not saying although I very rarely let people know my innermost thoughts and feelings on any given subject. In other words, just because I do not reveal that I know something, does not mean that I do not know it. This probably sounds strange yet familiar to most people because we all hide our feelings to a certain extent. When we are communicating with the Spirit World, this comes in very handy. If, for instance, I wanted to pass on a very personal message to someone from their loved ones in the Spirit World and we were with others at the time, I would need to express the information in a way that was comprehensible only to the person for whom it was intended. This becomes easier once you are used to it.

Because all these signs and senses are hard to get used to, people tend to give up trying. I am asking you to have patience. If any of this is not making sense to you at the moment, I assure you that it does get easier. If listening to what people are not saying sounds a bit deep and unusual to you it is understandable because you have not been so obviously guided in life by the Spirit World like I have.

It was only a few years ago that I became aware that not everyone sees the Spirit people. Since that realisation I have bombarded them with questions and I am pleased to say they have answered them! I did learn at about twelve or thirteen that thoughts are living things and that if you asked sincerely for something to happen it would.

On first meeting Mr R one of the things I noticed was his close shaven beard, stern look and staring eyes, which could be misinterpreted as hard. He may be hard but he is fair. He answers every question I ask, as long as he feels I cannot come up with the answer on my own. For example, if I have mislaid something, He will tell me where it is only if I have made every effort to find it and have failed. This brings me to a question I am often asked by people who are developing their Spiritual side: 'I do not know whether it is them or me? How can I tell the difference?' This is not an easy one to answer in simple terms, so I asked my Guide to answer it. His reply was: "My child, there is a simple answer to all your questions. If you were capable of taking a look at your brain it would read just like a map. Do you understand?" I smiled as the thought crossed my mind and replied, "Yes, I do".

Mr R immediately started talking again: "Good, I am sure that you will have noticed that I always stand behind your right shoulder whenever you are talking to me through your senses."

"Yes I have" I said, with a rush of excitement that spurred me to answer aloud, which is unusual for me, knowing full well that Spirits communicate telepathically and do not need you to voice your thoughts. "I stand on your right" he continued, "Because we communicate with people, who have not yet passed over to Spirit, by using their brains. Everyone's brain has a left and right portion, each of which control the opposite side of the body. Now then, on the left hand side of your brain there is a part we call the subliminal. This is towards the front, above and slightly forward of the ear. Because we use this part to communicate with people who are unsure that we are here, we stand behind them because the subliminal part is at the front, and to the right, because the relevant part is to the left. You see opposites attract in this situation, making it easier for us to communicate."

I knew that he had stopped to see my reaction. I also knew that there was no need to answer. 'Subliminal messages were used in advertising for many years in time gone by. For instance, a word saying the name of a product that a company wanted to advertise would appear in front of the newsreaders' face on television. This word would be made up of tiny dots, which, though invisible to the human eye, would be picked up by the subliminal part of our brain. Then, when we saw the product for sale, we would be tempted to try it without knowing why. This is no longer allowed in advertising because it is considered to be a form of brainwashing. In fact it is illegal.'

At this point he gave me one of the half smiles I had become familiar with and went on, "However, this is one of the main ways for us in the Spirit World to communicate with you when we cannot make you aware of us in any other way. This is why people sometimes get an idea in their heads for no apparent reason. The information is supplied in such a way that we are sure that it will be heard, not that we mean to tell you what to do, just to guide you. Everyone has a personal responsibility for himself or herself. In other words, they are in charge of their own life, not us. We cannot take this responsibility away from you and you should not want us to."

He was making sense of the things, which had previously been hard to understand but I still did not feel that he had answered my question. Before I had a chance to say so, he continued. "The answer to your question, my child, is within each individual. When you feel you have received information from the Spirit World you must immediately put your senses backwards by placing this thought in your mind: 'Who is it behind me saying that?' By doing so you automatically put the information where it came from, behind you. Straight away you will become aware of something else, maybe purely a sense of someone or something being there. Now place a new thought in your brain: 'Are you male or female?'

These may sound simple but once you have trained your brain to respond in this way then and only then, are you beginning to take notice of a sense to which we in the Spirit World have easy access. I promise you that the information which I have just passed onto you from the Spirit World does make a lot of sense.

At first I had to practise what he had told me, because I had grown used to communicating with these people so naturally, I did not realise how it was done, like many of you. Although to begin with the opportunities to practise this method will be few and far between, please stick with it because, I promise you, it does get easier with practise. You will also find that the more you use this way of linking with the Spirit World, the more they will talk to you. After all, if you were to talk to someone and receive no reply would you keep up a one-sided conversation for very long? I suspect not.

I have asked you to do two things, although simple; they can be frustrating to start off with. Practise them at every chance you get. Just to remind you, they are: When you wake up in the morning, ask yourself, 'What is today going to be like?' If you have time to write down any thoughts or feelings you experience in the response to this you will be surprised how much it can help. You will suddenly become aware that you actually know quite a lot and this realisation will boost your confidence that you can do this.

Every time a thought comes into your head for no apparent reason, send your thoughts and feelings backwards. Do this by simply placing questions into your head about who is communicating with you, instead of just thinking, 'Why did I think that?' or 'Was that me?'

Remember that trust is the hardest part of getting to know the Spirit World. You will find that trust in the knowledge that the Spirit World exists will come to you more easily than trusting yourself, or in the fact that you can do it at all. One more piece of advice which you will find helpful is do not think whilst you link. This is not easy, in fact you will be surprised how much of a habit it has become to think. And habits are hard to break. Instead of pondering what you have observed and why, try focussing on who it is and how they have managed to get close enough to communicate with you.

One of the most important steps with your development at this point is to stretch your senses. This means paying attention to the five familiar senses we all know about, which may seem strange considering that it is Spiritual development that you are aiming for. I assure you, though, that they will help in the long run.

You need two people for these exercises and I will talk you through them as if two people were following them. It is important to follow these steps in the given order, resisting the temptation to skip one here and there. I can assure you this is for your benefit not mine, the Spirit Worlds or anyone else's come to that. For the first exercise you will need:

* An ordinary scarf or similar (for use as blindfold)

* A set of headphones through which you can play music.

* A wall with space for one person to stand up against it.

* At least two people.

Now we can begin:

Both remove your shoes.

Decide which of you will wear the headphones and blindfold first (you both get a turn).

One of you now puts on the blindfold and headphones with music playing so that you cannot see or hear anything happening around you. It does not matter what kind of music as long as you can hear it and it is loud enough to drown out the sounds of the room.

With the help and guidance of the person who can see, the blindfolded person stands facing the wall and places the open palms of their hands against it.

After giving the blindfolded person a moment or two to relax them, the person who can see quietly steps behind their partner, moving as close as possible without actually touching them.

Then they slowly and quietly touch the blindfolded person on the shoulder. This should be repeated several times, altering the timing and or the shoulder they touch so that the blindfolded person cannot tell when and where the next touch will be. During this process, the blindfolded person should say when they feel the touch or when they are aware that they are about to be touched. Both partners should have several goes at being the one to test their senses. When the experiment is finished, both of you should make a note of the results, recording the date and time (this will be important later when you will need to check your progress).

This exercise is good for heightening the use of our senses. Or to be fully alert in order to protect us from any approaching danger from behind but since we rarely make use of this ability, it tends to weaken. Reawakening this faculty not only strengthens these senses but also makes it easier for us to sense Spirits when they are close to us thereby taking us a step closer to spirit linking.

In these early days of training our senses the headphones and blindfold should be our almost constant companions, whether separately or together. Most people would benefit from some time wearing a blindfold, it would sharpen their senses.

According to my Guides in the Spirit World every Medium is 'Clairsentient'. Some are 'Clairsentient' alone whilst others are 'Clairaudient' or 'Clairvoyant' as well. Some, like me, are lucky enough to be all three. These words actually mean clear sensing, clear hearing, and clear seeing in that order. They are all expressions familiar to those following a spiritual path. Clairsentience, or clear sensing, is by far the hardest form of Spirit communication to learn and to understand. It is also the most important. This is because it is the easiest for the Spirits to use, providing them with many ways of transmitting information to our senses. If someone from the Spirit realm stood close behind us we would sense a presence even if we did not know what it was or why it was there. People who are not sufficiently Spiritually developed to read the signs tend to describe this sensation in various ways.

They may report a sudden quivering sensation radiating all over their body and often describe it as a 'spooky' feeling. This is unfortunate because the word 'spooky' conjures up all sorts of false ideas about the Spirit World and its inhabitants' intensions.

An experienced Medium, on receiving this shivery sensation, would immediately be aware that someone from the Spirit World had stood next to them. That person, I can assure you, is only announcing their presence and expressing their love. A student, on the other hand may not be sure what to think. They might say that more likely than not, the Spirits are with them, but that is all they could be sure of because they will not be used to their own bodies or using their senses which are, after all, among their bodies most important functions.

At this point it is time for you to involve a third person in the exercise if possible. Repeat the exercise as before but with two people approaching the blindfolded person from behind, these two people moving simultaneously. They should approach on either side, each touching the shoulder nearest to them. Once the blindfolded person has got used to this happening, go back to just one person touching them on both shoulders and see if it is noticed.

The blindfolded person must call out straight away when they are aware of anything, no matter how subtle the awareness. They should also state which side they feel the touch. With practise you will all be at least a little bit aware when someone is approaching you from behind, and then it is time to change the exercise completely. That may seem a strange thing to do but I assure you that it will help to heighten your senses and take you a step closer to knowing when spirits are with you.

As far as Clairaudience is concerned, many people do not realise how difficult it is for Spirits to produce the sound and very few know how they do it. Quite often, when people are meditating or linking with Spirits they suddenly begin to cough uncontrollably. It is not because they have got a cold coming, it is because Spirits make sound by vibrating our own voice boxes. Whilst they are doing this they intend to come in very close to us, creating a tickling sensation that makes us cough. There is a simple remedy, just ask them to stand back a bit! It is because Spirits use our voice box to 'speak' that Mediums say that they feel that they have not heard the sound with their ears but as a voice, usually emanating from a place slightly forward from their throat and a little to the right.

Chapter Six.

A Changing World.

November 9th of the year I turned fifteen is one date I will never forget. My parents had been out for the evening and, at about ten thirty, whilst I was making the most of my rare free time and watching 'The Invaders' on television my father suddenly burst in. Mum was about to give birth to the baby she was expecting. I was to run to my friend's house next door but one and ask them to call an ambulance. Arriving breathless at their door, I found that my friend and her parents were out. However, my friend's nineteen year old brother was in and overcoming my initial embarrassment at having to broach what I felt was a delicate subject with a male, I asked him to make the call and scurried home.

To my delight my brother Martin was born the following day. But death too reared its ugly head: on that same day we found our budgie, which had been part of the family for a long time, lying dead. Then, to make matters worse we went outside to feed our rabbit only to find him dead too. That may sound fairly trivial to an adult but it is no laughing matter to a fifteen year old that is afraid of dying. Now I was preoccupied with birth and death all at once; dealing with feeling happy and sad at the same time. That is something I still find hard to this day.

The following year my friend from next door but one suddenly lost her father to the Spirit World. He simply went out to work, had a heart attack and never came back. My friend was especially close to her father and I was close to him too, having spent a lot of time at their house. The experience changed her, she grew up almost overnight and I was left once again to cope with the aftermath of bereavement and the changes it brings. Life never follows the same pattern once a death has occurred; the changes can be minor or dramatic, but they are changes all the same. Somehow life goes on although in a different way. Later that year another neighbour died suddenly after collapsing in a bus shelter, a girl we had all played with as we grew up. She was only eighteen.

It was as if my whole life was taken over by people dying, making me feel very confused and afraid of death almost to the point of feeling guilty for still being alive myself. Over the years, whilst all these things were going on, I had come to rely more and more on my conversations with three particular people in my life: Mr R, 'who is the most important of all,' Amy and of course the nurse.

Leaving school was something of a mixed blessing for me. A year earlier, on the evening of Chris' last day at school (she is thirteen months older than me), we were sitting on the back garden seesaw that dad made us, just chatting about life in general. As darkness began to fall she told me how excited she was at the prospect of getting a job and having some money of her own to spend. Of course I was pleased for her but wished that my turn would hurry up and come along. After all, we had done most things together all our lives.

Although we were still close, Chris was of course living a different life now. She was going out with Derek, her first boyfriend, to whom she married. A year later it was my turn to leave school, but by now my feelings had changed. I was not too sure about getting a job or about leaving either. Actually my father had asked me not to get a job for a while because my mum needed help with my baby brother, the housework, cooking and shopping. At first I did not mind this too much because my baby brother Martin was a gorgeous little child and I loved him from the start despite the fact that the rabbit and budgie's deaths had coincided with his birth.

I quite enjoyed taking my sister Hazel to school, bringing her home and picking up the shopping on the bike my father had bought me for my fourteenth birthday. I was very proud of my brand new light blue bicycle probably because it had been bought for me and was not the usual hand me down.

One evening I was about to watch Coronation Street when my sister asked me to make her a cup of tea, to which I replied that I was watching television and that she should make her own. She replied that since I was the only one who did not work that it was my job to make the tea, which annoyed me intensely because I had been on the go all day, like every other day in fact. That evening I told my father that I wanted to get a job. He was quite surprised and asked me why. I explained what had happened and said that although I could see my sister's point of view, I worked hard all day without pay. Dad told my sister that if he gave me permission to get a job I would get one straight away. Indignantly she retorted that I would not. Dad's response was to say, "Alright then Bean (this was his nickname for me), you can get a job."

The next day I did just that. I found myself a job and had my sister to thank for moving me forward in life. We went out together quite a lot after that, sometimes in a foursome with our boyfriends. I believe that this was the Spirit World's way of changing my life and bringing my sister and I closer. If so, they certainly succeeded!

Starting work was a refreshing change even though my lack of qualifications at that time meant factory work was the only kind available to me. Dad gave my sister and I a lift part of the way to work and we would complete the journey by bus. Although we worked in different places they were quite close to each other, so we always met up to travel together back to where dad could meet us and give us a lift home. Dad said this was safer than us having to carry too much money with us to work, so I would carry just enough for the return bus fare and no more. Then, the sudden death by heart attack of an exceptionally nice and Spiritual colleague called Henry Smith came as a great shock to me. I was particularly affected by his death because he had always been kind to me. They had a collection in his memory at work and although I had only enough for my bus fare to donate, this was more substantial than usual because dad was not meeting us that day and I had enough to pay for two bus rides. I gave this and walked home with my sister.

This incident made me aware that when death occurs, no matter how slight the impact, if you are connected to the person who has passed; lives all around are affected by their death. Obviously, the closer you are to them, the more your life will be affected.

Another evening, on leaving work, I had to travel home alone, because my sister had changed jobs and my father was off work through illness. I made my way to the bus stop on this cold, dark, foggy and rainy night, thinking as I went about Coronation Street and television. This was because a character called Val Barlow had received an electric shock from her iron and that night we were to find out whether she was dead or alive. I was keen to get home to see it!

Typically, like so many of the best laid plans, this one went wrong. I saw a bus approaching and squinted against the fog and rain in an attempt to see if it was the one I wanted: the 114. Just as I was thinking, 'thank goodness for that', on realising that it was my bus, the people in the queue shoved me forward. Stumbling up onto the vehicle I dropped my money into the driver's tray and made my way to the back where there was just one seat free with its back to the window. I sat, people watching, as the bust drew away, happy to be on my way home at last.

After I had been on the bus for about twenty minutes it began to empty and I moved to a window seat so that I could look out. Rubbing the condensation from the window and peering out I could see fields and trees but, worryingly, I did not recognise any of them. I was on the wrong bus! Panicking, I jumped off the bus without thinking at the next stop, only to find that I was in a small and completely unfamiliar village. There was a phone booth, but of course I was penniless.

Although fifteen, I was still very naïve, as you will see from what happened next. I dialled 999! The police were exceptionally kind and understanding and told me to stay put and wait for a policeman to come and help me. When the constable arrived he took me to the police station, which turned out to be a little house just across the road. Apparently I had caught the 116 by mistake and ended up in Kingsbury. The police decided to take me to the nearest bus station which was Tamworth, and told me to give the bus driver my name and address and he would let me onto the bus and pay later.

It was very dark by now and all thoughts of Coronation Street were forgotten. Feeling a little afraid at being alone in a strange place at night, never having travelled far before, I was very pleased when at last the bus pulled into the station. I was not so happy when the driver told me that because I had no means of identification he would not let me board without any money.

At that moment a police car passed. I flagged it down and told the policeman about my predicament. He very kindly lent me half a crown (about twelve and a half pence in today's money). And smilingly gave me his name and the address of his police station so that I could return it. I hurriedly boarded the bus, which eventually dropped me near Sutton town centre, about two miles from our house. I ran most of the way home and, as I turned from the gully way, halfway up the street into Lingard Road, where we lived, I saw lots of people. They started cheering.

It turned out that they had got up a search party to look for me because I was never late in coming home. They were extremely pleased to see me, particularly because of a recent news story about a girl of my age who had gone missing and had been found murdered. My father was angry at first because I had not thought to make a reverse charge call to our neighbours. I explained that this had not occurred to me and, when he saw how scared I was, he softened, gave me a hug and told me to come home and have my tea. I was so relieved to be home that I did not mind my family being a bit put out at having had to miss Coronation Street.

As usual, when I was afraid, the nurse was at hand and I said to her, "I do wish my family could have seen Coronation Street". She just smiled and comforted me. But to everyone's surprise it was announced the next day that they would be re-showing Monday night's episode of Coronation Street because reception had been impaired by the poor weather. Just as the announcement finished the nurse fleetingly appeared, smiled and was gone. Needless to say we all got to see the programme after all!

I sent the money back to the kind policeman as promised and received a lovely letter back, thanking me for my honesty because he had not expected to hear from me again. So that is what he had been smiling about! I will leave you to draw your own conclusions about the programme being shown again, but I am sure you know what my interpretation of events would be!

The nurse in the Spirit World about whom I have talked has been there with me during many situations and she has played an important part in my life and those of my children. When changes, sometimes, drastic ones, happen in my life, she has always tried to help me to understand their meaning.

To help you get used to differences, both here and in the Spirit World, simple exercises are occasionally necessary. This next exercise can help you to notice subtle changes on your senses. As well as a blindfold, you will need several household objects, such as a key, scissors etc. To keep things simple, I will refer to the group members as 'A', 'B' and 'C'.

Person A should put on the blindfold (you can be seated for this exercise.)

Either B, or C, passes an object to A, Who examines it by touch.

Person A then describes what they think the object is and what it is made of. B or C then writes down this response, noting the accuracy or otherwise of A's description.

Each person takes a turn at being blindfolded and describing various objects. The objects must be presented in a different order each time-or ideally, should be different objects altogether, so that memory cannot interfere.

As I have said before and will probably say again, thinking is your worse enemy whilst you are trying to link with the Spirit World. So I repeat: DO NOT THINK WHILST YOU LINK. It is a good code of practise to adhere to.

This last statement may sound odd but let me give you an example. Imagine that I ask you to memorise the room you are in because, in a moment, I am going to blindfold you and ask you to walk across the room unaided, and sit down in the chair opposite. When I blindfold you, the chances are that you will do very well in the experiment. Imagine then that I repeat the exercise several times using different subjects and allowing the rest of the group to watch. Each subject would appear more confident than the last, but if when it came to their turn, I placed a chair in front of them after the blindfold was on, they would walk straight into it. It would not cross their mind that something might be blocking their way. This is purely because thought came into the situation whilst this repetition was taking place, changing the situation from what it was to what they thought it might be. This alone made them fail the exercise. I hope that this helps to define the points that I am trying to make. These people would definitely have used a little more caution whilst crossing that room, thereby paying more attention to the realities, if thought had not come into the equation.

Whilst I was training to be a Medium I tended to pay full attention to everything because I realised how much I had missed as a child, having failed to appreciate even the possibility of the Spirit World's existence. At this point I must interject my own line of thought, just to say that friends are invaluable assets to your development, you need them to practise with and on! Without my friends I would not have persevered and I owe them a lot.

One day, a practise sitting with a friend was going extremely well until I asked her whether her mother had fallen down the stairs at some point before she died. She replied immediately, 'no she did not.' This surprised me. Why, then, was that scene so clear to me? She looked equally puzzled so I asked her, "well, if that is the case, why am I seeing a clear picture of your mother sitting at the foot of the stairs amongst a pile of shoes?"

A big smile came onto her face as she answered; "now I understand!" I was pleased that at least she understood, but nevertheless puzzled. She went on, "when my mother was a small child she would spend hours sitting at the foot of the stairs playing with the shoes that were kept there. When she grew elderly and senile, her thoughts reverted to childhood and once again she would sit at the bottom of the stairs playing with shoes!" This incident taught me a valuable lesson: DO NOT THINK WHILST YOU LINK.

I am sure you can see how easy it would be to make that kind of mistake. All I did was to change the information I was given by adding my own interpretation. This changed the whole message, making the information appear wrong when in fact it was correct. I was wrong. The moral of this story is: never try to work out why the Spirit World is showing you what it is showing you. Just tell it exactly as it is. If you do this, you will be surprised how accurate your messages will become with practise. This is important for the person receiving the sitting but even more important for the loved one who is communicating from the Spirit World. They are coming through with a desperate need to let their loved ones know that they are here to visit, bringing support, love, guidance and whatever else is needed.

Sometimes when people visit a Medium, whether it is on a rostrum during a public meeting, or in private, they do so because they have a great need to believe that we do not die but live on in the Spirit World. Their life at that moment may be going through a bad patch or perhaps they have lost someone important to them to the Spirit World. Yet their upbringing leads them to be sceptical about our beliefs, perhaps to the extent of seeing us as evil. The way to begin to change those beliefs is to convince them that maybe their loved one really is here. Notice that I use the words 'maybe' and 'might'. This is because that is how you start. As their confidence in you and what you are telling them grows, they will begin to realise that there is nothing evil about it. We do, after all, work with love.

It is important to point out that the Spirit World lives in the same space as we do, just on a much faster vibration, which the human eye cannot see. To speed up our vibration, we need to concentrate great love on the unseen or unknown as people call it. I hope that when you have read this book and practised a few exercises you too will know that the Spirit World really does exist and they really do visit us.

Mediums are often asked why it is that most of the great Mediums of our time have suffered, both physically and mentally. The usual answer is that Mediums need to have sympathy and empathy for the people with whom they come into contact. Pain comes their way so that they will understand how it feels to suffer when dealing with people with similar problems. Although this answers the question, it does not make much sense to me. I would not trust a Spirit World that made me suffer just to make me understand. So I asked Mr R for the real reason. His answer sat more easily with me: "A lot of people are born with the ability to be Mediums but the time has to be right for them to actually use the gift. The way to link with the Spirit World is by sending great love from within, which in turn relaxes you deep inside and raises your vibration. When a person is unhappy, they naturally send their thoughts deep within themselves which in turn relaxes them deep inside. They do this in the hope that everyone and everything else is shut out, which of course is the very action necessary to change our vibration. Because this person has dealt with a lot of sad, scary or lonely moments they naturally learn how to change their vibration at will. I would like, however, to explain that when exceptionally good things happen to us, they have the same effect. For instance, those who are lucky enough to see a new born baby just after birth that is, within a day or two, will know what I mean when I say that as you look at the baby everything and everyone in the room seems to disappear for a few seconds as you gaze at this little miracle. This is because you have naturally changed your vibration. Unhappy times are more obvious because people tend to remember them more than they remember the tiny miracles. It is not because the miracles are less important, it is purely because heartache leaves a lasting impression which is easily recalled at other sad times."

This answer satisfied me because I know for a fact that I would often be aware of these Spirit visitors whilst I was unhappy, worried or feeling alone in a very large world. You see, a Medium works well with Spirits because he or she has already suffered, not because the Spirit World has made him or her suffer.

If you are following the direction in which we are heading, I hope that you will be aware that I am trying to teach the retraining of your natural ability to sense without physically using your ears. Next, I would like to introduce you to an exercise, which uses the sense of smell. For this you will need the blindfold, as before, and some aromatic substances such as soap, perfume, coffee or curry powder. Now follow these steps:

Put the blindfold on person A.

B or C should now hold one of the strong-smelling substances directly under A's nose. A then describes what substance it is, while the others write down those responses. Even wrong answers are important and need to be remembered.

Repeat the process with several different substances.

Now take something with a strong smell and hold it close behind A's head without touching. This is to test whether they are aware of a smell coming from behind them.

This may sound silly but is important because Spirits quite often stand close behind us to be within our auric field. They also regularly put a waft of aroma into the air to tell us something.

If A is not already sitting on a chair with room to walk around it, they should be gently moved to such a position. This is because you need to approach them from all directions. Remember that Spirits can do this wherever we are. Walls etc. are not a problem for them.

Now it is time for B or C to hold the next item further away, repeating this with several of the aromas.

As B steps up with the next odour, a cup of coffee for instance, C should whisper loud enough for A to hear, 'that tea smells good.' You will be surprised how difficult it is for you to adjust immediately. This adjustment is, of course, necessary as you decide whether it is your nose or your ears offering the correct answer. I promise you that whilst Spirit linking you will need to do this sort of thing all the time although it does get easier with practise.

These exercises must be repeated using different odours and or in a different order for B and C. Remembering, of course to write everything down.

You will be surprised how often this causes confusion. You will also be surprised how certain you are that you are right when you are actually wrong. If you do falter before answering the question, it is still worth noting because your hesitation shows doubt, which shows that you were thinking. If someone from the Spirit World impresses something on your brain it is very straight forward until you start to think about what you already know. Then you change the message and get it wrong. This is why some Mediums say that they cannot give someone in their own family a message. The truth is that they can, it just becomes a lot harder because their own knowledge interrupts the message. So you see, these exercises are vital training in linking properly.

The mistakes that arise are not the fault of the person in the Spirit World but ours because we falter before expressing what we have received. Some of you may be feeling a bit daunted by all this, to say the least, but please do not let it put you off. The more practise you have, the more confident you will get and the easier it all becomes. Practise, after all, makes perfect in Spirit linking just like everything else! I can also assure you that the Spirits will help you when they can. So please learn to trust them and yourself. As I have said before, trusts in them and in your-self are the two hardest things to learn.

As I mentioned aromas before, I should explain that one of the easiest things for the Spirit World to do is to release an aroma that they hope we will recognise, into the air. For instance, if it is likely that you would remember that your grandfather smoked, then it is natural that if you smell cigarette smoke in a room where nobody is smoking, you will think of him. This is also a very easy way for them to communicate with a person who is not generally aware of Spirit.

I am sure many of the people who are reading this book will have at some time, been out for the day and stopped to buy fish and chips to eat in the car? You eat the food and throw the paper away in the bin, before setting off to finish the journey. But I guarantee that the next time you get into the car after it has been locked up for a while, it will smell of fish and chips. This is because the molecules that, make up the car, such as the steering wheel, seats, roof, etc., cling on to the aroma releasing it again as soon as there is any movement like us getting into the car. The smell is then picked up by your nasal passages.

Every person has an aura around them, as I have said before, which is a magnetic field. If someone from the Spirit World releases an aroma towards somebody's aura and then that person moves, the smell is released and picked up by the person's nasal passages, just like the fish and chips in the molecules that make up the car. The only problem is that after a bit of thought many people decide that it is their imagination. This is a terrible shame when their loved one has tried so hard to communicate.

Chapter Seven.

Happy And Sad Feelings.

It is now time to return to the Sense stretching exercises. Sadly, most people who Spiritually develop do not like clairsentience because they think it is the hardest element to learn and understand. If only they would give it enough time I am sure they would find it as easy as the rest. Yes, I did say easy. We are the ones who make things difficult! If we try too hard, it becomes more difficult because we are not listening to our Senses, which appear to be silent. Once again, therefore, I am asking you to listen to what people are not saying, this time the people concerned are in the Spirit World rather than here.

As I have already said, all Mediums are Clairsentient. Tackling the use of your Senses, therefore, is vital if you are to move forward. This form of communication can be used in many ways but first of all we need to get used to the idea that we can feel sound as well as hear it. We can also see it. I am sure that most of you will have noticed some people who cannot hear what another is saying without seeing their face. On the face of it, they are lip reading. But this has nothing to do with it. The real reason is that when facing the direction from which the sound is coming, they can Sense the sound vibration. I have never forgotten, one afternoon whilst I was taking a church service, I found that I could not see or hear the Spirit World but could only Sense it. I was horrified because I had always found this way of linking very difficult. That night I told one of my Guides off about this, only to be told in turn by Mr. R: "My child, you are not using all of the gifts that you have been given in order to communicate with us properly. If you learn how to talk to us through Clairsentience we will return the other two methods. This, I promise you, my child." I was amazed by this but went out of my way to learn and practise communication by Clairsentience very quickly. I now find this method as easy as seeing or hearing the Spirit World, although I must admit that it makes you work harder.

At this point I would like to suggest again that you try to communicate with your Guides for a few minutes every night as you are about to go to sleep and again each morning when you wake up. It does not matter whether or not you are aware of them because they will be aware of you. Equally it is not a problem if you fall asleep whilst you are doing this or if you are rushing around getting ready for the day. You do not need to talk aloud or stop what you are doing. They will hear you and eventually make you aware that they are communicating back.

You will be impressed by the results of this next exercise once you check them. You need at least two people, A and B, standing about three feet apart.

A should stand facing B but B should stand sideways on. In other words, A should be looking at the side of B's face and body.

A should mumble under his or her breath, a sentence of their own choice. This should not be a whisper but it should not be too loud either.

Now B should try to repeat that sentence.

Person B now turns to face person A.

A now repeats the sentence they said before or a different sentence if the first one was heard.

Now A and B change places.

Remember to write down the results.

It is amazing how many people cannot hear a low voice whilst facing away from its source. Yet the same person hears perfectly well when facing the sound's source. For me, most of the exercises came naturally because they were all part of growing up. As I have said before, I quite liked spending time with my younger sisters and brothers. There was baby Martin and four year old Gordon at home and Hazel, who was only five but went to school. Keith and Kenneth then aged ten and eight were also at school at that time. Hazel had a little boyfriend who lived in one of the police houses at the top of our road because his dad was a policeman. His mum and I used to chat whilst taking the children to school, after which I would cross the road to do the shopping and then go home on my bike.

Although the greater part of the day was taken up with housework and looking after children, I really did not mind. In fact I even enjoyed it. What I did not enjoy was my dad and sisters' return from work because I was then expected to wait on them hand and foot. This meant that I rarely had time for myself and never got to watch a television programme from beginning to end. Sometimes I would give up on television and take my bike outside, not to ride it, but to sit on it at our gate talking to Amy.

The Christmas of 1970 was a happy one. However, unknown to us life and Christmases would be different from then on. On the morning of January 4th, time for my brothers and sisters to go back to school after the Christmas break, Ken, then aged eleven, woke up with his whole body swollen. He did not even look like himself.

Mum said he could not go to school and made a doctor's appointment for that afternoon. But by the afternoon the mysterious swelling had subsided so she cancelled the appointment. The next morning, however, the swelling had returned and Ken was packed off to the doctor, from where he was dispatched straight to the hospital. It was his kidneys. He never came home. He died on February 26th.

Chris and I had been planning a double wedding for March 20th but now I wanted to cancel. However, before I had the chance to say so, dad decided that we should go ahead as planned because that was what Ken would have wanted. I did not admit to dad, I would have been happier not to go through with it. My husband to be, though, persuaded me to leave arrangements as they were so as not to upset my father further. He was, after all, grieving for the loss of his son. My father liked my 'would be groom' even though I was not entirely convinced that I loved him. Nevertheless, my aspiring husband assured me that I would grow to love him one day and that in the meantime he had enough love for two! If I was unsure at the time, I did end up feeling that he was right. Later on I felt much happier about things, as he had said.

Once again, though, we were all trying to balance feeling happy and sad at the same time. I had hardly got the hang of this the first time round. But this time it was not just pets, but my brother who had passed away, something I never quite got over. And I am sure I am not the only one who feels that way.

This was the first time that the person who had died was actually from my family; in fact, was from our home. Although I was hurting just as much as everyone else, I felt that I should be brave for mum, dad and the rest of the family's benefit. I kept wondering whether I would ever see these missing people again. Part of me always thought that I would. Actually I had seen my grandmother but thought I had imagined it because I had been scared of her and had not cried when she died. The second person that I saw from the spirit world is the nurse, on whom I have relied heavily as I have said before. She has always been around in times of trouble and the time of Ken's illness and soon after his passing was no different. His passing changed my life considerable because of the way it affected my family.

My father had often told us as children that he was an atheist. Yet he also told us stories about growing up as a choirboy as I have said, his mother was very religious and forced God upon him throughout his childhood. This did not convince him to believe. It had the opposite effect, until my brother fell ill and was clearly dying. Then my father prayed. Since atheists, by definition, do not pray, my father could not have been one. This realisation made me rethink his position and mine in an ever-changing world.

My father was a strict man back then and was always in control so I suspect that my brother's death brought about all kinds of new feelings in him. Suddenly he was not the master of one of his children's fate and there was nothing he could do about it. He could not help and he could not begin to put things right.

My brother's death affected him a great deal. He changed in the way that he reacted to everything and mellowed a great deal. My youngest sister, Ann, who was born after Ken's death would talk about a father who was much gentler, more easygoing than the dad I, had been used to. It is hard to believe the two are the same. Sometimes it is in situations like this that create problems when a Medium is trying to pass on information from a loved one in the Spirit World. For example, if my father was giving a message to my youngest sister the Medium would feel that he was a strict and strong-minded man. Ann would refute this. This was not her experience of him but it actually described him well. It is not that she lied, both versions are true. Similarly, Chris and I spent most of our time together as children yet we have very different memories of the same dad. This is just because we are different people with different opinions. In fact dad favoured me, so I saw him in a different light.

A Medium would, therefore, need to tell us different things to jog our memories despite the fact that dad would be exactly as he always was. I am only saying these things as an illustration of one of the many problems a Medium is faced with.

Mum and dad used to tell us true stories about the times when they lived with my grandmother shortly after they were married. They had one of the upstairs rooms and spent quite a bit of their spare time in there. One day, while they were in bed, they heard a banging noise coming from the wardrobe. They both sat up abruptly, looking at each other, puzzled. When nothing more happened for a few minutes they settled back down and tried to sleep. Then suddenly the whole bed jumped into the air as if someone had given it a powerful kick from beneath. This happened a few more times until Dad lit a candle (grandmother did not believe in electricity). Cautiously emerging from the bed he peered underneath it and into the wardrobe but there was nothing and nobody to be seen. The next day they arranged to go and live with my mum's sister!

I left the family home at the age of eighteen after marrying my first husband, and left all thoughts of my haunted bedroom behind temporarily.

Being married changed my life as well as those of others. It must have been a difficult time for my parents, first losing a son for what they thought would be eternity and my sister and I both leaving home at the same time. It must have felt as though they had lost half of their family. For the first two months of married life my new husband and I stayed with Chris and Derek. My husband was beginning to show signs of violence. I would have left him then if I had had somewhere to go. My father's point of view on the subject would have been, 'You have made your bed. Now you can lie on it.' In other words there was to be no going back. Having moved in with my husband's brother and his wife in Tamworth for a further month we became eligible for a council house there.

Moving into our house was very hectic as these things always are. The stress was exacerbated by the fact that I was pregnant, having been talked out of my desire to put off having children for a while. I worked very hard preparing the house for the new baby. She was due on December 22nd but decided to put in an early appearance after I fell down the stairs with a little help. Born on St. Andrew's day, November 30th, Dawn made life seem a whole lot better. Having had her straight away turned out to be a very good decision. That Christmas was a happy one because it was Dawn's first, but at the same time sad because it was the first without Ken, remembering the happiness of the previous Christmas: and how we had no idea of the problems ahead made the difference between the two hard to deal with, but of course, we coped.

It was after moving into this house and deciding to pack some things away in the loft that things started to flood back. Our house proved to be haunted and at that time I did not realise that I could do something about it. Nor did I realise that being just nineteen and living with my husband was more of a hindrance towards my learning this fact than a help, due to the psychic energy I was creating. Whenever my husband walked into the kitchen our small brass ornaments would fly off their shelf opposite the door and hit him. He was afraid to go upstairs alone, convinced that there was someone there. I would laugh at this, although I had to admit I often heard footsteps or bangs and that the lights were forever switching themselves on and off.

One day my husband had spent the money he was supposed to have used to pay the electricity bill. Needless to say the first I heard of it was when they came to cut the electricity off. I was very upset. He had really let us down this time. We went to bed early to keep warm, taking a candle upstairs with us. The candle had been extinguished for about ten minutes when, very cold and upset; I remonstrated with my husband again. How could he have done such a thing when we had a young baby to look after! As usual his response was to shout at me and at that very moment the candle lit up again of its own accord, the bedroom door opened and slammed shut with a bang and the room went suddenly extremely cold. My husband leapt out of bed and tried to open the door. It was stuck fast so he jumped fearfully back into bed and cowered under the covers. He had nowhere to hide as the covers were whipped right off the bed. The bottom draw of the dressing table repeatedly opened and closed and suddenly an old man appeared, walking across the room holding an old fashioned 'Wee Willie Winkie' style candlestick with a lighted candle. He walked straight through the wall of the fitted wardrobe and, instantly, everything returned to normal. If only I had known that the psychic energy I was producing was allowing all this to happen, perhaps my life would have improved a lot sooner. In other words, I think my husband would have left me there and then!

A few months later, we were sitting in our lounge with the light on when suddenly the bulb blew. Or at least that is what we thought happened. The room had two light sockets, one at each end, but the other bulb had gone the preceding day and we had removed it. I told my husband to get one of the two bulbs in the hall. But when he stood on a chair to change the bulb in the lounge he found that the socket was empty. "It must have fallen out. It will be on the floor," I said. Once the light was back on we searched the room but could not find the bulb. It was a mystery. The next day, whilst I was doing the housework, I found it at the opposite end of what was a rather long room, in a corner behind the armchair. To have travelled this distance it would have had to bounce several times without breaking. This was surely impossible. But it definitely got there somehow!

One evening, my husband had gone to the pub as usual. I was heavily pregnant, and sitting downstairs listening to music, when I thought that I heard footsteps coming from upstairs? I walked up the hallway to the bottom of the stairwell, and as I looked up the stairs, the front doorbell rang behind me. Fortunately two friends had decided to call round for a coffee and too keep me company. After letting them in, I explained what I had been about to do when they arrived.

Sally's eyes opened wide as she said: "ooooh." Bursting into laughter, to which we all joined in. After which we decided that we would all go upstairs and investigate. The girls pushed me forward, towards the stairs saying that it was my house, so therefore I should go first! I tried to object, saying that I was the one who was pregnant, but they pointed out that I was the one who would be left in the house once they went home. So in the end, I had to agree. We began to climb the stairs, and sally started to giggle, I put my finger to my lips, and whispered: "Shhhhh."

There was a deadly silence as we climbed the stairs. In this house you went to the top of the stairs and came back on yourself past all three bedrooms, to the bathroom. Just outside the bathroom door, there was a trapdoor in the ceiling to the loft.

We were all staring around the landing when we heard a noise from above. We all looked upwards with startled eyes. At this moment the girls screamed and turned tail to run down the stairs. As they ran, I stood staring at the loft opening with my mouth agape. I definitely saw the same two eyes glaring down at me from the trapdoor, as I used to see in my childhood home. I returned downstairs and asked the girls if they had seen anything, and they both retorted at the same time: "The loft door moved". I asked whether they had seen anything else, but neither of them had. Not long afterwards my husband came home from the pub, a little the worse for wear, as usual. My friends went home, and I was once again left to wonder about the man up the loft.

From then onwards, there were frequent occasions when footsteps etc came from upstairs. It gave me the feeling that I was permanently being watched whenever I was upstairs in that house. Things happened downstairs too, but there was a different feeling, upstairs. At least when you were downstairs you did not feel as though you were being watched. But upstairs it was an eerie feeling to say the least, even from my point of view.

After Dawn was born, things became even more eerie and creepier in that house. However, I could not help but notice that things always seemed to quieten down when my husband was out of the house. Then just before he was due home, it would start all over again. Looking back to those times now, I often wonder how different things would have been, if I had realised that I could and did communicate with the dead.

Maybe my husband would have been forced to behave differently towards me, or at least I would have known that the man up the loft was in fact dead, and trying very hard to convey to me, the way, in which he had died.

Now, that I know that I am able to communicate with the Spirit World, I know the difference between the people in the wardrobe, and the man up the loft, for instance. Spirits haunt spaces; they do not generally haunt people.

Those people in the wardrobe were haunting the space where our home had been built, because of a past connection with that space, whereas the man up the loft had lost his way and not gone all the way home to the Spirit World like those Spirits who were haunting the space.

He needed help from someone who appeared to be able to see him, which I obviously could. He needed this help to convey to the living world that his death had occurred but he could not find his way home. He is one of few lost Spirits who actually realise that they have died. It is more usual for a lost Spirit not to have realised that they are in fact dead!

When I moved house again to my present home, the man up the loft was still very apparent. In fact to this day, my loft has latches on it, to lock it shut from the outside. Although I have since helped the man to settle at home in the Spirit World, knowing that his death had been acknowledged for which he was extremely grateful.

Those latches on the loft trapdoor are a reminder to me, of a time when I was unfortunate enough not to realise that I had the gift to enable me to converse properly with the dead, in fact maybe even better than I converse with the living? I am sure that my close friends would agree with this point of view.

Unfortunately my life had taken many bad turns before I was to reach the point where I knew why this man was following me around to whichever house I lived in. Thus enabling me to help him and for my life to change enough to bring something that resembled happiness, without having to rely on the living who always seemed to let me down.

I am forever trying to see the good in all the living people whom cross my path, even when I can clearly see their bad side beginning to reflect in their actions. Yet with the dead I am always shown the bad side first, which I think is good because then the bad cannot creep up on you bringing the hurt that frequently happens when becoming close to the living, and not seeing them for who they really are until you are too close to walk away.

If only the living were as straightforward as the dead. Yet those who have moved on to the Spirit side of life are the ones that most of us are afraid of. Whilst giving the living the benefit of the doubt until they prove us wrong. This is purely because of the unknown factor that presents itself in connection with the Spirit World. Although people do not tend to be afraid of the unknown, and sometimes dark, side of living people's characters, they do not give Spirit the same grace.

The point I am trying to make is that if we look hard enough, or are unfortunate enough to draw the wrong type of people to us, then it is not only the dead that present an unknown factor, but sometimes it can also the living. We should therefore try to give our Spirit friends and relatives the same chances as the people who are living in their physical body. In my experience they quite often care for us even more than the living.

After many ghostly happenings we moved house back to Sutton Coldfield where I was born. My husband spent more time out of work than in and would only be employed in short spurts, mainly after I had threatened to leave him if he did not find work. He found himself a job in the boiler house of the local hospital. The problem was that he had to work nights one week in three and was afraid of being in the boiler room alone at night this meant that on each week that he worked nights I had to wait till everyone else there had gone home and sneak into the boiler room to keep him company. Whilst there I often saw a man walking through and stopping as if to stoke the boiler for which there was no need because it was automatic. My husband, though, could not see the man, but only hear him, which frustrated me because I could not see how he could be missed. Of course, I did not realise at that time that he was in Spirit. My husband was petrified. But he had the perfect excuse for walking out of yet another job! Not that he ever really needed an excuse.

Sadly, many of the ways in which the Spirit World communicates with the people who are still here, can be misunderstood, so they are passed over or even ignored. This is not because the person receiving the information is necessarily uninterested but because they put it down to imagination or intuition: that questioning, "Is this me?" This is a fairly common feeling. Whereas the question they should be asking is: "Is It You!!"

During the months that followed I was fortunate enough to meet some very special people who helped me on my way. Because I had been in touch with the Spirits all my life without knowing it I was able to practise sitting for anyone who would let me, mainly friends and friends of friends. It is important for anyone wanting to develop their Spiritual side to practise constantly.

Our Guides and Helpers in the Spirit World are like teachers; there to help us with our lessons. And like the teachers at school they will not move on to a new lesson until we have perfected the one we are working on after all, if a job's worth doing, it is worth doing well, so why not aim to be the best. Bear this in mind while practising your development and your Spiritual side will become a natural part of you and everything you do. This means that you as a person and your role as a Medium will have the fact that you are ordinary etched on your heart and soul. This will ensure that your ego does not take over and prevent jealousy of others having any place in your work. Believe it or not, once jealousy of another Medium that is doing better than you comes into play, it actually lowers your vibration so you will not be able to link with Spirits as effectively.

In my opinion, this is because we use the top three 'chakras' whilst linking to the Spirit World and the lower ones whilst using negative emotions such as jealousy and hate. "What are chakras?" you might ask. You can buy books which explain them but for now all you need to know is that we have eight main chakras:

1. The base chakra, which is red in colour and is found at the base of the spine.

2. The sacral plexus chakra, which is orange in colour and is found between the base of the spine and the navel.

3. The solar plexus chakra, which is yellow and is found at the navel.

4. The heart chakra, which is green is found in the centre of the chest near the heart.

5. The throat chakra, which is blue and found in the throat.

6. The brow chakra which is indigo is found at the bridge of the nose.

7. The crown chakra, which is violet and found at the crown of your head.

8. Last but by no means least is a pure white chakra which is situated about a foot above your head.

Chakras are part of the etheric body, not the physical. We actually use the throat, brow and crown chakras to help put us on the right vibration to be able to see, hear or sense the Spirit World around us. This is because we use them for opening our third eye.

Now I would like to introduce you to another exercise which will help you if you are interested in developing your gift. I call it a gift not because it makes us special but because, like any other talent which we are born with, this needs nurturing. After all, a concert pianist is not born playing great music but their ability is most definitely there, waiting to be developed and nurtured.

For this exercise you will need to be in a quiet, semi dark room or space, I say semi dark because you need to be able to see the glow of a torch. As well as a torch, you will need three circular pieces of coloured paper, one blue, one indigo and one violet, at least ten centimetres in diameter.

1. Decide who is going to be A and who is going be B.

2. Sit facing each other about two feet apart.

3. B now holds the blue circle in front of their chest, facing A.

4. A now focuses on the blue circle whilst trying to visualise the colour blue and nothing else.

5. B now shines the torch at A's throat, holding the torch above the blue circle which is still held in their other hand.

6. A (trying to ignore the torch beam), must concentrate their thoughts on the blue circle whilst picturing the colour blue being transferred into their throat. In the meantime, B counts slowly to a hundred in their head. On reaching a hundred the torch is switched off.

7. Now B exchanges the blue paper for the indigo. B repeats 4, 5 and 6 as before with the torch beam directed at the bridge of A's nose instead of the throat. A also needs to concentrate on the colour indigo going into

their brow chakra, which is just above the bridge of the nose.

8. Now follow the same steps using the violet circle, this time with the torch pointing as close as possible to the centre of the top of A's head.

9. B now holds all three coloured circles together, showing part of each colour. This time the torch needs to be shone directly onto the three pieces of paper not onto A.

10. A now pictures all three colours blending together to combine into one, stretching from A's throat, through to the brow, through the face to the top of the head.

11. It is now time for A to explain to B everything that has come into their thoughts during the process. This information does not have to be connected with the colours or to the experiment itself, although it should be recorded if it is.

12. Finally, repeat the whole process in reverse order. This is purely to allow both A and B to strengthen their abilities.

These exercises should not be rushed. In fact it is probably best to spend as long as you can on them. Repetition is always a good idea if we want our brain to become accustomed to acting out a set of rules which we put into it. After all, it is our brain that we use to link and communicate with the Spirit World.

Chapter Eight.

My Guides Working With Me

Talking of Guides working with me may sound out of context, so I will explain how these Guides work with me and one another to bring through Spirit communication. We all have what we call a 'Guardian Angel', who is with us from the moment we are conceived. Mine is, as I have said before, a Russian gentleman. I know him extremely well, having known him all my life. I guess you could say that I am one of the lucky ones because I do actually know him, unlike most of us who are never aware of our Guardian Angels. He is, however, just one of several Guides. As the leader, he stands just behind my right shoulder, towards the centre whilst two more Guides stand behind him on either side, placed in order of seniority. Behind those two are three more Guides, one in between them and one either side. Behind them stand another four Guides and behind them another five. To picture this, imagine an inverted triangle with fifteen people inside it rather like the snooker balls set up in the triangle for a snooker game.

These Guides work together as a team at all times when I am linking to the Spirit World. Without them I could not work as I do. People tend to think that Mediums like myself call up the dead and assume that this is why we are able to contact the Spirits for them when we are doing a sitting or a service. This is not true.

As soon as an appointment to see a Medium has been made, the Medium's Guides set about their job of contacting people in the Spirit World who might want to speak to the people concerned. The Guides know exactly who will be attending the service or sitting, sometimes before we know ourselves, so the friends and loved ones of those people can be notified in advance. Whether or not the Spirits concerned will get in touch will depend on whether they want to, as well as on a number of other factors.

These are guides who can find out any information from spirit if asked. Or anyone who has died.

Guides at this level ask spirit visitors questions, and convey the answers to us, if we are unsure.

It is usually at this level that friends or relatives who have passed guide us. This is to bring balance.

With us forever, but not all the time.

Constant help and direction.

Guardian Angel or Main Guide. This guide is the most powerful, and is with us all our life from the moment of conception.

For instance they might be busy at the specified time, perhaps being with someone else they are close to here on Earth. That other person might need them more than you do at that time. They have a lot of other things to do too so their non-appearance does not mean that they do not love you or wish to visit you. It probably just means that they are too busy or occupied elsewhere for the time being.

Sometimes even Mediums' lives become too emotional or difficult for them to be able to function normally, and that is when our Guides are really put to the test. A true professional carries on wherever possible because people have made an appointment to meet with their loved ones in the Spirit World. The people who have passed on have also made the effort to be there, so if the Medium does not turn up, he or she has let both sides down.

As you can imagine, it is not easy in times of trouble to carry on regardless, and that is when we need our Guides to come very close to us and take us over. This should make it doubly clear to you that there is nothing special about Mediums. They are ordinary people. Like me: in fact, as ordinary as they come and proud of it!

People tend to look at Mediums in one of two ways. They either put us on a pedestal, where we do not belong or they keep their distance because they think we are weird. It is a shame they do not grasp that the only reason they feel that way is that we are dealing with the unknown, and that every time part of the subject is explained properly it becomes normal, logical and ordinary. In other words, explanation removes the sense of weirdness or the spectacular.

One Monday afternoon, after attending a service at Sutton Coldfield Spiritualist Church, I arrived home by taxi, being too ill to drive at the time, to find Dawn and Dean in a panic because the house was on fire. My son had put a pie in the oven and forgotten it. The kitchen had caught fire and the fire brigade was on its way. Although the damage was quite bad, it was nothing compared to the one five years previously. The firemen saw to it that Dawn, Dean and I were taken to hospital in an ambulance because we were suffering from smoke inhalation.

They assured me that they would lock the place up safely when they had finished and, whilst we were gone they put the burnt out fridge, freezer and oven in the back yard in case they re-ignited. The floor had been burnt away, the kitchen cupboards were badly scorched, the door leading into the kitchen was half burnt and its glass shattered and everything, everywhere was blackened.

My other daughter, Toni, had been away visiting friends but had come home early, arriving before we got home from hospital to find the place in this terrible state. She panicked assuming that we had all been killed in the fire, so it must have been far worse for her than for the rest of us!

The one thing about this episode in our lives that served to amuse us all was the fact that the pie which Dean had placed frozen in the oven and which had consequently caused the fire, was still frozen. We all had a good laugh about this at a later time.

Later, when Toni had calmed down, she explained that when she had first walked into the house the door between the hallway and the lounge was open, which usually meant that someone was at home. She was also sure that she had heard someone walking about in the kitchen. That is until she entered and found all the mess. Even so, she insisted that she had also felt a breeze wafting through the lounge when she first went in.

I believe that the Spirits were keeping an eye open for us that day because Dawn had been asleep and Dean engrossed in the television when the fire broke out. Dawn had been woken up abruptly by what she thought was a nightmare and went into the kitchen for a drink of water when she, of course, discovered the fire. I also feel that it was Spirits in the house when Toni arrived home.

The following Christmas, my friend and I were in the middle of a service, and I was in the middle of a link, when all the lights went out, plunging us into total darkness. Evidently the Christmas tree lights had shorted out the electricity supply. Like a true professional, I decided to carry on in the hope that we would get the lights back soon. I dragged out the message I was in the process of relaying but soon realised that this was turning it into a private sitting so I needed to move on to the next link. I could not even see the congregation, apart from some vague shadowy figures in the front row, and they could not see me either so I asked the Spirits for help. On my Guides' instruction, I asked whether there was a lady seated one row from the back, next to the wall and described her appearance and clothing. There was no reply so I repeated the description again, no answer. "Have I got that wrong? Is there no one fitting that description in that seat?" I asked. Very quietly came back the reply, 'Yes it is me.' 'Thank goodness for that,' I said, ' I thought I had gone blind and deaf for a minute!' this raised the vibrations because it made everyone laugh and I continued the service.

At the end, by which time the lights had been fixed, I was having a cup of coffee when the lady who had received this message came up to me and explained that it was her first time ever in a Spiritualist church. She added, ' My friend talked me into coming but I was very nervous because another friend told me that you sit and hold hands in the dark. So when the lights went out it scared me. I did not know what to think! It also shocked me that you knew what I was wearing even though it was too dark to see. Then you shocked me even more by telling me things about my grandfather that I had never told anyone!'

We laughed at this and I told her not to listen to the rubbish that she had been told but to judge for herself. I also commented that, 'the only time I would sit and hold hands in the dark would be with my partner, and I am sure he would not mind.' This also got a laugh. That lady is a Spiritualist to this day and I am sure that this is a happy memory for everyone who was there that day.

Last year my husband and I were placed in a position where there was a power cut at Bangor Spiritualist Church just as the service was due to start. Luckily the president managed to find four candles and once again I was holding a Service in the dark, but at least on this occasion there was a little light to be had. The room where the service is held is quite wide and the four candles were placed one on the organ so that the organist could see to play. One candle was on our table so that we could be seen as clearly as possible and one at each side of the back of the room. I looked out into the semi darkness and said: "Is there anybody there?" This achieved what I had hoped for and lifted the vibrations by putting everyone at ease and making them laugh.

At a certain point in my life I began asking the Spirit World lots of questions. They always seem ready to answer, if not always straightaway. For me, it is important that things have some sort of logic to them, and I am a firm believer that if you can do something you can teach it. You need to find a common sense, ordinary way to tell people about your subject so that they too can understand its logic. This is what I set about doing next. I asked Mr R. how the Spirits link to us and he explained that it is by using our brains. That is when he gave me the instructions for this workshop, which is a good one for trainees to follow.

At first view this exercise might look quite difficult, but do not give up because it is easy once you get used to it! As I have already explained, our Guardian Angel stands behind our right shoulder in order to be in the best position in which to work with us during our communication. The very first part of our brain that Spirits need to connect with for sensing to begin is the subliminal part. This is situated just above and forward of the left ear. All Mediums use this part of the brain because all Mediums sense Spirits whilst linking, whether by seeing, hearing or feeling them or, like me, using all three.

At the first stage of linking we may get a thought into our head, for instance the name: 'Tom'. This name on its own is not much because all sorts of questions then pop into the Medium's head, and of course most of us could find a Tom somewhere in our lives, past or present. So this alone would not stand up as evidence. Then we might ask: "Is Tom dead or alive?" Good question! but one which would be difficult to answer at this stage if you did not know what you were doing. One of the first things that the would be Medium needs to learn is the difference between a thought and a subliminal message because, as I have said before, the golden rule is do not think whilst you link. As soon you begin to think you might change the whole message; thereby making a true message appear to be false. The only difference between the two concepts is that a thought is solid and takes time to form whereas a subliminal message is lighter and appears very quickly. It is only with practise that we can learn to tell the difference. It is also useful to know that a thought tends to stay with you and a subliminal message does not.

Now say, for instance that you have learnt to tell the difference and you know that the Spirits have indicated the name Tom. The next question has to be: "Is Tom talking to me or am I just being told the name Tom?" This is very important because if you say: "I have got Tom here." and it turns out that Tom is still alive and well you have got it wrong. However, if you say instead: "They are talking about a Tom?"

This is a little better but it still does not establish for sure, if the Tom in question is here or there. Because you are only getting a sense, rather than a concrete thought, it is important to make sure that you have made a note of all the information available to you. If you are more aware of being back in the place in which you were standing when you received Tom's name, then he is alive. If, however, you are more aware of the Spirit side, Tom is in the Spirit World. Remember that you are only sure that the man you are talking to in Spirit is Tom if he says so. This is because even though you are certain that Tom is in the Spirit World you could be talking through an intermediary in the Spirit World.

If you then take the connection further into your brain you will begin to use the reflective part of your brain, which is situated on the opposite side of your head. This should help you to see a clear mental picture of anything that the Spirit World wants you to know about. I should point out that it will not always be the picture you expected to see. So do not be tempted to say what you had expected instead of what you are actually seeing. This, again, would change the information and make the message wrong despite the fact that the Spirit World has tried to communicate something correct. I say that you should get a clear picture in fact it sometimes looks like a photographic negative. You might say that is not exactly clear, but if you think about it, a negative contains just as much information, just as accurately as the finished print. To extend the metaphor, the difference between the two mental pictures is that the 'print' is easy for our eyes to see properly. The 'negative' on the other hand requires us to use an invisible eye, which is brought forward by love. In other words, if we care enough to pay proper attention we can see just as much, if not more, on a negative as we can on the finished photograph. Love and attention are all you need and do not forget that the Spirits are providing most of that love!

1 would like you to close your eyes for a moment and picture a beautiful golden stairwell stretched out in front of you. At the top are the people you love most and who have gone on to the Spirit side of life ahead of you. They are walking down those stairs smiling brightly. There are about thirty stairs and they have quickly descended twenty seven of them in anticipation of talking to you. However, having reached that far, they find that the bottom three steps are missing and they cannot finish their journey to you. All they are asking you to do is think of them with as much love as you can so that the three missing steps appear and you can connect. Their love was, after all, strong enough for them to negotiate the first twenty seven steps so it is not a lot to ask for you to return enough love for the last three.

The next stage of our brain, which is used whilst linking to the Spirit World, is the comparison part which is roughly in the centre of the head, on the edge of the left hand side. Assuming that you have already decided from the information you have received that Tom is in the Spirit World it is now time to work out whether the person you are communicating with is Tom himself. To do this you must sense this person in comparison with yourself. Are you sure that it is a man? If like me, you are female, you will soon learn that a man senses differently to a woman. Make that decision first: 'Yes. It is a man.' Ask yourself: "Is he taller or shorter than I am? "You might conclude that: 'He is slightly taller.' Remember that since you know your own height, so you now have an approximate idea of this mans height. I am five feet three and a half inches tall and this man feels as though he is about four or five inches taller. He is therefore about five feet eight inches tall.

The next question to ask yourself is: "Is he fatter or slimmer or about the same size as me?" You might then conclude that he is slimmer in the body except for the fact that is stomach is bigger. Now it is time to find out: 'Does this person have more or less hair than I do?' He has less in fact not as much at all. So I hope that you are beginning to see how much you can find out just by comparing that person with yourself. We have found out that the man visiting us from the Spirit World is a slimmish man who is a bit rotund around the middle and is about five foot eight inches tall with a fair amount of hair loss. Already we are beginning to build up a picture of the person to whom we are speaking.

Now is the time to ask inwardly: "Did Tom look like this?" You would be surprised how, at this point, if you are not communicating with Tom, you will be aware of another person, even if only for a moment. You now know whether or not you are talking to Tom. This information can all be gained in a matter of seconds and I assure you that as soon as you say one thing the person concerned will make you aware of the next. So the trick is to start talking and do not stop! After you have established all the information that you can from this point, which gives you a subjective 'negative film' image, it is time to use your brain's 'individuality' area, which is situated by the bridge of your nose. At this stage more complex information can be brought into play, referring to things you understand simply because of who you are. For example, if you are a mathematician you might receive mathematical information.

If on the other hand you had a bit of a mental block about maths, there would not be any point in the Spirits trying to pass you information you would not understand. Similarly, if you come from a large family, Spirits would know that you understand the issues involved in large families.

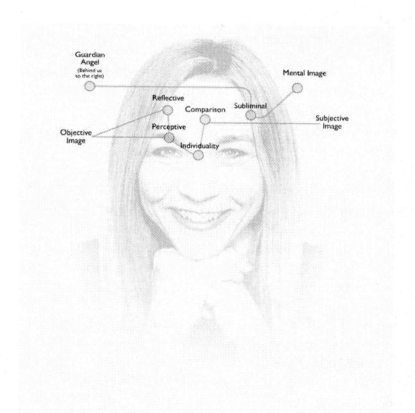

Brief description of how Spirit use our brain to communicate.

Workshop on different links to Spirit.

The class split into three groups, dependant on what colour stone they have got? Pink, Blue, or Green. This is done leaving a gap between each team. We now have a blue team, a green team and a pink team, who are separate from each other. A meditation takes place, making links through the brain. As the part of the brain is reached, that your group colour covers, the leader will say, for instance:

The blue team will stop listening now and concentrate on what Spirit, are trying to communicate to them. It is at this point that communication with the Spirit World should take place. The leader then brings the class back and asked them to sit together. Now asking each one in turn what colour bead they have, which is purely to allow them to know, who their message is for. This is defined by who has the bead of the same colour. After the first person's partner has been defined, they are then asked to give each other their message. The leader explains things as they go along giving help where it is needed. After which this is repeated with each couple until all have given their message. It is always with amazement that the people realise, that the person can understand their message from the Spirit World. This usually comes about because during this exercise they do not have time to think whilst they link.

One of the problems at this stage of linking with the Spirit World is the way in which it is misunderstood. There is a particular part of the brain, just above the right eye, that is essential in comprehending the information, which we receive. The trouble is that we do not make that connection and therefore do not fully understand what we are being told. However, having already stimulated the third eye (which is just above the bridge of your nose), you have reached the stage where you can see the Spirits objectively, especially if you look at things laterally using the reflective part of your brain again.

Seeing Spirits objectively is like seeing them as solid entities just like you would see people or objects. It is very important to use your brain in the right way, hence the importance of brain stimulating exercises to our Spiritual training. The workshop a few pages back will help in this, but it is no good on its own! You will need to practise what it suggests and meditate whilst you are doing so.

There is an exercise, which may help, when first starting out with stimulating different sections of your brain and that may help you to practise starting and stopping at different parts of the way. This is important in order to understand what you are feeling and why. You will find it better to work with a group, it teaches you discipline as well as giving you more people to practise on. As before, you need to meditate, running slowly through the links with the brain as shown in the workshop on how to use your brain,

At first you will find you can only pass on information you received during the meditation but eventually you should be able to link on further, giving information as you speak. Practise is the only way to build your confidence in yourself and in your Spiritual work.

Chapter Nine.

Are They Dead Or Alive?

Teaching my husband Mike to link with people on the Spirit side of life was a pleasure. He started off just sitting in on my sittings without saying anything. But soon he would occasionally interject the odd piece of information and, if the person who was having the sitting did not understand, I would tell him to go back for clarification. Of course, I would always let the person concerned know that if they were still baffled at the end of the sitting by anything that Mike had told them then I would sort it out for them!

People always thought that I was rather cruel when I kept on repeating, 'ok, go back and get some more.' In fact I was being cruel to be kind, as they say and the upshot was that I never had to sort it out for him!

One such incident in particular sticks in both of our minds. Whilst doing a sitting, Mike told the lady in question that he was aware of an old man who kept putting his head up the chimney. He had nothing else to mention but a pocket watch and a few other items like money…that kind of thing. Losing confidence, his commentary tailed off into the admission that: ' I know this sounds mad, I must be getting it wrong!'

The lady laughed and explained that he was not mad at all. In fact he was quite right. When her grandfather died, his wife and family could not find his things. They searched and searched until one day her grandmother remembered that he was always messing about up the chimney breast, being unused, the hearth was never hot. Acting immediately on this vital piece of information they looked up the chimney and found his secret hidey hole a loose brick, behind which was revealed grandfather's pocket watch, cash and a number of other sundry items. So you see, you should never discount what you are told, no matter how silly it sounds, because the Spirit World always have a good reason for bringing a piece of information through. It usually makes sense to the person receiving the sitting very quickly. Next to 'Is it me or Spirit?' I believe one of the hardest things to learn has to be: 'Is this person whom Spirits are telling me about dead or alive?'

Once again, this takes a lot of practise. Do not forget, though, what I said earlier, you can learn to sense whether they are with you in the here and now or in spirit. For people like Mike who mainly sense the Spirit World it is slightly harder because they only see a picture within their mind rather than a Spirit person standing in the room they are in.

One day, a lady was referred to me by someone at the local hospital. All I knew about her was that either she had just lost someone close to her or they were dying of cancer at the time, but I was not told how that person was related to her or where the cancer was. On the Monday morning of the week in which I was due to see her I noticed that I had put her name in the diary twice, on two consecutive days. I had never made this mistake before, yet when I looked for her telephone number so that I could check, which was the correct entry I found that I had made another mistake. I had neglected to take her number! And she lived about an hours drive away. Again, this was the kind of mistake I never made.

I thought about the problem and discussed it with my husband. We decided that we would have to go to see her on the first night and, if it turned out that she was expecting us the following night, we would just have to do the trip all over again! So we set off that evening hoping we had got the right night, if not it was a consid-erable waste of time and fuel! An hour later, we pulled up outside the address we had been given. I looked towards the house and could see a lady standing in the window crying and fiddling with something in her hand. I was a bit apprehensive knocking on the door, not being sure whether I was supposed to be there or not. The lady I had seen in the window answered the door looking a little surprised. "Yes? Can I help you?" she enquired.

Now I knew we had the wrong day, because surely she would have guessed who we were if she had been expecting us. So I smiled and replied, "we are Jean and Michael Kelford. We are Mediums and we have an appointment with you." Her puzzled look said it all, but anyway she answered, "It is not today. It is next month!" This really surprised us we were half expecting to be a day early but not a month!

"Are you sure?" I replied, "we had the appointment written down twice, which is unusual, in fact it never happens. But we have nothing in the diary for this time next month. This never happens!" "Yes, look I will fetch my letter from the hospital," she said, looking slightly flustered as she walked off towards the kitchen. Sure enough the letter gave that day's date but for the following month. I apologised for the mix-up and said we would return next month. But she said that since we were there, we might as well do the sitting now.

Her young son had died recently after suffering with bone cancer and she was delighted when he came through with a lot of information about himself, his mum and dad and other family members. She told us that the session had helped her a great deal and added, "Can I tell you something?" "Of course you can, anything," I replied without hesitation. She smiled a beautiful smile that made you feel sad that she had so little reason to smile at the time. "You know when you arrived tonight?" "Yes. You were in the window" I replied, smiling reassuringly. She smiled again and began, hesitantly:

"I had a bottle of pills in my hand and I had just said out loud to my son, if it is possible for you to hear me and you do not want me to kill myself to be with you then give me a sign. At that precise moment, your car pulled up outside and you have given me some beautiful proof that my son is all right. And I take this to be his sign because of the misunderstanding about the date. You arrived at exactly the right moment to save my life thank you both very much!"

Both Mike and I felt very humble as I explained to her that she should not thank us but her son in the Spirit World for answering her prayer in a way which she could not doubt. Then I added, "He wants you to carry on with your life and be as happy as you can because he loves you and does not want to be responsible for making you unhappy. Please try for him. You will never forget him or stop missing him but I promise you that with time the sadness that you feel now will be anaesthetised. When that happens you will be able to carry on with your life, safe in the knowledge that one day you will meet him again and you will all be together."

I do not think we will ever forget that day. You would think that when you link to Spirit every day like we do, they would not be able to surprise you any more. Just when you start thinking this, they come up with something like this, totally out of the blue. And to say that they shock us is probably the biggest understatement that we will ever make.

During that same sitting, Mike described a man in the Spirit World who had a beard, rode a bike and worked for the railway. The lady and her husband, who had since arrived home, tried very hard to place him and could not, until I said to Mike, "Are you sure he is in the Spirit World?" Before he could answer, the lady's husband said, "We can think of a man like that, my uncle but he is still alive." "Has he been off-colour recently," I asked, "because Spirit are sending him healing."

He seemed quite excited by this because his uncle had only told him that morning that he was feeling unwell. We all laughed about the fact that Mike had put his uncle in the Spirit World before his time. I explained that he should have known he was still alive by the way that he was presented to Mike; that is, as being in the here and now. This was the last time Mike told anyone that someone was dead when in fact they were still alive!

As Chris and I were going through the chapter headings of this book to ensure that the pages on the content page were correct, we came to chapter nine's heading which is entitled 'Are They Dead or Alive?' when suddenly the words 'Chapter Nine' jumped as if on their own to the left of the page from the centre of the page where they should be. Interesting considering the title of the chapter don't you think?

Chapter Ten.

Learning To Let Go

After my stepdaughter Jenny had been in the Spirit World for almost a year, she realised what a bad state her dad was in. Her face had appeared in one of our wedding photographs, which was a giant step forward for Mike into believing that there is no death and that Jenny really is all right. Unfortunately, Toni had the photos and they were in her car when it was stolen. Sadly, when the car was finally recovered, the photos were gone. Mike was so upset about losing this picture of Jenny; this proof that she was still alive, that he had a nervous breakdown.

Quite often, when the face of someone who is in Spirit appears on a photograph, it does not show up when you take another print from the same negative. On this occasion, though, it did! Not quite as clear as before, but perfectly discernible all the same.

One of the hardest things for us to do is to let someone we love go when they have passed over to the Spirit World. This does not mean that you cannot think about them any more, in fact quite the opposite. You should think of them and talk to them every day. By talk to them, I do not mean speaking out loud because that is not necessary. They communicate with telepathy (reading the mind) as Mediums do when they pass messages to you from the Spirits. The Spirits can read every thought, they know when you are thinking about them and why!

I should say at this point that Mediums only read the minds of people in the Spirit World, not those of people here. It is a good idea to try to Sense whether Spirits are near at hand whilst exercising to open our third eye. Once you have trained yourself to open your third eye properly you will also pick up an image of the person with whom you are communicating. As I have said before, your third eye is found just above the bridge of your nose.

Try the following exercise regularly, do it sitting down or lying down, with your eyes closed and pretending to be cross-eyed. In other words, look at the bridge of your nose with both eyes while relaxing with eyes closed. At first, most people find that although it is dark (because their eyes are shut), they can see a patch of fog or dim light within the darkness around the bridge of their nose where they're concentrating their vision. This is because they are seeing the glow of the bright lights that shine out of the Spirit World. Whilst I am linking to Spirits from the rostrum, I can only see the person in the congregation for whom I am linking and the Spirits. Everything else is in a light blue mist and that is all I can see.

The vortex of energy mentioned in the last exercise is what created that blue haze. If everything else around you is in a mist so that you cannot see it, you will concentrate much more effectively on the things that you can see. It is just like when you are driving a car in the fog. You concentrate on what is in front of you to avoid hitting anything because you cannot see anything else. People often apologise for a noise or disturbance during a service. But the truth is that when you are linking properly with the Spirit World you do not see or hear anything else. You are only aware of this mist, the person with whom you are speaking and the people in Spirit.

Workshop on opening the third eye.

Close your eyes and picture three discs central to your face as in the picture below.

These discs are in an inverted triangle.

The disc over the mouth is blue.

The disc over the right eye is indigo.

The disc over the left eye is violet.

Now picture all three discs are spinning clockwise. However, you need to remember that because they are within you they are in reverse order.

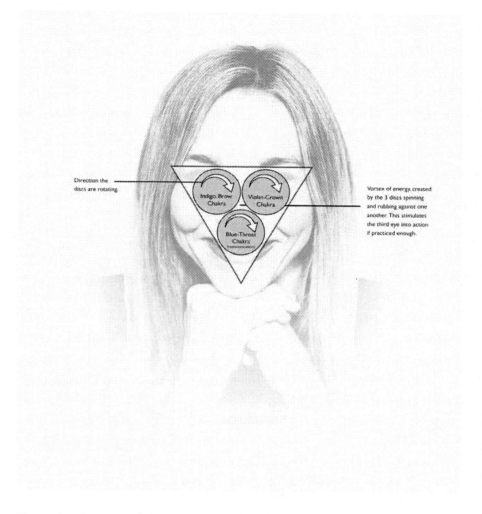

To make this easy, imagine these discs spinning in the direction of your left ear or imagine a clock covering your face with the dial facing outwards with its fingers working normally.

As they spin they will create a vortex of energy in the small triangle in the centre of these discs. This is caused by friction as the three discs rub together where they connect to each other. Now try to picture the small central triangle. This will stimulate the third eye because the part of your brain that controls it will be gently stimulated. This will in time cause your third eye to operate effectively.

Workshop on linking using the third eye.

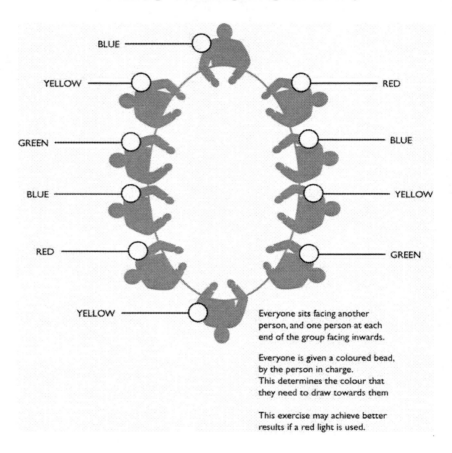

BLUE

YELLOW — RED

GREEN — BLUE

BLUE — YELLOW

RED — GREEN

YELLOW

Everyone sits facing another person, and one person at each end of the group facing inwards.

Everyone is given a coloured bead, by the person in charge. This determines the colour that they need to draw towards them

This exercise may achieve better results if a red light is used.

First of all we close our eyes and follow a meditation to open our third eye. This is done following the principle below.

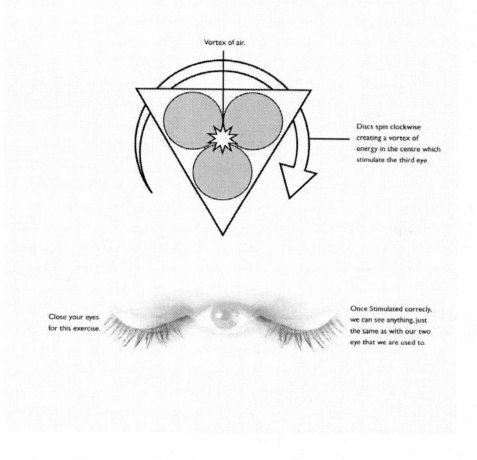

Vortex of air.

Discs spin clockwise creating a vortex of energy in the centre which stimulate the third eye.

Close your eyes for this exercise.

Once Stimulated correctly, we can see anything, just the same as with our two eye that we are used to.

Everyone now opens their eyes and looks at the person opposite, at the same time concentrating their eyes towards the bridge of their nose, this will also stimulate their third eye. They now must think of the colours being used in the group. For example, in the group above, the colours are Red, Blue, Yellow, and Green, therefore, they must think about these four colours.

Next we close our eyes again, asking Spirit where the colour is, that is the same one that we are holding. Sometimes there is a flash of colour leading to that person, or they may be just drawn to someone, or if they are lucky they will be told a name.

Everybody now knows, who they think their message is for, therefore they should all close their eyes again for a short meditation on stimulating the third eye by picturing their Guide gently massaging the bridge of their nose. They will then be left for a moment to gain any information they See, Hear, or Sense, from the Spirit World.

On opening their eyes everyone should be observant of anything they might See, Hear, or Sense, to add to their communication. It is now time for everyone to exchange messages, but of cause they must be aware that two people at the ends of the group, have duplicate colours to someone within the group, therefore, may have a message from their loved ones in Spirit, this could create a cross link?

One evening whilst I was doing a service with an excellent psychic artist called Sue Wood, a close friend of mine and her friend arrived late after getting lost. I was in the middle of a link when they came in and, although they had to walk right down the aisle in front of me, I did not see them. It was only as I stopped between links that I noticed her sitting there.

Whenever I talk to my family about the Spirit World and my previous knowledge of it, they realise why certain things happened in my past. My brother Keith always makes me laugh when the subject comes up. He will tell me all about an incident that has happened to him in connection with someone who is in Spirit and I tell him, "I am not surprised that you can do it. Mediumistic ability is in the genes!"

"I know, Sis. That is why I do not wear them!" is always his reply. It is just fear of the unknown, so I just laugh it off! I have Spiritualism to thank for having met two very special people in my life: Grace and Sue I met this mother and daughter one day when they were part of the congregation for one of my nervous early appearances on the rostrum. Grace looked up at me and beamed a beautiful smile at me, she could see how nervous I was, and that the link I was bringing through at the time was making me very emotional. Her smile helped me a great deal. I will always remember it as one of those acts of kindness that can take you forward in life. It certainly did that for me! It was a very special act from a very special lady who always smiles from the inside.

The love that she gave to a stranger that afternoon was, and is, exactly the kind of love the Spirits need to connect with us. I am very happy that this stranger became a friend. Sue has also become an invaluable friend and is now well on her way to becoming a brilliant Medium. She says that she wants to be as good as me. I hope with all my heart that she becomes a lot better because the Spirit World needs good Mediums and I have every faith that Sue will continue developing her links with the Spirits in the very special way that she has begun. Susan Bragg is definitely a name for people to look out for in the future!

She has come on in leaps and bounds since the day I suggested that she join my development class. I thought she would make a very good Medium but she was not so sure:

"Because I have had a lot of sittings from you and you have never been wrong I trust you, but I think you are wrong this time!" I corrected her, pointing out that it was not me that was always right. It was the Spirits. Without them I would not be able to tell her, or anybody else, anything! I also assured her that they were not wrong this time. Since she could not link at all when she first started the class she is actually doing exceptionally well. She is already practising sittings on her friends and anyone else who will let her, just as I had done in my early days! In fact she made her debut in November (2001) at one of the churches with Mike and I! She was extremely good as I suspected she would be.

This came about when Sue's plan to get Mike on the rostrum backfired. One Sunday, Sue and another student friend called Caroline came to church with us to observe my work. The two girls went into the church to save seats for themselves and Mike in the congregation. Sue was chatting to the booking secretary, telling her that she should try getting Mike up on the rostrum because he is very good. She said this because the preceding year, whilst staying with friends in Newtown, Wales, I took the service at the local church and Kay, our hostess, suggested that Mike went up on the rostrum. He refused at first, despite the fact that he is a brilliant Medium in his own right these days. He was quite happy to give sittings to anyone in private but, like all of us, he was still intimidated by the exposure of the rostrum.

"Why don't you just go and sit on the rostrum to see what it feels like? You do not have to actually do anything." said Kay. "All right then - but I am not going to do anything," Mike replied with conviction. "That is what he thinks!" interjected Mr R. Obviously I was the only one to hear this last comment, so I just smiled to myself. Once we came to the part of the service that called on the Medium to give proof of survival I gave some of the evidence and then turned to Mike. "Have you got anything?" I enquired. Mike met my eyes, went red and said, "Yes, I will have a go." He got up and gave messages from the Spirit World to three people from the congregation, all of which were understood and taken on board. I was so proud of him!

The next weekend, in Belfast, he turned to me and said, "You do the morning service and I will see if they are aggressive. If not, I will do the evening service with you." The morning service went really well, so he agreed that he was on in the evening one. I should explain that some congregations are more difficult to work with than others, Mike was just checking that these people were not going to be difficult deliberately. That does happen sometimes!

Tragically, Mike suffered a heart attack that very afternoon and ended up in hospital instead of on the rostrum. He had not been on a rostrum since. Sue had asked the booking secretary not to repeat to us her suggestion that Mike mounted the rostrum, but she did. Mike's response was "she can talk, she is very good herself...She should go up." The booking secretary turned to me and gave permission for them both to go up with me. I said that it was not fair to expect them both to do so at such short notice. Could they instead come up the next time I was due at the church, in November. She agreed, but Mike panicked and said he would not. "Okay then, can I bring Sue and another student?" I answered. "Okay, I will do it." Mike exclaimed before she could reply. "You are booked, came her swift response!" I had no idea why he had changed his mind, so I asked him. "If Sue got onto the rostrum before me I would never live it down!" he chuckled. I joined the laughter but Sue was not quite so confident when she found out. In the end, though, she did agree to pluck up her courage and go on like a true professional!

I will always be proud of Sue both as a friend and as student or any of my students as long as they do their best in their work with Spirit. She has not been on the rostrum again YET!! However, she does practise sittings whenever she can and is doing really well. She works for Spirit like a true professional already and I know that you will see more of her, especially if I have a say in it.

Mediums are very important to the Spirit World because without them Spirit could not communicate to their loved ones whom they have left behind, accept for on rare occasions when their loved ones are able to link personally.

My stepdaughter, Jenny who as I have already said is in the Spirit World, really enjoys making a link to people still here. She learnt the lesson, more or less straight away that it was easier for her to make a link to someone here by using the energy that water provides.

She in fact made her first link back to me whilst I was in the bathroom and she had only been passed to the Spirit side of life for two hours. Her appearance came as quite a surprise to me because of the fact that I was preoccupied with the grief that I was feeling at the time.

As I am writing this, Jenny is here and wants to help. Since going to the Spirit World, she has brought two poems through before, to help people here to deal with their grief. This is yet another poem that she wants people to hear:

Coming Home.

I opened my eyes to the brightest light
The most wonderful feeling of peace, and love,
It is not how you would think there was not a fight,
You are just there with the angels above.

I was not alone, and I was not afraid,
There were beautiful colours and flowers,
I would have been in a lot of pain if I had stayed,
Still unaware of my strengths and my powers.

I met my grandmother, and family once more,
I also met my sister, and my friends,
Today life began for me it was the opening of the door
It definitely is not where life ends.

When I was alive, I wanted to fly,
I would have given anything for some wings,
If I had known then, I would have wanted to die,
Because death as given me these things.

After saying hello to people I knew,
And also to those I did not,
I looked around at the beautiful view,
The pain in my life, all forgot.

Then came the time when I could visit again,
And went to visit Jean and my dad,
She said Spirit worked well by water, not meaning rain,
So when she came to the loo, I was glad.

I explained I was happy, and had learnt how to fly,
So she could explain this, to my dad.
People were alive, and did not really die,
So the people we love should never be sad.

The place we live is a wonderful place of peace,
But we need your love to help us to visit you there,
Our love for you can only increase,
For this is the best way, to show how you care.

To light up your heart, reach within to your love,
Then the shadows in your heart will brighten,
As the night shines bright with the stars up above,
I also shine to try to help your heart lighten,

I am surrounded in Love, and feel at home in Spirit,
My pain and heartache has gone away,
Our love together will help me to visit,
So please send me a light every day.

Chapter Eleven.

Ghostly Experiences

One of the things I like most about being a Medium is that you can meet many new people and also help your fellow man even if your health is not too good, like mine. Clearing ghosts scares many people but it is just part of everyday life for Mediums like myself. If there is a problem with ghost activity we are happy to go along and try to solve it. What a lot of people do not understand is that, ghost activity, is generally created by a Spirit who has got lost and failed to make the transition to the Spirit side of life as they were supposed to.

Sometimes however, ghostly experiences come about just so that Spirit can lead us onto the right pathway in life. For instance they know that it is essential that we should meet certain people to take us forward in the right direction. The next true story is one of those occasions.

On 21st September 2002, I was at Ottakar's book shop in Walsall Town Centre, signing copies of my first book 'Oblivious but true' when a lady came into the shop and told me that she had already bought and read my book and had found it very interesting so when she heard that I would be in Walsall where they lived her daughter had asked if she would call in and ask me if I do private readings. I gave the lady my telephone number which I wrote on the back of a bag containing a birthday card she had just bought from the card shop because I did not have any of my business cards with me on that day.

A few days later I returned home to find a telephone message on my answer machine enquiring about sittings. Before I had time to react to this message my telephone rang and on answering it I was asked if I could do anything to help because the young lady on the other end of the telephone was concerned about ghost activity in their home. She was afraid and did not know what to do. I assured her that I would probably be able to help but said that I was leaving the country the next day to work in Spain for three weeks. I promised however, that I would ask Spirit to try to calm things down with the Spirit activity in their home until I returned from Spain when I would visit their home to try and alleviate the problem for them.

Three weeks later the day after my return home, my husband and I went to the family's home. It turned out to be the home of the lady whom I had given my telephone number to on her birthday card bag. Not only was we able to help with the ghost activity but the activity had calmed down from the day the daughter spoke to me on the telephone and started up again three weeks later the day before my visit. The lady of the house, who turned out to be my now very good friend Chris, explained to me that a few weeks before she first met me in the Walsall book shop she had been shopping in Sutton Coldfield Town Centre. She went on to explain that she was passing Ottakar's book shop one Saturday when she decided that she would go in and have a look at the books in the Mind, Body, and Spirit section of the shop. As she looked through the books she picked three or four different ones up which she held in her hand whilst trying to decide which one to buy. She was drawn to my book so decided to buy it and took it home to read.

A couple of weeks later Chris went into Ottakar's book shop in Walsall to order a book written by another Medium that she wanted to buy. Whilst in there the lady serving behind the counter told her that there was a Medium Author coming into the shop to do a book signing session soon and she should look out for the details which would be advertised in the shop soon. The following week Chris once again called into the book shop to buy a book for her husband. Whilst in there she was told that there would be a Medium in the shop on 21st September at twelve am. She said that if Chris waited she would fetch the book and tell her the Author's name. As soon as Chris saw the book that the young lady had fetched to show her, she realised that she had already bought and read the book which was mine. Once at home she told her daughter 'who is a very special young lady' about my forthcoming visit to Walsall. Her daughter asked if she was calling in to see me and Chris answered that she did not know because she was due to visit Holland with her husband and was due back the day before I would be at the bookshop so was not sure whether she would feel like going into Walsall the day after travelling.

The day came round when I would appear at the Walsall book shop and Chris' daughter asked her mum once again if she would call in and ask if I do sittings. Chris told her daughter that if she was still in Walsall at twelve am and I was on time then she would call in and speak to me. But she did not feel that I would be there on time because she felt that these things never started punctually. She finished her shopping at approximately ten past twelve and decided to wonder down to the bookshop but did not expect me to be there. I however, am always punctual where possible and was already seated talking to people when she walked into the shop. There were in fact two ladies in front of her in the queue so she waited to speak to me. This was to be the start of an extremely good friendship between Chris, Mike and myself. A friendship that Spirit had brought about for many reasons including the fact that Chris was to develop her Spiritual gifts, which she had always had but been unaware of to a certain degree.

It was my pleasure to be introduced to and get to know a special couple called Nicola and Ivan who live in Las Vegas, America. At first this was through conversations via the telephone, after which I had the privilege of meeting them at their home in the USA.

Nicola tends to have a catch phrase when talking to me which is 'Hello Mamma Jean, I have a question'. This always creates a laugh because the day that she does not have a question will cause me to worry.

Questions are a good thing for anyone who wishes to learn any topic, but especially when learning Spiritual Development as Nicola is and progressing extremely well. Nicola is a brilliant student because she takes advice and also criticism on board and acts upon it when necessary. You do need to do this if you would like to develop your Spiritual gifts.

Nicola and Ivan will be visiting England where she was born in the not too distant future, and when they do it will be my privilege to introduce her to working with Spirit from the rostrum alongside me as she as asked. She already works one to one with people, giving readings from Spirit and the rostrum is inevitably the next step for which she is more than ready and capable of taking. I am sure that she will rise very well to the occasion.

Chris' mum Ethel is a very special lady who has been aware of Spirit to some degree for most of her life. Recently she sadly lost her second partner to Spirit. Chris' dad had passed four years earlier.

In July of last year Ethel' partner Charles decided out of the blue that instead of celebrating his eightieth birthday in September when he became eighty, he and Ethel should celebrate their birthdays together on the tenth of July which is her birthday. So they set about arranging a party for that night which I was privileged to attend. It was a fantastic night and everyone there had a great time especially Charles and Ethel.

Unfortunately it was only to be a couple of weeks later that Charles past suddenly to Spirit after a very short illness. Chris, and Ethel and I came back from the hospital that evening feeling a bit low because of losing such a good and special man from our lives. Chris made teas for herself and her mum and of course coffee for me. 'Anyone who knows me knows that I only drink decaf coffee and lots of it.' And we sat discussing Charles, his life and of course his sudden death as people do when someone first passes to Spirit.

Ethel stated that she wondered when Charles would put in an appearance from Spirit. As she said this I suddenly became aware that Charles had joined us and was in the room. He approached us from my left and I quickly told Ethel and Chris that he was there, when at that point he reached out his arm and knocked the flowers which were in a vase on the coffee table in front of us. They swayed wildly from side to side and I retorted can you see that!

Chris was seated on my right next to me on the settee, and Ethel was seated on an armchair to Chris' right facing the end of the table. Chris became very excited straight away because she could see the flowers shaking about which she knew they could not do on their own, even though she could not see Charles himself like I could. Sadly that time Ethel had missed it but she was really pleased anyway because it showed that he had arrived home safe and reappeared within an hour or so of passing to Spirit. This was to be the first of many appearances that Charles would make which is not surprising considering he is a very kind and Spiritual man.

A couple of weeks later Ethel decided to use up the film in the camera so that she could have the photographs which were taken at their party developed. As she was taking photographs from her kitchen the camera went off with a sudden flash and took a picture of the kitchen door in Ethel's bungalow. Once the pictures were developed we were all surprised to see that in the centre of what is a brown door there was what looked like a shiny patch. In this shiny patch you could clearly see faces so we put the photograph onto the computer to enlarge it and to our amazement you could clearly see that one of the faces was definitely Charles' face.

As I explained before, Ethel is exceptionally psychic therefore she is capable of taking photographs of those in the Spirit world because that is what it takes to make the energy strong enough for Spirit to show themselves. If you are in doubt about Spirit, then seeing their image appear on a photograph that is taken after they have died goes part way to convincing you that there is no death.

146

Being a Medium has some very exciting and memorable moments, but it also has some funny or unusual ones that we will never forget.

I met and became friends with a very special and Spiritual young lady called Simone Roth Bryce. This is a very Spiritual and unusual true story which Simone approached me about.

Simone and a gentleman called Paul went on a travelling holiday sight seeing around New Zealand. Paul was visiting the country for six months and Simone met up with him for the three weeks whilst she was out there. The couple hired a car and started their sight seeing in Christchurch after which they travelled to a small town called Akaroa. It was during this visit that they went for a walk through some woods and up a hillside, where they came across a cemetery.

Because Simone loves cemeteries, they decided to go in and have a look around. She read lots of headstones, until one headstone seemed to jump out at her. This headstone stuck in her memory it was the grave of a lady called Jean Mckillop. The only other thing that she remembered about Jean was that she passed to Spirit at 59 years of age.

Simone remembers vividly that she constantly spoke to Paul about this lady and could not get her out of her mind. So that night she decided to write a poem about Jean Mckillop, in her memory. Here is the poem.

Jean Mckillop.

Jean Mckillop a lady that was,
But can no longer be seen,
She now lies in the ground,
Under a big pine tree.

Her headstone is broken,
The wording is faint,
It says she died at fifty nine,
Yet the message is still quaint.

It says not how she lived,
Or how that she became to be,
A lady of such mystery,
Lying quiet underneath that big pine tree.

Sleep now Angel,
Your work here is now done,
Its time to lie and rest,
Lie back, feel the warmth from the sun.

At night the stars will shine,
And the moon will last its spell,
Spirits stir and become lively,
And it will be your time to tell.

Your company will be accepted,
By the Spirits that lie with thee,
There'll be many a story told,
Underneath, that big pine tree.

The tree will cast its shadows,
The branches they will sway,
And if you listen closely,
It's as if the breeze has something to say.

It's the story of Jean Mckillop,
And the friends that she has made,
There is something quite mysterious,
About where you're finally laid.

So when your time is running out,
And a last breath you finally take,
The last breath should be, that a big pine tree,
Shelters your resting place.

By Simone Roth Brice.

Simone says that Akaroa is a beautiful town that she nicknamed 'wish town' because there were lots of little 'fairy wishes' (plants) flying around in the air. The ones many people used to catch as children and make wishes.

After travelling for three weeks, Simone and Paul returned to Akaroa for the last two nights of their stay in New Zealand. This was because Simone loved it there so much and because she had not stopped talking about Jean Mckillop since their first visit to the graveyard.

The couple spent these evenings in a bed and breakfast and as they entered the room Simone noticed a book on the coffee table called:

'A Thousand Things To Do And See Before You Die.'

This was the very book that Simone had been reading in London before leaving for New Zealand.

A man called Barry who owned the bed and breakfast where Simone and Paul were staying for those last two nights, showed the couple around his garden. In this garden were mirrors, which caught Simone's attention because her uncle's garden in London has mirrors in it. Yet she had never seen this anywhere else.

Simone says that she did not know why Jean Mckillop had such an effect on her. A big enough effect to inspire her to write the above poem about a lady whom she had never met or so she thought!! That is until she came to see me for a reading and it became apparent that Jean Mckillop is one of Simone's Guides in the Spirit world.

Simone thanked me but my thanks and love, go to her a very special person whom I am proud to know and call a friend. I know that she intends to find out more about her Spirit Guide Jean Mckillop, and will spend large parts of her time in New Zealand where she effectively heard the call of Spirit.

I am sure that you will agree that once again this is proof of coincidence being God and the Spirit World trying to have a quiet word with Simone who is now a very large step further on her Spiritual pathway. Good luck Simone, on your travels both material and Spiritual and many thanks for sharing your wonderful experiences and new found talents for Spirit linking, and poetry with us.

Whilst conducting a service in a Spiritualist Church recently, a young gentleman in his late thirties came through to speak to his mother. He went on to say that he had been bludgeoned around the head and shoulders and had also been stabbed several times. He described blood bubbles coming up his throat and choking him. He told me to tell his mum that he was sorry for all the distress that he had caused her through his life and subsequent death. He was extremely emotional, as you would imagine, and gave information about people involved in his own lifestyle. For obvious reasons I do not wish to divulge all the details, but he did say, "Tell Mum, it is tomorrow and I will be there."

At this point in time his family could not understand what he meant. However, the following morning it was announced on television that, two men had been arrested in connection with the murder and would appear in court that morning. This was obviously what he had been trying to tell the family and to reassure them that he would also be there. He wanted his family to know that he was at last in peace and to say, "Mum I love you, and I really am sorry. Do not worry about me, I am okay, and at peace."

Anyone who wants to develop their Mediumship should remember that they are in charge of their own body and brain at all times, so they should only allow Spirit the amount of access that they are happy with. It is also important to accept that strength of mind and connecting with the Spirit World are two different things.

For me, things that go bump in the night could never be scary because they are normal for me. I could never be afraid of Mr R and would be terribly worried if he was not on the stairs, alone or in company, when I went to the bathroom at night.

Everyone is psychic to some degree but not everyone can become a Medium. You can, however, help your own life and those of people around you to go more smoothly by developing the psychic powers you have. Practise, practise and more practise is the answer. It helped me and I assure you that it will help you. I wish you all the best of luck on your path to Spiritual development. And remember, the thing to keep in your head is: "I can. And I will." Then, I assure you, you will have a chance of it happening for you just as it did for me.

Chapter Twelve.

The Man Up The Loft.

Both the sound of rustling and the loud laughter booming down from upstairs were very common sounds to me. I had been aware of them many times during my lifetime, yet I was still uncertain of why they occurred. One day however, whilst my sister Hazel and my niece Mikaela were staying with me, Hazel was about to go upstairs when she heard a rustling sound emanating from the wall and rushed back into the lounge to inform me about it. After investigation I assured her that I did not know any more about the noises than she did. She however, would not go upstairs to the toilet alone just in case, and neither would the others!! We all decided to go up together to visit the bathroom before leaving the house to visit our mother. When we all went upstairs, I am sure that I was the only one who looked up towards the loft hatch, I knew beyond a shadow of a doubt that the noises were coming from there. However, it was not until this occasion took place that I realised, the rustling sound in the wallpaper always linked with the man in the loft's appearance, of either body or sound.

I decided not to say anything at that moment, because I did not want to scare my children or my niece, and I knew that at that point in time Hazel would be more afraid than they were. Therefore, it was not the time for honesty about someone who lived in, and as part of a world that most people could not see and usually chose to believe did not exist. I had always been bought up to believe that silence is golden, and working with Spirit brings about a silence all of its own. This helps to sharpen any sounds that Spirit produce. I had always had the ability to disappear mentally into this silence and pick up connective pieces of information from and about the person here whilst also connecting to the Spirit side of life.

As we stood in the hall that day listening to the rustling noise, I could also hear whispered voices trailing off the sounds from the wall, and connecting to the change of vibration that was coming from my sister. She was obviously a little afraid and I was picking this up from her vibration.

I believe that many people in my position believe that they are using telepathy at times like these and would think that I was in fact reading Hazel's mind. However, I know that what was actually happening was that my psychic powers allowed me to read the vibration that she was giving off and then with the help of Mr R, who translated the vibration to me. Yes I did know what she was thinking, although not because I was reading her mind, but due to the fact that I was reading her vibration and the changes it brought. This in turn made me raise my vibration high enough for the Spirit World to fill in the gaps.

Spirit, were expressing concern about my sister at that time, meaning that her presence created an upsurge in the psychic energy within my home. The man up the loft understood my sister's vibration as well as he did my own, because of the fact that she was born in the same house that I was born in, being the house where his existence as a Spirit visitor began, due to the fact that he used to live and work on or close to the land where our childhood home was built. On that day he was trying to demonstrate that he was available to help if his help was required. It was to be soon after that when I would find out exactly who he was and why he was following me from house to house, and from loft to loft. I am sure that Hazel does not realise how much her visit helped my 'development in knowledge of Spirit communication' to this day. Yet it was from this visit that I moved forward in my quest for knowledge of the Spirit side of life, and why I was able to begin to communicate with these dead people so easily.

It was to be a few weeks later after Hazel had returned to her own home that I decided it was time once more to investigate the visitor from the loft. As I have said before, I would often be aware of Spirit visitors whilst either in the bathroom or toilet. It was a Saturday night and the children were finally in bed and asleep, therefore all was quiet. I decided to spend some time relaxing in the bath, which meant that I would be in the water until it became cold. After about ten minutes of lying relaxing in the peace and quiet of the water, with my eyes closed, I became aware of the rustling sound that we had heard a few weeks earlier. Then however, it had been coming from out on the stairwell, whereas this time the noise was coming from the bathroom walls and landing ceiling. I opened my eyes and called: "Dawn, Dean, Toni, is that you?" These are the names of my three children whom were the only other people in the house at that time. A silence came back apart from the rustling sound as before.

Although I thought that maybe the rustling was due to the steam from the bath making the wallpaper shrink where it was pasted to the wall. I was now sitting bolt upright in the bath, listening intensely for any sounds apart from the rustling. Nothing! At that point I noticed that Mr R was standing on the landing with his arms folded looking up towards the ceiling. He had a very serious expression on his face. I naturally followed his stare, with a curiosity that helps if someone wants to gain information from the dead. I was amazed by what I saw next. It was as though a round television screen had appeared in the ceiling above me. The scenes that I was watching were in full colour. These scenes did, however, move very quickly as they unfolded from one picture to the next just as though someone had pressed fast forward on a video machine. I was fascinated and suddenly became aware that I was not afraid, just curious as to what I was seeing, and why was I seeing it? It was at this moment that the old man whose face had appeared from up the loft of each home that I had been in since childhood became very clear. His eyes were small and beady, and I thought that he looked tired. His hair was grey and scruffy and unkempt in appearance. He had shallow cheeks, and I realised that for the first time I was looking at him properly and his serious gaze came back in my direction. Therefore, he was checking me out too. All through the years whilst we had been aware of each other's existence we had equally tried to avoid too much contact with one another. Yet here we were, communicating a feeling of safety to each other, from which neither of us wanted to back away because we both felt safe in each others company. I was suddenly aware of the fact that the bathwater had turned cold, which did not seem possible until, that is, I looked up at the bathroom clock and realised that almost three quarters of an hour had passed by. How could that be? I had only been watching the man in the loft for a few minutes, or had I? All had gone quiet and returned to normal and I returned to the task at hand, whilst trying not to give the incident another thought. Well, at least for that moment in time anyway.

My thoughts would constantly drift back to that incident over the next few days. I could not help but wonder what the man was doing up the loft and why he was always around wherever I lived, but most of all why did he suddenly seem to be so friendly and less aloof. From that day on, whenever I was in the bathroom with the tap or taps on I would first of all become aware of the rustling sound and then looking up, although I could not see him I could feel his presence there. Yet it no longer bothered me, it just made me more and more curious instead. I regularly liked to lie and soak in the bath because it usually helped to ease the aches and pains in my back. It was only on certain days that I got the opportunity to soak for a long period of time whilst either alone in the house, or at least at a time when all the children were asleep in bed and therefore the house was in silence.

It was to be the following Sunday before my opportunity arose again. I ran the bath and settled in as usual with my eyes gently closed, however, before doing this I checked the time on the clock which was just above my head. It told me that the time was almost a quarter past ten. I made a mental note of the time and was thinking about this when the rustling noise began. Opening one eye, I looked in front of me. The room looked very misty, much more so than I would have expected to be created by the steam from the water in the bath. I slowly cast my eyes upwards towards the ceiling and there once again was the appearance of a circular shaped image, and leering down at me once more was my new found friend, the gentleman from the loft.

Over the days prior to this happening, I had thought long and hard about what I should look for if I had the opportunity to gaze upon this magical scene again. My decision was that I should try to find out what else I could see besides the man whom I usually concentrated my eyes upon on these occasions. I could see an old barn type building which appeared to be a bit ramshackle. As I watched, engrossed in the sights I was seeing, I realised that without averting my eyes I was once more staring into the pupils of the man up the loft. It struck me for the first time that the only emotion shown by those eyes was fear. Yet how could that be so when he had spent the last few years following me from home to home? Therefore, how could he possibly be afraid of me? It did not make sense. At that point I shivered and became aware that the bathwater was once again cold. My eyes went straight to the clock, it was two minutes past eleven, yet like a repeat of the previous occasion it only seemed minutes ago that this whole event had started to occur. In reality approximately three quarters of an hour had passed by.

As the following days went by my mind concentrated on these events whenever my brain was free enough to spare the time for idle thoughts. I thought about the man in the loft, who had never attempted to hurt me in any way. My only worry where he was concerned, was to find the answer to the questions that had bugged me for years. Those questions were:

1. Why was he following me from home to home?

2. Why did he always reside up the loft?

3. Why did he catch my attention and then just stare at me without saying anything?

4. Why did the sound of laughter always appear

whenever he was about to show himself?

And finally,

5. Why did the wallpaper rustle and the loft-hatch bang,
   even though it was latched?

Maybe these things were just his way of catching my attention,
however, I did not think so.

It was Friday evening and my children had gone off to choir
practise as usual, they all sang in the local church choir. A friend
had taken them and was going to pick them up because I had
recently undergone major surgery and was not fit enough to drive
at that time. My friend was also taking them for a burger
afterwards, which meant that I would have at least three hours to
myself and it was therefore the ideal time for a long soak. I ran the
bath as usual and clambered in after mentally noting the time.
Relaxing, I closed my eyes and lay waiting for the familiar noises to
start. I waited, and waited, but to no avail. The noises did not come
as they usually did. After about five minutes I opened my eyes and
stared intensely at the ceiling, I was willing the man up the loft to
appear but he did not show himself. This puzzled me more than
him appearing and not saying why. There was nothing I could do at
that point apart from accepting that he was not going to appear at
that time. His reasons were a mystery to me, but would soon
become abundantly clear. For my part, I was becoming obsessed
with thoughts of the man up the loft, his intentions if he had any
and finding time to soak in the bath in the hope that he would put
in an appearance and solve the mystery for me.

Once again it was to be Sunday evening when my next opportunity
arose. This time however, I had only closed my eyes for a few
seconds before the old familiar noises started. I slowly opened one
eye followed quickly by the other and sure enough, he was there. I
could see the old ramshackle barn once more, but this time I

realised that the man appeared to be separated from the barn which I obviously could not understand.

I was once again lost in the stare of his beady eyes as he leered down at me. Then a shiver ran down my spine as the realisation hit me once again that the bathwater had turned cold just as it always did on these occasions. After this, I came to the decision that I would need to change events if I was ever going to find out more about the man up the loft or the ramshackle barn for that matter. Because the coldness always overcame me at about the same stage of the story thereby stopping me from finding out anything else that Spirit were trying to portray to me. In other words, each time he appeared whilst I was in the bath my train of thought would be altered by the human fault of becoming cold along with the bathwater. This meant that I would never be able to understand the full story unless I found a way to avoid this happening.

I thought back long and hard of the many occasions over the years that he had shown himself. This allowed me to reach the conclusion that I had not always been in the bath when these sightings had occurred. So therefore, the water was not necessarily a contributory factor as I had been assuming, yet I had definitely started to gain more information at these times. I thought back to the time in my last house when my friends and I had investigated the noises he had produced. This made me realise that as soon as any suddenness of movement or action had taken place on my part the man had disappeared. I knew beyond a shadow of a doubt that I would have to stay still and relaxed, trying not to make any sudden moves if I was ever going to learn more about my permanent un-paying lodger. This was when the idea occurred to me, that it was possible, if I lay in the bath without any water in it then, maybe I would be able to gain more information. I was no longer bothered by the fact that I had a strange visitor in my loft, just curious as to why he was there.

Friday evening I put my plan into action. As soon as the children had left the house and I had waved them off down the road, I went upstairs and settled in the bath. Unfortunately, I just lay there in great expectation to no avail, as my visitor did not appear. Maybe I had got it wrong? I was sure it was not the only time that he had not appeared because he did not show himself last Friday either. This got me to thinking that perhaps Friday was not a good day for trying to communicate with my visitor. I would try one more time without any water on Sunday night. This came around quite quickly and I settled into the bath once the children were asleep. I could always be sure of them settling early on a Sunday in readiness for school the next morning after a busy weekend.

Closing my eyes, I waited patiently. After a few minutes I opened one eye and glanced first up to the ceiling and then over to the clock. It was five past ten and there were no signs of the man up the loft. Deciding that I should give him more time I relaxed once more and closed my eyes gently. After only a couple of minutes I could hear the walls around me starting to rustle. I felt quite excited with the anticipation of what I might see in the next few minutes but knew that I must only make gentle movements if I was going to see my unusual lodger. I waited momentarily, whilst I tried to calm down from the excitement I was feeling. Then once I felt relaxed enough, I gently opened one eye followed shortly by the other. There in the ceiling was the familiar view of a round open space, showing the all too easily recognised picture of a ramshackle barn. I scanned the view that I was seeing carefully, making full use of both eyes by watching both sides of the picture at the same time. After only seconds of doing this, I began to notice a shuddering effect taking place within the picture. I tried not to adjust my eyes but kept them trained on the scene in front of me. To my amazement the picture began to move just like being at the pictures and watching the screen in front of you showing a film.

As usual I started off seeing the ramshackle old barn, which was on what appeared to be slightly overgrown farmland. It was as though suddenly I became part of the picture I was watching, instead of just seeing the scenes in front of me.

Next I was aware of being taken through a rickety door that creaked as it opened. There was straw strewn all over the floor, which grated under my feet as I walked. At that point I noticed the familiar face of the man up the loft whom I had seen many times over the years. He looked agitated in his appearance. He was turning his head from side to side as if in panic, staring around him as if looking for someone or something in the barn with him. He clambered up a ladder leading to the top of the barn where the straw bales were kept. The barn door suddenly creaked. It was as if I was standing in the centre of the room, yet was an invisible entity within the barn. I could see dust falling through the gap in the wooden rafters above where the man was now peeping through, there was a shaft of light sifting through from God knows where, because it seemed to be very dark and black up there apart from this. The light made the dust more visible as it gently floated to the ground.

At that moment, my daughters' bedroom door wrenched open, jarring me back to reality as I glanced quickly towards the bathroom door then back to the ceiling which was just that, a ceiling as it had been before. I felt really frustrated by the fact that for once I was beginning to find out more about the man up the loft, yet now I was not certain whether I had been dreaming or not. As quick as I could with my aching bones, I pulled myself up and clambered out of the bath heading towards the door on time to see my daughter crossing the landing to go to the bathroom. I smiled across to her as I asked: "Are you alright darling?" Rubbing her eyes with her right hand she stretched out her left arm to place it around my waist. Looking up at me, she answered: "Mum, I dreamt that there was a man hiding up the loft. I woke up and thought the ceiling had a hole in it. I smiled down at her planting a kiss on her forehead. Knowing that she was already a little nervous about ghosts, and things that go bump in the night, I decided that it would be better to let her think that she was in fact dreaming, even though I knew that if we were seeing the same thing, then we could not be both dreaming, could we? Over the next few days the scenes of that night played over and over in my head. I knew that it was important for me to investigate the matter further as soon as possible, yet I also decided that it was probably safer to do it whilst alone in the house in case Dawn or indeed Toni or Dean overheard these events taking place.

Friday evening seemed to take forever to come round, but that was to be the next time that I would be in the house alone. However, it came and went because once again nothing happened when I tried once more to switch off and tune in to the scenes within the ceiling. After giving the subject some thought I realised, that whenever I had tried to make contact with the man in the loft on a Friday nothing ever happened. It was as though he disappeared on a Friday night, reappearing on Saturday through to Monday morning. I now realised that looking back over the years, I would either see or hear this man on Saturday, Sunday or Monday morning, when things definitely seemed to get worse as far as things that went bump in the night were concerned. Yet on the several occasions recently that I had had the opportunity to try to connect to these events on a Friday evening whilst my children were out of the house at choir practise, nothing ever happened. This meant that I would now have to wait until the opportunity arose for me to try to relax and link into these events whilst in the house alone. The only opportunity for this to happen in the foreseeable future would be to wait until the children were at school on Monday morning and I would once again be alone in the house.

I suppose if anyone had seen me settling into the empty bath fully clothed on a Monday morning, they would think that I had lost the plot, but you need to understand that at that point in time I did not understand as much about the existence of the Spirit World as I do today, otherwise I would have just tuned in from wherever I was. For these scenes to be shown to someone like myself who was psychically aware, without me knowing how to tune in at any time and indeed anywhere, to be told the information I needed to hear, then it was necessary for certain things to be in place to help that psychic ability to kick in. First of all, it was necessary for me to be in close proximity to the trapdoor to the loft where the Spirit of the man in the loft could access my psychic awareness by creating a similarity in my mind. Secondly, it would be easier for the Spirit World to create a psychic impression into my brain, if these images were created at a time that coincided with the original events. This knowledge once I was aware of it, did explain a lot to me.

Monday morning came round at last, and the children were safely in school. I made my way upstairs and after checking the time settled myself down in the bath. I smiled to myself as I settled down and closed my eyes, thinking how this would look to most people. Sure enough, within minutes the scenes started to roll, I watched with a certain amount of impatience as I viewed all the scenes that I had already seen the last time that I had experimented on viewing the man in the loft. My interest picked up however, when once again the barn door opened with a creaking sound and I could see the shaft of light with the dust particles floating down. A large brown boot was visible coming through the door. The lofts wooden ceiling above me creaked and the brown boot ran forward towards the wooden ladder that led to where the man was hiding. The owner of the boot was a swarthy looking man in need of a shave. His clothes were dirty and his shirt tail was hanging out. I watched with expectation as I waited for him to notice the man whom I knew was hiding up the loft amongst the bails of hay.

He did notice him and in one quick movement, he lunged his heavy frame towards the man up the barn loft who was at that time desperately trying to hide from his assailant. There was a slight scuffle and the swarthy man threw the man over the edge onto the barn floor below. He laughed out loud, a really loud deep laugh that I recognised to be the booming laughter sound that I had heard for many years. He climbed back down the ladder and ran across the barn and out through the door. I could hear his laughter fading away into the background as he made his way across the field. Minutes later there was a rattling sound, which I now understand was the man from my loft getting to his feet and pulling on the door of the barn which the other man had pulled shut behind him. I realised that these noises were familiar to me. I had heard the rattling of the door on many occasions since childhood. I had also heard that laughter on several occasions at the same time, but not every episode of rattling was joined with the laughter, and where was the rustling sound that usually accompanied these events?

I was just thinking about this when I was aware of darkness all around me, after which it became light and darkness followed again. Once the light returned, I heard footsteps approaching and the creaking of the barn door opening. The barn was burnt to the ground because the land was being prepared for houses to be built on it. Now I was beginning to understand. The man up the loft had used the roof of the old barn to sleep in until the fire was ignited, and as he was already weak from hunger and thirst, the smoke was to be the end of him. The rattling door was this poor soul trying to attract attention from a passer by, which, were few and far between. The rustling walls were created by the sound of the flames licking around the building, and the laughter was the sound of his aggressor making his escape. However, it did not explain why he had appeared in the loft of my childhood home, or why the man in the loft was following me from home to home wherever I lived. It was also hard to understand why sometimes he appeared whilst on other occasions he did not.

I was going to make it my business, not only to find these things out, but also to know who the man up the loft was. Although I was not sure how I was going to achieve this outcome. Over the following days, thoughts of all these questions travelled through my head. However, it was to be several weeks later that I was to gather information, which would grant me realisation of the truth connecting these facts together to give the whole story about my permanent Spirit visitor.

I woke up one morning, feeling as though I had been awake all night. I remembered my dream of those sleeping hours vividly, as though I had really taken part in the scenes, which had taken place in that dream. I propped myself up in bed and almost drifted into a state of semi consciousness as I contemplated the events that I remembered so clearly. The room around me began to fill with the mist like substance that I had seen on many previous occasions. I then saw a clear picture developing in front of me. At first the scenes were upside down and although I could see the people moving their mouths as if they were talking there was no sound coming out. I relaxed further and to my amazement the picture in front of me flipped upright and I could hear the sounds that were necessary to understand the story behind the scenes that I was watching. It was at this moment I realised that the dream, which I had dreamt the previous night was somehow magically being explained to me in a way that was easy to understand.

This was also the moment when the realisation hit me that I could find out the answers to anything, which I required to know. Although I soon also needed to accept that these answers were always very straightforward and explicit. It was only wise to ask the questions that you genuinely wanted to know the answers to; because once you know something you cannot erase it from your memory.

The first questions that I experimented with in my newfound way of discovering knowledge, were to be:

'Why did the man in the loft first appear to me in my childhood home?'

'Why did he follow me from home to home, wherever I lived?

And finally:

'Why did he only appear on some occasions and not others, even when the situation seemed to be the same?'

As I sat up on the bed semi propped up by the pillows watching the scenes flashing before me, I started to think about these things and the picture seemed to go back to the beginning. It was as though I was watching a movie that had been switched to fast forward. The story was one that I recognised straight away and the scenes in the barn were being replayed in front of me. I watched in interest and then the thought suddenly struck me that I was being shown farmland with an old house and the barn, whereas prior to this occasion I was only aware of the barn. This thought passed clearly through my mind, when suddenly Mr R stood at the side of the bed with his arms folded, looking down at me. He spoke suddenly: "Your childhood home was built on the land of an estate. It was farm and wasteland for the most part apart from the manor house that is."

I jumped up, losing sight of everything within that smoke like substance, including the mist itself. I felt a little disgruntled by this to say the least. So immediately settled back onto the pillow and relaxed once more. This time however, I was aware that I could interrupt the scenes and ask questions and get answers to my enquiries. Therefore, I immediately asked: "Why did the man in the loft first appear in the loft of my childhood home?" Again Mr R moved up close to the side of my bed. This time he spoke more gently. "He first appeared at your childhood home because he worked on the farm estate that used to occupy the land where your parents' house was built. As a Spirit, he is haunting the space in the hopes that he can right a wrong and alert someone of his death by telling someone of his demise." I thought for a moment then asked my second question, which was: "I can understand that, but why then does he always show up in the loft of any home I live in?" He smiled, a smile that I now know means that he is pleased with my reaction, as he replied: "He has been aware of you since you were a young child, therefore he knows that you can see him and feels that you may be able to help him by letting him reveal to you how he died so that he can go home and rest in peace."

Now it was all making sense apart from the fact that on occasions he did not appear whilst on others he did. Before I had the chance to ask my next question, Mr R read my thoughts and answered:

"He was in the barn on Saturday evening, where he remained until Monday when the building was set ablaze. This is why he only appears on those three days, to influence your mind to a time span." I became quite excited at this point and jumped up, once again changing my vibration. It took me sometime to learn the lesson of not making sudden movements whilst linking with the Spirit World. Although I have to admit that it is not quite so important to me these days, because I am capable of quickly changing my vibration back again, as easily as opening a door.

Chapter Thirteen.

Learning To Understand My Shadows

From my earliest memories people have made comments about my eyes. Your eyes are the windows to your soul and therefore, speak realms about who you are. Only last night after finishing a service in front of approximately ninety people, a lady approached me and asked; "Can I say, that my friend and I think that you have got the most amazing eyes." I smiled brightly, as I answered "thank you very much. People often tell me that, but I cannot think why" Without hesitation she remarked: "Your eyes which are grey, turn blue each time you make a link with someone from Spirit. They open wide and go the most amazing pale blue, just like your jacket. We could not take our eyes off them."
I, of course was wearing a pale blue jacket that particular night but it does not seem to matter what colour I am wearing, as long as I am confident in what the Spirit World are conveying to me. This is because I am in fact using my eyes in two different ways at once. I am looking at the congregation with my normal eyes then expanding them towards my third eye, to enable me to see Spirit. This is the look that people see, and are surprised about. At times it is just as if there is a video recorder playing inside your head and you need to watch these scenes to be able to get the full picture of what you are being told. My sister Hazel said that she has often been accused of staring at someone when she was in fact doing the same thing and watching the recordings in her head, which were portraying messages from the Spirit World.

This sometimes creates a problem when this is happening and you suddenly snap back to reality, meaning that you are then looking the person straight in the eye, whom the message is for. This can and does sometimes get misunderstood. My father used to get quite angry if he saw us looking at one another whilst he was talking. His favourite saying at these times was: "I can see you, eyeing each other up." Therefore, whenever he was annoyed we were afraid to look in the direction of anyone else in the room because we would be in trouble. He had in fact grown up in a world where he at times was given information in this way. In reality Spirit were communicating with him but he assumed that he was receiving thoughts from people's heads and that they were communicating with one another through telepathy. Because this confused my father, he became nervous whenever he was angry due to the fact that he thought that if we looked at one another then we could gang up on him just as people had when he was younger. He in fact became a little obsessed by this factor, and therefore felt more in control if we did not look at one another. That way we could not communicate with each other behind his back, or so he thought. For this reason he always made us look him in the eye when he was speaking to us. He often declared that you should never trust anyone who did not look you in the eye when they were talking to you. To this day I believe this to be true and therefore do not trust anyone who does not look me in the eye whilst I am speaking to them.

When I first started to be aware that I was communicating with the Spirit World, I found it easier to gather all the information that they were giving me with my eyes shut. This was purely because with my eyes closed I did not become distracted by the things that belong to the here and now. I once spoke to a Medium called Margaret about this matter because she is a lady whom I respect a great deal. She said that if it was easier to keep my eyes closed then keep them shut, however, for me it was not that simple for the reasons that I have just given you. I knew that my dad would turn in his grave, 'so to speak' if I was not looking people in the eye as I spoke to them. It is the same when someone who is extremely psychic knows what another person they are with is thinking, or about to say. Mike and I frequently communicate with each other without saying a word. This part of our gift can come in handy when someone is not what they appear to be. This is not because we read peoples minds, it is because we read their vibration,which alerts us that a thought process is taking place that would be of interest to us, and then our Guides translate these vibrations to us. We then know what the person is thinking. My eyes are in fact, no different than anyone else's, I just use them differently. This is mainly due to the shadows in my heart. Each time that someone comes to visit from the Spirit side, they come with love. A Medium needs to return that love in order to make the link complete. This is what shows in the eyes when they join with the third eye and the heart at the same time. This in turn serves to widen the iris of each eye just the same as when we look at something we like or are interested in.

Each time that Spirit step up close to us, they are standing within our auric field and this tends to act like a magnet, which pulls us towards the Spirit and them towards us. If we stop at this point to feel for our heartbeat, we will notice that it is beating slightly faster. However, as soon as we relax with this feeling we become peaceful within just as if we have been anaesthetised. Those of you whom have undergone surgery which required a general anaesthetic will agree that it feels as though only seconds before you were receiving the injection yet it may have been two or three hours. You are not aware of anything, which has happened during that time. Whilst linking with the Spirit World from a rostrum it is very similar. One minute you are starting a service and then all of a sudden you are being called to time. During this time you are generally only aware of the Spirit people and the person within the congregation to whom you are speaking at any given time. This is because time loses all prospective, just like you have been anaesthetised. It is like this at all times for those in the Spirit realms, which is the reason why time is not important to them, because it has no meaning.

In the Spirit World every year that passes here is the equivalent of a month in Spirit, therefore, when someone from Spirit says that something will take place soon!! to them that is within two years. Because two of our years are only two months in their time, this makes it soon. Every time that I stand upon a rostrum ready to commence with a service I become extremely nervous. This is because although I know that Spirit would never let me down, I also know that if by any chance they did, I would be up there in front of all those people with absolutely nothing to say or do. Therefore, I begin to shake as soon as I am on my way to the venue and am shaking away quite a lot by the time that I arrive and of course, even more when I stand up in order for the service to commence.

This, as I have said, is partly due to nerves and anticipation of the unexpected things that may or may not occur but it is mainly because Spirit are coming in close ready to communicate during the approaching service. This affects the way that our body is reacting and we perceive it as being nerves when sometimes there is another explanation for these feelings. This reason being that Spirit are actively altering our vibration, which in turn changes our metabolic rate. They do this to allow us to link more easily to the vibration which they are on.

If I was to ask you to stand by a wall where you were able to see the shadow cast by your own body onto the wall, and you stood there watching your own shadow when suddenly another unexpected shadow appeared that was approaching you from behind, I am sure that you would probably jump or gasp with surprise. The reason for this is obviously because someone or something that was totally unexpected had appeared and affected your thought process with a shock reaction. At this time your heartbeat would speed up because of the adrenalin rush produced by the surprise element of something appearing which was different than you had expected. This, therefore brings into play your: 'Fight or flight response,' which we all have to try to protect us from danger. i.e. The element of surprise affected your heartbeat because the reaction caused by the surprise view of another shadow was different to the reaction you were already experiencing viewing your own shadow. Your body in turn prepared you for self protection, which would allow you to either fight or run.

When someone steps up close into your auric field, it has a similar response. Because the Spirit World are on a faster vibration than ours when they come up close, it is very similar to the surprise element response that made us react to the approaching extra shadow. In other words, although we could see the extra shadow approaching, we were caught out by the surprise element because we did not know what it was. This affected our bodily reactions because both sensations were different, thereby creating the adrenalin rush. We would equally be caught out by the surprise element and lack of expectancy when Spirit step up close to us, thereby causing the same adrenalin rush.

A service usually starts with an opening prayer, which is said by the Medium and it is during this time that it is most likely for people to be able to tell that I or any other Medium are nervous, due to the fact that our voice may be a bit shaky. This is because as soon as Spirit, move in close to make their links for the people in the congregation or give an address of philosophy, the Medium becomes very relaxed almost anaesthetised. Because it is now Spirit who are holding the service the Medium becomes unaware of their own surroundings except for Spirit and the person who is receiving the communication so therefore they are no longer nervous. Practise makes perfect with everything that we attempt to do in life. Common sense therefore tells you, that the more you link to Spirit the easier it will become. To me, communicating with the dead is as easy, if not easier, than conversing with the living. Even before I can see a Spirit visitor I am aware of a fluttering sensation within my heart. I often wonder how many people mistake this sensation for there being something wrong with them. Knowing now what I know about linking with the Spirit World, I realise that the two most important parts of our body that are used when making these links are our: 'Heart and our Brain.'

It is true that without our brain Spirit could not make the links which are necessary in order to hold a conversation with us. Students often joke that this must be the reason why they are having trouble linking, because they have not got a brain or it is too small. My husband Mike would use this as a reason in the beginning. However, every living person has an active brain whether they use it or not. Obviously brain capacity alters with each individual but we all have one so therefore are technically able to link with those in the Spirit World. It is also true that if we were not capable of showing love from our hearts, then the most important link between Spirit and ourselves is missing.

When I was first training to become a Medium, I would know without doubt whilst on the rostrum that Spirit were definitely there even if I could not see them. This was because of my faster heart rate and an overwhelming feeling of love which was surrounding me. My problem was that because I am lucky enough to see Spirit objectively or clearly, I had trouble knowing who was dead and who was alive. As a young child I was definitely not aware that at times I was talking to dead people. This could prove to be quite a problem when it was time to give proof of survival because I could try to link a Spirit person to another Spirit person instead of a live person. It could also make the congregation feel that I had lost the plot and did not know what I was talking about if I said: "Can I come to that lady in the front row?" pointing to an empty chair as I did so, but of course the chair would not really be empty. There would be a Spirit person sitting in it although most of the congregation could not see that person.

My Main Guide, who as I have said before is Russian, explained to me that it is necessary at these times to use our senses. If whilst reaching our thoughts and feelings out towards the person who is in our company, we feel our heart at the same time, then we will learn to notice the difference. All living people and animals feel solid to our senses because we also sense solid they will not immediately affect our heartbeat unless we are afraid or heavily attracted to them. However, someone who is already in the Spirit World will sense light. This will have the effect of unbalancing our heartbeat thereby speeding it up. This occurs because they sense light and we sense solid, this alters our bodily reactions.

I should also explain that if we are afraid or heavily attracted to someone, then it will feel as though our heart misses a beat. This does not happen when we connect to a Spirit person, it just speeds up. If, at this point we close our eyes briefly whilst feeling our heartbeat, we will become aware of the shadows in our heart. These shadows are in fact Spirit trying to communicate by stepping up close within our Aura.

We should close our eyes and then relax thoroughly, which in affect will start the process of opening the third eye by drawing back the curtains which are drawn between us and our Spirit. It is at this point that people often talk of seeing shadows, shapes and colours. This is because they are starting to be aware of the love vibration coming from the Spirit side of life. As a Spirit communicator sends love across to our heart, it makes a wavy type patterned vibration just like you would see whilst watching the side of a bonfire close up whilst it is burning.

As this vibration is watched by the third eye, colours can be seen to emanate from it. To the human eye it appears just like a rainbow bridge reaching out from your loved one in Spirit, straight to your heart.

There is a lot to learn if we wish to communicate with those people who exist in the world of life after death. One of the first and most important steps is to know our self well. This can only be achieved by concentrating on how we react to certain things happening. It is also necessary, if we are to know the difference between what is us and what is the communicator. Because it is easier for them to make the right connections with our brain our Guides communicate most from your right hand side. Remember, they mainly use our:

'Brain, Heart, and Aura', in order to talk to us in a way that we are in with a chance of picking the message up.

As soon as Spirit make their first connection with our auric field, we are likely to be aware of them whether we realise it or not. Sometimes this can be recognised by a feeling of becoming slightly more alert. If we watch for that feeling occurring, then we will quickly become accustomed to knowing how it feels when our Guides are letting us know that they are near. Most people who first try to be aware of Spirit, do not realise how hard it is for their loved ones to summon up the energy required to make a link with us possible. This can lead to many misunderstandings. People presume that because it is as easy as picking up a telephone here on the earth, then it must be just as easy to communicate whilst in Spirit, because the person or people they love, love them too and would want to contact them if it were possible. This is of course true and creates a situation where confusion exists. One of the questions I get asked a lot as a Medium is: "Why is it that the person I love most in Spirit is usually the last person to come through when I know that they would be excited about my visit to a Medium and would want to talk to me?" The answer to this question is a fairly simple one. Once a Medium makes a link with a person here and their loved ones in the Spirit World, the energy between Spirit and that person starts to build up. The more positive links that are made with the person here, the stronger the energy gets, which enables Spirit to give more information. This is because the only way that Spirit can make a sound that the Medium can hear, is by vibrating the Medium's voice box. Therefore, common sense tells us that the person you most want to hear from will wait until the energy has built up, enabling them to talk more which will help them to prove that they are definitely here. This means that they are often the last person to come through or even time it wrong, leaving it too late and therefore do not come through at all, because they run out of time. This is purely because the Medium is human and is aware of time and the size of his or her congregation whilst imparting Spirit messages, meaning that he or she will sometimes move on to the next recipient before the Spirit has a chance to convey their message and presence to that person within the congregation. This factor should always be remembered because people intend to think that the reason for this is lack of love, when in fact it is the opposite they love you a great deal and so are prepared to wait for stronger vibrations giving them the chance they need to communicate properly.

A lot of everyday people come into Spiritualism searching for proof that someone they love who has died, lives on. This to me is the truth because in reality there is no death, therefore these people do live on. However, sometimes people need to know for themselves because they are afraid of dying, or quite simply they are searching for peace because their life is in a mess in one way or another. Spirit are sometimes able to help at these times because by proving that they have an insight into our future, they can restore faith into a person who feels that they are in a hopeless situation, with no sign of a light at the end of the dark desperate tunnel that they feel they are in. Knowing that our loved ones will meet us once more when we die, and also having knowledge of the beauty and love that is available in the Spirit World makes people less afraid of dying.

Chapter Fourteen.

Aura Cleansing To Link.

The following workshop is a way of making a few points about Spirit linking easier to understand. People in general are more inclined to believe in what they can personally see or hear, whereas we are less likely to believe what we are sensing because feelings are easier for us to put down to our imagination than sightings or sounds.

This workshop deals with what we can see. For this workshop to work, it is necessary to have a dark room with a clear white wall or screen placed at the front. A bright light needs to be placed about two feet in front of this wall or screen, shining directly onto it. The seats should all be placed behind the light facing the wall, allowing everyone to view what is taking place. Now it should be explained to those entire present how to see an Aura this is done by looking directly at a person's face and straight past on both sides at the same time. This accomplishes using both eyes separately but at the same time, this in turn opens the third eye.

At first there should be a meditation, which will cleanse everyone's Aura, and put everyone within the group on the right vibration to see Aura's. During this meditation, words will also be spoken by the leader who is leading the meditation, which will place everyone on the right vibration for the next part of the exercise. Everyone must sit relaxed with their eyes closed and their legs uncrossed. The reason that their legs should be uncrossed is because they may be in the meditative state for several minutes. If this is the case, someone's legs may get pins and needles or cramp, so bringing about the desire to move. If this should happen then people tend to fidget a lot before uncrossing their legs, which not only makes them uncomfortable but can also disturb other members of the group. It is also important to remember that during any meditation, if the desire to cough should present itself then the

176

person should do exactly that, cough, because it is less likely to disturb the others at this stage whereas, if the person waits, then a huge coughing fit may take place and this could really disturb everyone present.

Aura Cleansing Meditation.

As we sit in the peace and the love of this group of like minded people here, accompanied by those in the Spirit World, I want you to picture a disc at the base of your spine. The disc is Red in colour all over. As you are aware of that disc, the colour starts to spread sticking to the inside edge of the disc presenting a hole in the centre, so that it looks like a small red tyre.

Up through the hole in the centre of this Red disc, comes a Golden Yellow cord stretching upwards.

Approximately two inches further up your body, I want you to picture another disc, which is Orange in colour. Again the colour starts to spread, clinging to the inside edge of that disc producing a hole in the centre so that it looks like a small Orange tyre. The Golden cord that has already stretched up through the hole in the centre of the Red disc now stretches up through the hole in the centre of the Orange disc.

Approximately by your navel, I want you to picture a third disc, which is Golden Yellow in colour. Again the colour starts to spread filling the whole of the disc, but there is no hole in the centre of this disc. However the Golden cord still stretches up from the centre of the Orange disc and still goes through the centre of the Yellow disc.

Further up in the region of your heart, there is a fourth disc, which is covered in the colour Green. The colour begins to spread sticking to the inside edge of the Green disc, forming a hole in the centre of that disc so that it looks like a small Green tyre and the Golden cord stretches up through from the Yellow disc to the Green disc and through the centre.

In the region of the throat there is a Blue disc. The colour blue spreads out sticking to the inside edge of the Blue disc, forming a hole in the centre of that disc so that it looks like a small Blue tyre and the Golden cord now stretches up from the Green disc through the centre of the Blue disc.

Approximately just above the bridge of the nose, I want you to picture another disc which is covered in the colour Indigo. This colour starts to spread out over that disc sticking to the inside edge of that disc, creating a hole in the centre so that it appears like a small Indigo coloured tyre where the Golden cord stretches up from the centre of the Blue disc, going up through the centre of the Indigo disc.

Now, I would like you to picture another disc at the crown of your head. This disc is covered in a Violet colour. This colour is spreading across the disc sticking to the inside edge of that disc, forming a hole in the centre so that it looks like a small Violet coloured tyre where the Golden cord stretches up from the centre of the Indigo disc and through the centre of the Violet disc.

Finally, I want you to picture a disc which is approximately one foot above your head. This disc is covered all over in White and there is no hole in the centre, however, the Golden cord still stretches up from the centre of the Violet disc pushing through the centre of the White disc, going approximately six inches above this disc where it showers down beautiful Golden raindrops all around your body. These raindrops are showering the front of you, the back of you and each side of you, so that the whole of your aura is showered in them and you can feel these raindrops all around you. I am now going to leave you for two minutes whilst you enjoy the sensation of these beautiful Golden raindrops all around you. So now I will leave you for a couple of minutes.

Through the White Disc

Through the Violet Disc

Through the Indigo Disc

Through the Blue Disc

Through the Green Disc

Through the Yellow Disc

Through the Orange Disc

Through the Red Disc

Gold Cord

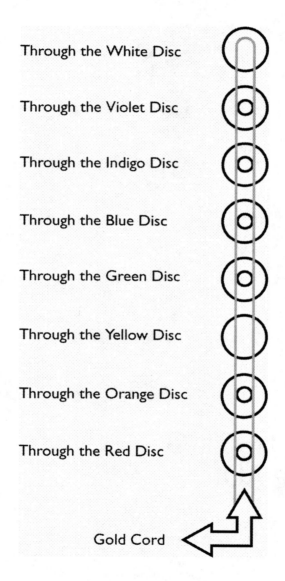

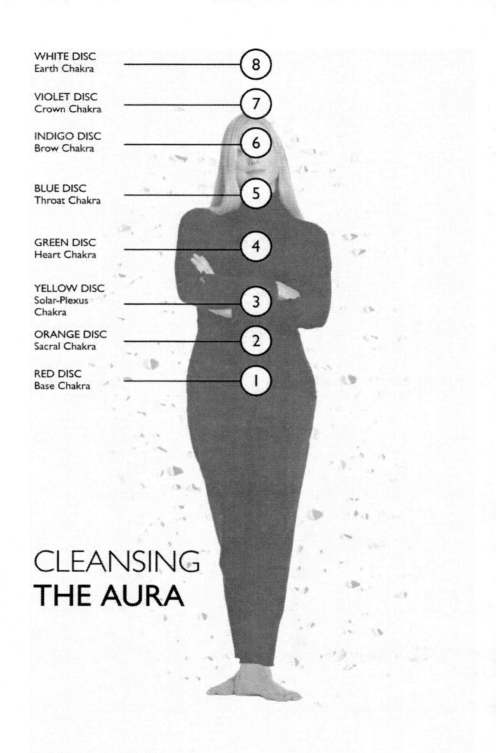

WHITE DISC
Earth Chakra — 8

VIOLET DISC
Crown Chakra — 7

INDIGO DISC
Brow Chakra — 6

BLUE DISC
Throat Chakra — 5

GREEN DISC
Heart Chakra — 4

YELLOW DISC
Solar-Plexus
Chakra — 3

ORANGE DISC
Sacral Chakra — 2

RED DISC
Base Chakra — 1

CLEANSING
THE AURA

Now as you are aware of the peace which is all around you from these Golden raindrops, I want you to be aware that they have stopped falling. You can feel the Golden cord slipping down through the centre of the White disc, the Violet disc, the Indigo disc, the Blue disc, the Green disc, the Yellow disc, the Orange disc and the Red disc. Now you are totally relaxed and feel at peace with yourself and the rest of the world, especially those on the Spirit side of life.

After approximately two minutes the leader should start to speak once more. This meditation is to cleanse the Aura and as I said before: 'Is important at the beginning of this exercise.'

This Aura cleansing can be done regularly as it is good to have your Aura cleansed periodically anyway because we all come into contact with trials and tribulations in our life. Sometimes the troubles belong to the people connected to us but we take them on board whilst trying to help these people. All these things are then retained within our Aura and just like everything else it needs clearing from time to time. However, for this particular exercise, it becomes important to have our Aura cleansed as we go into the meditation, then carrying straight on forward with this exercise whilst still meditating.

This helps because we are already on a very inner relaxed vibration due to the cleansing which gives us the perfect opportunity to heighten our vibration even more. This is essential if we are to be able to be on the right vibration which is necessary to stretch our Aura enough to see it on the outside of our shadow. As soon as the leader has said 'Now you are totally relaxed and feel at peace with yourself and the outside of your shadow' or: As soon as the leader has said 'Now you are totally relaxed and feel at peace with yourself and the rest of the world, especially those on the Spirit side of life.'

She/he should carry on with: Now I want you to be aware of a feeling that the whole outline of your body is glowing, emanating a second shadow, which glows around your own shadow. You can now feel that extra shadow which is your Spirit within, stretching outwards from all around you. Now in your own time I would like you to return to the group and to the room. So please, in your own time, return to the group and to the room.

Now the leader should check to make sure that you are all back and alert. Now is the time for the leader to ask for a volunteer and if there are not any produce one who has agreed before hand, to step in should it be necessary. This person should then be asked to stand facing the wall or screen with the light shining directly behind them.

At this point the group should be able to see not only the clear shadow of that person on the wall or screen but they should also see a light shadow around that person, which is their Aura.

After several of the group have had a go at this and all are happy that they can see the shadow of a person's Aura, then it is time for a second meditation. The same instructions and rules apply as with the first one.

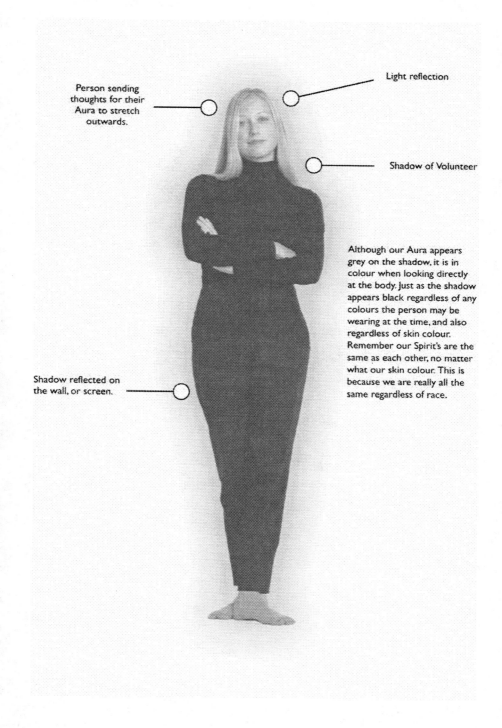

Person sending thoughts for their Aura to stretch outwards.

Light reflection

Shadow of Volunteer

Although our Aura appears grey on the shadow, it is in colour when looking directly at the body. Just as the shadow appears black regardless of any colours the person may be wearing at the time, and also regardless of skin colour. Remember our Spirit's are the same as each other, no matter what our skin colour. This is because we are really all the same regardless of race.

Shadow reflected on the wall, or screen.

183

Meditation To Bring Our Spirit Guides Closer.

"Once again, I want you to be aware of the peace and the love of the Spirit World around you. You are feeling perfectly relaxed, safe and at one with yourself, the group and the Spirit World. I want you to be aware of an energy coming from close behind your right shoulder. This is your Guardian Angel who is coming close to guide you .As you are aware of this energy, I want you to try to be aware that a hand has been placed gently upon both shoulders. I would also like for you at this point, to pay attention to your heartbeat. You should be aware that it is slightly faster than normal. This is simply because your Guardian Angel has come up close within your Aura.

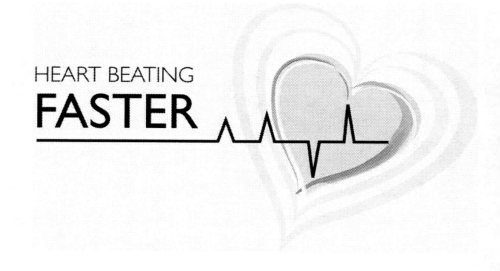

You should also be aware of a fluttering sensation inside your stomach; this again is a normal reaction to your body sensing two different vibrations at the same time." These are all very natural sensations because Spirit use the vibration of love to link with us, and anyone who has been in love will know that these three sensations are quite normal whilst feeling the sensation provided by great love, for anyone or anything.

"As you are aware of these sensations taking place, I want you to picture the face of the person whom you love most in this world (either here or in the Spirit World) smiling at you. I want you to be aware of the feelings, which are brought about by this person whilst relaxing, and feeling the hands upon your shoulders.

Now I am going to leave you for a couple of minutes to gather in the love which you are receiving from this sensation and the person behind your right shoulder. So now I will leave you for two minutes." The person in charge of the group during this meditation should watch everyone within the group whilst this time passes. This is purely to make sure that no one is in difficulty, which rarely happens. But the group leader should be aware if it does, to bring that person back to the group safely. After the two minutes have gone by, the person in charge should say:

"Remembering the love that you can feel at this moment, I want you to be aware of the hands lifting off your shoulders and the person taking a gentle step backwards. You can still feel the love of this person close by and feel extremely safe and relaxed. Now in your own time, could you please return to the room and to the group. So please, in your own time could you return to the room and to the group."

Once again it is important to make sure that everyone is back from the meditation and alert to what is being said before asking each person what they were aware of, so that explanations can be given.

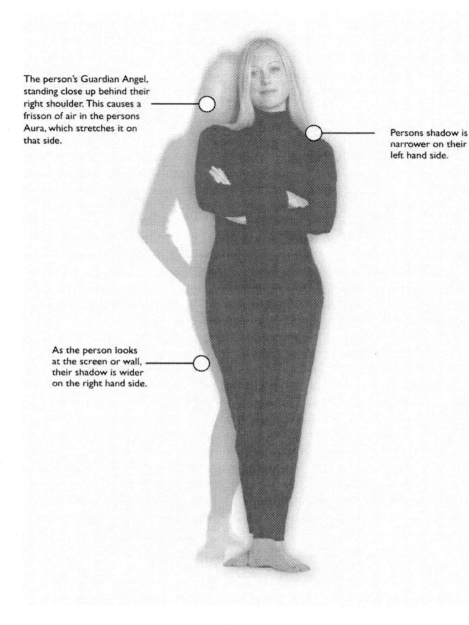

The person's Guardian Angel, standing close up behind their right shoulder. This causes a frisson of air in the persons Aura, which stretches it on that side.

Persons shadow is narrower on their left hand side.

As the person looks at the screen or wall, their shadow is wider on the right hand side.

Once again a volunteer should be asked for to stand in front of the light so that their shadow can be seen clearly on the wall or screen. There should now be a wider shadow on the right hand side if the meditation has been carried out correctly. This is because your Guardian Angel is standing close enough to create a frisson of air within your Auric-field, making that side wider which shows on your shadow.

Several volunteers should be asked to stand in front of the screen or wall because this will show that it is the same for everyone who was involved in the meditation regardless of how experienced they may, or may not be. It is also good for as many people as possible to view their own Aura at the various different stages. People tend to be amazed by the fact that not every shadow is identical, which I would hope goes part way to prove that there is no trickery involved. Once again it is time for everyone to relax and close their eyes so that the next meditation can begin.

Meditation to invite Spirit Visitors.

As we sit once more in the comfort and the love surrounding us, which is brought about by the people here and now and those in the Spirit World, I want you now whilst your eyes are closed to look towards the bridge of your nose with both eyes. You may now be aware of white shades within the darkness that you can see or different colours or even people and/or scenes there in front of you. As you are watching these things with both eyes looking towards the bridge of your nose I want you to be aware that the person behind your right shoulder reaches out their right hand and gently rubs just above the bridge of your nose with their finger tip. As this is taking place, any of the above that you are seeing should start to become clearer. This is because your Guardian Angel is stimulating your third eye. You are beginning to feel sleepy but comfortable and relaxed as you now begin to picture the face of the person or people you love most in the Spirit World. As you are doing this, the atmosphere within the room appears to be changing, because you are surrounded in love.

187

I am now going to leave you for a couple of minutes to concentrate on the scenes and people there with you, asking you to remember everything that you See, Hear or Sense, to bring back to the group later. So now I will leave you for a couple of minutes.

Once again the leader should watch the group whilst those couple of minutes pass by. 'For those who are not over experienced' it is a good idea to watch each member of the group individually one at a time as though you are trying to see their Aura as was explained before. This will stimulate the leader's third eye thereby allowing them to see more. Then, remembering everything that you have Seen, Heard or Sensed, I want you to return to the room and to the group. So could you please return to the room and to the group. When the time is right the leader should start to talk softly building up volume slightly as they go along. This is to avoid making any of the sitters jump unnecessarily. Now as you are aware of the different things that you have Seen, Heard or Sensed, I ask you to bid farewell to those visitors for the time being whilst letting them know that they are welcome to stay close by. Once again it is time to ask each person individually what they were aware of during their meditation. It is important to answer all questions where possible at this point. Volunteers should once again stand in front of the light showing their shadows on the wall, where this time it will be evident that the extra shadow is thicker on the person's left hand side. This is because of the shadows of the visiting Spirits, Relatives, Friends etc, who wish to communicate with someone in the room, moving close in for this purpose.

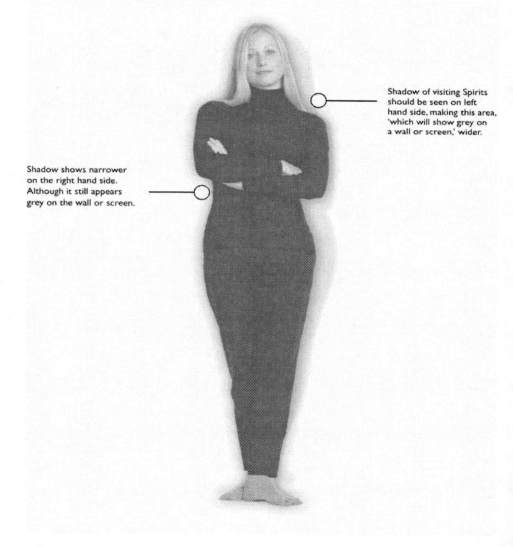

Shadow of visiting Spirits should be seen on left hand side, making this area, 'which will show grey on a wall or screen,' wider.

Shadow shows narrower on the right hand side. Although it still appears grey on the wall or screen.

Chapter Fifteen.

Haunted Houses and Ghost Clearing.

As fully trained and respected Mediums, Mike and I frequently get called out to clear a ghost. In other words, someone who feels that their home, workplace or any other building is being haunted by a ghost, calls upon us to show the lost Spirit how to find their way home.

We received a telephone call one evening from a young man who was extremely frightened because he said that he and his family were being haunted by a ghost who was causing a lot of problems in his home, thereby scaring himself and his family so much that they had moved out to live with his in-laws. So I agreed that Mike and I would visit his home to investigate, after which a date was set.

On the evening that we had arranged, Mike and I arrived outside the house ten minutes prior to the time that we were to meet the family. As I said before, they had moved out of the family home to stay with relatives because they were frightened by the happenings in their home. They were going to meet us at their home to show us round the house where we would hopefully be able to help with their problem. Dead on the turn of eight o'clock, 'if you will excuse the pun', the time we had agreed to meet, a car pulled up in front of ours, and two ladies and two men clambered out and walked towards the front door of the house we had been called to investigate at. We got out of our car and called out to them. It turned out that the younger couple were the owners of the house and the older couple were the young lady's parents whom they had been staying with. The couple also had two young children whom had been left with the man's parents so that they could meet us without worrying about the children. Introductions out of the way, we all went inside the house. It was a very old parlour type house and we found ourselves in an extremely small front room parlour straight away once in from the street.

There were two two-seater settees facing one another with about one foot of space between the two. There was a portable television in one corner and an electric fire in another. The other side of the room became a hallway leading from the front door, through past the stairwell to the tiny kitchen and bathroom. The young lady's mother went through to the kitchen to make a cup of coffee for us, whilst the couple gave an explanation of what had been happening. They explained that although there were problems with lights switching on and off and things of that nature downstairs, most of the problems were upstairs.

They went on to explain that whilst they were in bed at night they were always aware of a bad presence standing next to the bed. The room would go as cold as ice and the blankets on the bed would be thrown back off the couple. They were also aware of noises coming from up the loft. The gentleman who lived in the house that we were investigating, said he had been forcibly thrown down the stairs by something or someone that he could not see. We drank our coffee whilst at the same time sensing what we were feeling in the house. We had been instantly aware of a ghostly presence in the building as soon as we had walked in through the front door.

After quickly looking around the downstairs and being reasonably satisfied that there were no major problems in that area, we headed for the stairwell. The stairs were extremely steep and there were at least twenty stairs. Climbing these stairs would normally have me shattered and out of breath but due to the fact that the atmosphere was heavy because of the presence of ghost activity, I was puffing and panting and could hardly breath. At the top of the stairwell there was a large top stair, which was approximately three foot square. There was a bedroom door to the left and one to the right, and a loft trapdoor up above in the ceiling. We were told that the children's bedroom, which was the door to the left did not seem to have any problems but the master bedroom on the right created many scary incidents and so did the loft.

As soon as I had stepped inside the main bedroom, I felt instantly nauseous and dizzy, which are two of the classic signs that there is a lot of psychic energy around due to ghost activity. Once I had moved across the room by the window, the feelings got worse and the room suddenly became extremely dark as though someone had drawn the curtains, or the sun had gone in. Yet the truth was that none of these things had occurred. It also became exceptionally cold and the curtains started to flap as though the window had been opened, although it had not. At that point I was aware of a man who was scowling at me. He gave me the definite impression that he was trying to make me feel so uncertain that I would go away.

At this point Mr R stepped in really close, which made me certain that this man was not going to be easily persuaded to go towards the light that would take him home. With this the Spirit gentleman hid away so that I could only see his head peeping around the corner. He seemed bothered by the fact that Mr R was there. Although I suppose this is not surprising when you consider Mr R's stature and stern expression when he is not impressed, as was the case at this time. I crossed the room to where the man was peeping and he backed away. I asked Mike to join me and we concentrated very hard on persuading him to go to the light, which eventually he did.

He was an elderly man of eighty eight years of age whom had lived in the house for many years and was not aware that he had in fact died. He therefore, felt that the family who now lived there were intruders in his home. Before this man had died, he had nursed his sick wife when she had suffered from cancer, they slept in a bed which was situated below the window. He had been around the house for around eight years, since he had died suddenly of a heart attack whilst looking out of the window for the doctor to come and look at his wife who had taken a turn for the worse. However, the previous tenants did not seem to be bothered by him until just before they moved away. Then his presence and that of other ghost activity had scared them so much that they had moved out suddenly. The family had gained this information from their next door neighbours who knew the past tenants really well.

The puzzling element to all this was, what had happened to make the old man become so suddenly obvious to anyone who went into that bedroom and why had the young man been thrown down the stairs, if in fact he had? It took a while but we were eventually able to persuade this man that we meant him no harm and were trying to reunite him with his wife. He then returned to the light where he would be safely home. We now asked the man who lived there if he could get us a ladder, which would give us access to the loft. The ladder was placed up to the trapdoor in such a way that the foot of the ladder was directly facing the stairwell. This looked extremely dangerous to me, especially when you consider that Mike would have to go up to investigate because my health would not let me climb up into the roof myself.

I told the man who lived there that he would have to hold the ladder steady at all times whilst Mike went up into the loft and I climbed enough rungs of the ladder to peep inside, just in case Mike had any problems with any Spirits, remembering that the man who lived in the house was saying that he had already been thrown down the stairs by the Spirit entity. Yet we were going to be even higher because the ladder became a continuation of the stairwell. For Mike, this was the first time that he had been called upon to take the lead roll in dealing with a haunted space. He did, however, rise very well to the occasion.

Once he was safely up the loft and I was peering across the space with just my head up through the hole, we were shocked by what we saw. There was a chair up against a beam with chains all around it and evidence that candles had been burnt up there at various spots around the chair. We made sure that any Spirits had safely returned home to the Spirit World, then after checking the bedroom once more, went downstairs for another coffee and to discuss our findings.

One of the most obvious and pertinent questions that I asked, was: "Had they been up the loft during the six months that they had lived in the house and if so, had they removed or altered anything?" He explained that he had been up the loft and that he had removed some items because the knowledge that these items were up there bothered them immensely. This had now really caught my curiosity causing me to ask: "What did you remove, and where did you put them?" He explained that he had found an axe, a long bladed knife, a scalpel, a ouija board and two books, one entitled: 'How to Dissect A Human Body.' And the second was a book about Voodoo. He went on to say that he had thrown them in the canal because he thought that, that would get rid of them for good.

Now the picture was becoming clear. The previous tenants had obviously been playing around with the ouija board and other things that they did not understand and could not control. They had managed to call up a dark entity from the Spirit World and then were not able to get rid of it. They had then decided that the answer was to move house leaving the problem for the next tenant, or so they thought. This may sound logical to most people but the truth is that generally Spirit haunt a space, not a person. In other words most hauntings are produced when a person passes to Spirit and does not realise that they have died. They therefore, spend time either 'around a place they love, like the home they lived in or the place where someone they love, is' or they remain in the place they died, not being able to move on.

In these instances, the occupants moving house would result in the desired affect. That is, the ghost would be left behind and become the new tenant's problem. However, once a Spirit has been called up using a ouija board, without a trained Medium present, then, that Spirit is haunting the person who called them up and not the space they are in. Therefore, on these occasions, moving is not the answer because the Spirit would follow you wherever you go until a trained Medium has put them to rest. I can just imagine how many of you are now thinking well in that case why was the old man in the bedroom upstairs causing problems for these tenants when they had not called him up? The answer is a simple one. The immense psychic energy that was built up during the time the previous residents lived in the house, gave the energy necessary for the old man to be Sensed by anyone who walked in the space he was haunting.

As for the man being thrown down the stairs, once again there was a massive build up of psychic energy in that area due to the activities that had taken place in the loft whilst the trapdoor was open. The man of the new family living in the house was very psychic himself, although probably not aware of it. This created a great static type affect whenever he walked in this area of psychic energy. Because he was not aware of what was happening, he did not lower his vibration and became dizzy, therefore falling down the stairs. This means that he fell down the stairs and was not pushed at all. Because there is a feeling of great force at these times, it could easily be misinterpreted as someone pushing you. Which was unfortunately the case this time, but it was made worse by the fact that at the time he was at the top of a steep flight of stairs which caused him to lose his balance. There were no future problems with the house although unfortunately the same probably cannot be said for the previous occupants of the house, who had after all taken the ghosts 'that they had called up,' with them to their new home.

One evening whilst holding a séance in our class, we were surprised to see that my husband Mike had been over shadowed by a man in the Spirit World, who had the most piercing, staring, evil eyes of anyone that you could imagine. I should point out that when a Spirit over shadows a Medium, they come in really close so that the Medium takes on their appearance. This is purely to give their message from the other side and they cannot over shadow anyone without permission. Our body belongs to us, and we are in charge of it and responsible for it, not the Spirit visitor. This man stared around the table at each of us in turn. I welcomed him and asked what his name was, his reply came straight back: "I am not telling you. I do not trust you." This surprised us and I answered: "You do not trust me?" He was still gazing at each of us in turn as he replied: "I do not trust any of you." We were all looking at each other as I said: "Why?"

"Because I was hung for a crime that I did not commit, that is why. "With that he disappeared, which left us all sitting there amazed. He has, however, been back on several occasions since and we are beginning to collect some information about him so that we can check on his life here.

There are many different ideas and explanations for things that occur in our world but this is especially so with things, which connect our world to the Spirit side of life. Your Guardian Angel is a person who is assigned to take care of you throughout the whole of your earthly life. They are by your side or at least not far away, at all times from the moment of your conception.

During the same evening of the incident with the photograph going missing of Gemma that I mentioned earlier, we were also amazed by the way that the Spirits had managed to let us know that their presence was about. We started off with the six people who were present that evening, sitting in a circle, with a picture of someone who is now in the Spirit World tucked up their jumpers. After a short meditation which I as the leader led them through, I asked them all to rub the palms of their hands together briskly. This creates a frisson of energy within our auric field, which is a magnetic energy field we each have around us. This energy creates a spark that is like static electricity, which helps to demagnetise the psychic energy that is around. Then we all held hands making the circle complete. Everyone said that they could feel a burning sensation go through them, which was created by the energy field being demagnetised, making it easier for Spirit energies to come through to us.

Next we started with me giving part of a link from the person in the Spirit World, for instance: 'There is a man here who passed to the Spirit World with a complaint of his chest. His breathing became very erratic at the end of his life. 'The person sitting to my left then gave the next piece of information for the same gentleman. Going around the circle until all six had given some information about him. Then it was time to ask if anyone could understand this person as the relative or friend in their photograph, or someone connected closely to the person in their photograph. We then started again but with the person to my left starting and me finishing. We did this six times in all so as to give everyone a chance to find the link in the first place. During these links, the people on two out of the six photographs of people in Spirit were prominent.

Next we placed a small three legged tripod table in the centre of the group, with the photographs face down on top of one another on the table. We then turned out the lights and asked for those from the Spirit World to let us know that they were there. This was done after making it clear that we only wanted people who came in love and light. After a couple of minutes the table began to rock until it tilted and tipped the photographs onto the floor. We switched on the light to enable us to see to pick them up and found that two out of the six photographs had turned over and were now face up. These two photographs contained the pictures of the very people who had come through prominently before. I would also like to point out that the two photographs were not in the pile together. One had been placed second and one fifth in the pile. We took this to mean that the Spirit World preferred the table to be empty, so we turned off the lights and started again.

We each placed our fingertips gently onto the edge of the table so that our little fingers were touching the little fingers of the people on both sides of us. After a few minutes everyone began to feel a gentle vibration coming from the table. We were beginning to get a little excited about it when the table started to lift on one side, leaning towards Mike. We welcomed the Spirit visitor and asked them to tilt the table to the alphabet, thereby telling us who they were. At this they spelt B, E, A, S, E, Y. We were all looking puzzled and I commented that there was no such name, when Mike declared: "Yes there is, it was my grandmother's nickname." We were all shocked by this especially Mike, because it is after all a very unusual name.

The next person to come through just kept repeating the letter C, which we could not understand so they gave up. It was not until later that evening that I realised that we were using a table that once belonged to our brother-in-law Chris, who would have been passed to Spirit one year ago the following week. Next, we first of all got A and when we did not understand it, they kept repeating AA. We had trouble understanding this one too, that is until one of the group said perhaps they are trying to tell us the Automobile Association, and another of the group retorted or perhaps it is: "Alcoholics Anonymous."

At that point we realised that a person close to us who had passed away the week before, and whose funeral would take place the next day had died from a poorly liver brought on by drinking too much. We then asked her if she liked the flowers that we had bought that day ready for the funeral the next morning, which were in a room in the back of the house to keep cool. A loud bang came from the room out the back at that precise moment. There were other more private messages but what stood out the most for us all was the fact that the table had pirouetted on one leg for several minutes. I asked everyone to lift their fingers six inches up into the air off the table, which they did and the table stayed put for at least another two minutes. It would be impossible to move this type of table like that with your foot, and anyway two of the group looked under the table to make sure that none of the group were touching it.

Another unusual occurrence happened on a trip to Bangor in Wales. Mike and I were looking round an old second hand shop, because we collect Music boxes and Clocks. We came across a few small items which we liked. These things included a star shaped broach that was not worth anything and only cost twenty-five pence to buy but because Spirit assured me that a star with you meant that you were inviting Spirit to spend time with you, I liked this broach.

I took all the items up to the counter and asked the man if he would round the price off, up to two pounds and fifty pence because that was all the cash that I had on me. The price should have been two pounds and sixty five pence so therefore I was asking him to reduce the price by fifteen pence. He, straight away said that he would and took the items off me to put them into a bag. We returned to the car, placing the bag in the boot and resumed our journey to the hotel where we were staying. Once there, Mike and I looked in the bag to find that the star was missing.

I was very disappointed because as I said before, that was the item which I wanted the most and I would have preferred to go to the bank and get some money to pay the extra fifteen pence than not have the broach. However, there was not time for us to go back to the shop so I had to count my losses so to speak.

When Mike and I returned to the car again, we rechecked the bag and the boot for the star but it was conspicuous by its absence. As we were travelling home the following day, I commented to Spirit that I was very disappointed because they knew why I wanted the broach and should have made me aware that the man had kept it. When we arrived home and went into the bag again, lo and behold, there was the star broach, returned.

It is, I feel, time to bring in another development exercise. After reading the above, I am sure that many of you would be interested in a workshop linking together with a group and Spirit. I am therefore including the exercise involving the photographs.

Each person should have a photograph containing the picture of at least one person who is now in the Spirit World which should not be shown to the rest of the group. Now follow these simple instructions:

There should be a group or several groups of five or six people for this exercise to work properly. These people should sit in a circle using straight-backed chairs, sitting close enough to hold each others hands. Each person should now hide the photograph up their jumper or shirt, with the photograph facing their body. Now a small meditation takes place asking the group to relax and inviting those people in the photographs from the Spirit World to join you if they wish to communicate. During this meditation, the group should be left for two or three moments to send out their thoughts to the person or people within their photograph. After which they should be called back to the room and the group.

Now each member of the group should rub the palms of their hands together briskly to create the frisson of energy necessary, if strong links are to be received. Now all five or six people should hold hands with the person on each side of them. After deciding which person is to start, they must say the first words that come into their head. For instance, the first person may say that they have an elderly man with them who passed to the Spirit World, with an ailment to do with his chest. Next it is the turn of the person sitting to the right of the person who started the link. They may add something like: This man was about five feet, ten inches tall, and had a good head of white hair. This proceeds around the circle, each time going to the right of the person who linked before, until the entire group has had a turn.

Now it is time to ask whether anyone can understand the information given, either with the person or people in any of the photographs or a person connected to them. If you are linking together well, someone in the group will know of the person from the Spirit World that has been given. If there is time, the group should start the process all over again but this time starting with the person who was second the first time round. It is important not to forget to rub your hands together between each new link.

I can just imagine the questions that are going through your minds at this moment. The first one will be: why does the photograph need to be facing our body? The answer as usual is a simple one. Our Aura is our etheric body and therefore part of us. We generally face a person when we are speaking to them and we are asking the person in Spirit to communicate with us. It is therefore manners to face the person with whom we are wishing to communicate. This makes us, as human beings more able to connect to another person if following what comes normal to us. This means that we are more likely to link properly if that person in Spirit is facing us.

Another question, which is probably on your mind at this moment is: Why does the frisson of energy created by rubbing our hands together help make a link to the person in Spirit? Yet again, the answer is a simple one. We all have an auric field around our body which, is magnetic. This magnetic field draws things towards it or repels things away from it depending on whether they are compatible or not. This reacts just the same as a magnet will draw a pin towards it while facing one way and repel the same pin away whilst facing the other way. The frisson of energy draws Spirit towards it, helping them to communicate with the people here.

Whilst recently working in Scotland, Spirit managed to make me aware of them in what seemed like an amazing way, to not only myself and Mike but also to two friends of ours who were present at the time. A few days earlier Mike had bought me a pair of screw on garnet earrings from an antique shop in Warwick. I do not have pierced ears 'feeling that if God had intended me to have holes in my ears then I would have been born with them', therefore I usually wear clip on earrings, but Mike had spotted these screw on ones which, were beautiful. I decided to wear them to a service with a necklace which I had owned for years and happened to match the earrings. I was aware of feeling short of breath as soon as I put them on but put this down to the fact that we had been busy and I was not feeling too well at the time. The service lasted for an hour and a half, after which we went outside for five minutes so that the smokers could have a cigarette and I could get some air as I do not smoke, we then went down stairs to get a cup of coffee.

Mike and I chatted for a few minutes to some of the people who had been at the service and then our friend Patricia fetched the coffees and teas with Mike whilst our other friend Anne-Marie and I found a table. All four of us had been sitting chatting for several minutes when suddenly my right earring shot off my ear and flew straight across the table. This shocked us all because it obviously had not fallen, but had been thrown. After discussing this for a moment or two I took off the second earring and to my amazement started to feel better almost immediately.

Remember, that these earrings had been bought from an antique shop where we were told that they were made in 1951, so they were obviously second-hand. Jewellery invariably carries the vibrations felt by the person wearing it during the time the item belonged to them. I believe that the lady who had owned these earrings suffered with a bad heart which I was picking up by the shortness of breath, as soon as I put the earrings on.

This is called psychometry which is the reading psychically of an article. This can only tell us things about the past and present where the owner is concerned, and not the future. This is done by reading the psychic vibrations left on the article by the person who owns it or owned it and has handled it or worn it. Therefore, because the future has not yet happened, we are not able to pick it up from the item.

I dare say that a lot of you who are reading this book are thinking: Why didn't she pick it up if she links to Spirit. The answer is just that I link to Spirit thereby communicating with the so called dead. Whereas, this is psychic work, therefore because I was prepared for taking a service, I was too busy communicating with people from the Spirit World to notice that the reason why I was feeling unwell was in fact an effect, which the earrings had caused. My Guardian Angel, Mr R did not wish to distract me from the job in hand, which was of course communicating with the Spirit World at that time, so waited until after I had finished work before throwing the earring to catch my attention and let me know that the earrings needed cleansing from the previous owners psychic vibrations. Remember he always stands behind my right shoulder, leading him to throw the right earring off the right ear so that I would realise that he had done it and sure enough he was right, I did. Needless to say, I have not and will not wear those earrings again until they have been cleansed.

As I have said before, the Spirit World link with us by means of extending the normal uses of the parts of our body that come naturally to us. For instance, we cannot see our third eye even though it exists but we can see our two physical eyes. They use one to help activate the other into use. In other words, it comes naturally to us to use our physical eyes to see what is around us. Although most of the time we only half use them and do not extend them to their full ability. Spirit work however, needs us to use them to that full ability, whereby this in turn opens the third eye which is needed to both see and build up the ectoplasm required for seeing Spirit physically and not psychically.

Once again, I feel that it is time for another exercise, so here it is:

There needs to be two people for this next exercise, or a group containing an even number so that the people can be paired off. A chair is also needed for each person taking part. They should sit opposite one another with a gap of about twelve inches between them. This exercise may give better results if there is only light from a red bulb in the room, as people tend to extend the focal infrared part of their eyes better when sitting in a room with a red light. It would also be a good idea if each person had a tissue or handkerchief at hand during this exercise. Each person should make sure that they are fully relaxed, with their tissue or handkerchief either in their lap or their hand.

Now the couple should look into each others' eyes, making sure that they are using both eyes. This can be done by looking outwards with both eyes whilst concentrating on looking at both of your partner's eyes at the same time. Where possible there should be no conversation between the couple at this point. As you look into your partners' eyes, they should begin to glaze over and at this point you may be able to see shadows and images start to appear in their eyes. Keep watching, whilst keeping your eyes open as wide as you can.

As you watch, a bluish grey mist will start to appear in front of your partner's face, and tears may start to stream down your face. This is nothing to worry about, it is only your eyes getting used to the ectoplasm that is starting to build around both of you. If possible, try not to move position by wiping your eyes, just keep watching and concentrating whilst letting the tears fall. Keep your concentration on watching both of your partner's eyes, even if it gets to the point where you cannot see them any more.

Every person who attends my regular Spiritual Development Class will know that I believe that it is important for them to work themselves and not just listen to me talking or just watching me working come to that. For this reason, I set homework for my regular class members. By homework, I do not necessarily mean that they need to take a long time over it. For instance, I may give them the name of someone whom I know about and ask them to get as much information as they can about that person and find out whether they are here or in the Spirit World. This may sound difficult to a beginner but if they get used to knowing their Guide, and ask for that person's help, it is very easily accomplished.

There are two things that I tend to say from time to time, that seem to worry my class members for some reason. The first is, when I am giving them their homework, I might add: "There may be a red herring here." This tends to make them think, therefore creating a block on their Spirit link. They say that I am cruel but in fact I am being cruel to be kind because they need to get used to ignoring any information that they already know and just collect the information that the Spirit World are trying to communicate to them. This becomes important if you need to pass on a message from the Spirit World to someone whom you know fairly well. Practise makes perfect, therefore when I tell them that there may be 'a red herring', I am helping them to practise and therefore get nearer to perfect linking. The second thing that seems to bother students is when I am listening to what they received for their homework and I say: "Interesting." The reason this particular word bothers them is because they take it to mean that they have said something that I either know to be right or wrong and they are not to sure which. It is quite funny really because as soon as I say the word: "Interesting" everyone's eyes go wide and they look at each other and nod. This is especially so with Laureece because she has a very interesting turn of phrase most of the time anyway. This always creates laughter, which lifts the vibrations and as I said before helps the links go smoothly. My students say that the word 'Interesting' is my catch phrase.

On many occasions Laureece would complain that she could not do her homework. I would say: "You can", but she would retort "I cannot". It always reminded everybody of a pantomime, with children saying: "Oh yes you can" and the character shouting: "Oh no I can't." We often laughed about this even when she would telephone me in the middle of the week for advice because she would say: "Jean, I cannot do this homework." I would of course reply instantly: "Of course you can" but try to give her some advice anyway, even though I knew that she would be able to do it really.

My niece Michaela was lying in bed one evening when she looked up towards the window and saw a yellow orb of light hovering around the bedroom, on her right hand side. She then noticed that the orb changed colour and turned blue. When Spirit find it difficult to make their presence clear, they often use orbs of light to catch our attention. This is because light is reflective and can catch our view easily.

This particular orb was on her right hand side, which was indicating that it was her Guide that was trying to attract her attention. It started off yellow, which meant that her Guide was trying to educate her because yellow in this instance means teaching and learning. It changed to blue to let her know that Spirit wanted to communicate. A blue orb showing itself to a person here always means: "Spirit wish to communicate." Her Guide wanted to introduce her or himself to her. This was to be the beginning of her tuition to learn about being a Medium and Spirit linking in general.

Chapter Sixteen.

Murder Alley.

Psychic ability does not need to be acknowledged by the recipient to create the energy necessary for Spirit to show themselves to people here and now. My husband Mike has previously been a total sceptic and non believer in the existence of life after death. That is until he met and married me!! I therefore felt that it would be of interest to believers and non believers alike out there to hear some of Mike's true life memories involving a Spirit World that he felt did not exist!!

Mike was about six years old when he first saw the house and the street that he was to do the rest of his growing up in. It was a very long street with long rows of back to back houses on each side, which looked very scary, especially because the street was extremely dimly lit due to the fact that the lighting was the old gas streetlights. His mother and father had separated and Mike, his two older brothers, and his youngest sister Janet who was still a baby had moved to the new house with their mother and the man who was later to become their stepfather. Mike was uncertain because he had never met his soon to be stepfather before and he missed his older sisters who had stayed behind to live with their father.

On entering their new house for the first time, he was extremely scared as he looked around the dimly lit house, which also had gas lamps that were not very bright for its lighting. To a six year old being forced into a new beginning that he was not even sure that he wanted, could be quite scary on its own. The walls in their new home were painted with green distemper, which was a cheap type of paint used to help make the walls look clean by many people in days gone by when money was short, as it frequently was. The paint was peeling off the walls.

As Mike looked through the shadows created by the flickering from the flames of the coal fire, which was an old large black fire range, he became more afraid. The fire was supposed to be a welcoming sight for the new residents of the house but instead it served to make the room look even more, creepy!

There was a flight of stairs leading up to the main bedroom. The stairwell was dark and fairly spooky in its appearance but even more scary was the fact that the stairs carried on into an old attic just above the main bedroom which was to be a bedroom for Mike and his two brothers.

There were no gaslights or lighting of any kind, either on the stairwell or in the small attic room, which was to be his new sleeping accommodation. There was only the use of a hand held candle to light the way. Mike was terrified by this and desperately wanted to go back to his home where his father and two older sisters were. He could not understand why he could not be back with them and away from this horrible spooky place he was expected to call home.

He blocked out many memories of his formative years. Even now he cannot remember much about those early events which took place in his life, yet he remembers vividly how frightened he was in that house. The attic was and is the worst memory of the place he had to call home. As he lay in bed at night covered by as many old blankets and coats as they could find to keep out the biting cold that was a part of that room, and that whole house, he would watch the ceiling which sagged badly and always gave the impression that it would fall in on top of them at any moment. The bedding did little to stave off the cold, which was made worse by the dampness bedded deep into the walls and ceiling. One memory that has impressed deep into his mind is the fear he had of that house! Waking up screaming and shouting that he had seen someone standing by the bed which he shared with his brothers, or feeling someone or something had touched him from outside the bed.

One night stands out very clearly in his memory. On this particular occasion he was not in the attic, but in the living room. As he sat on the sofa whilst his mother had popped to the shops, his brothers were outside playing and his stepfather was as usual, over the road in the Public House, Mike must have fallen asleep. He was suddenly rudely awakened by someone touching him. He jumped up in time to see a tall, broadly built man who was dressed in black looking down at him!

Feeling absolutely terrified by what he was seeing, he summoned the energy to run to the door which would take him outside and ran for his life. Running up the entry by the side of the house, he banged urgently on the door of the next-door neighbour. His friend, who he often played with lived at this house. A largely built women whom was his friend's mother, answered the door. So Mike hurriedly blurted out what had happened. She was a person whom could look after herself and took him by the hand marching him back round to the house. Entering the living room she checked every nook and cranny before searching the rest of the house only to find that there was nothing or no one out of the ordinary in the house. She then sat and waited with Mike until a few minutes later when his mother returned. Being a very straightforward lady, she told Mike's mum exactly what she thought about her for leaving him alone in the house. Everyone assured him that he was just being silly and he must have been dreaming, but he knew different.

This street that he grew up in was a busy street where everyone knew everybody else's business. It was situated in Hockley, Birmingham. There were several Public Houses in the street and trouble would regularly spill out from one or the other of them, onto the roadway. Whenever, Mike was around at these times he would quickly cross over the road and hurry past. The street became known as 'Murder Alley', because during these altercations and at other times, there were a few murders committed in the street. Mike has gruesome memories of a man being taken away by the police after being told that this person had killed his wife with an axe. On another occasion, two old ladies were found strangled in their home on the street where Mike and his family lived.

Although there was not much money and life was hard in that street there were happy times too. Mike lived in that house in 'Murder Alley' until he was in his twenties. At this time everyone was moved out when the houses were pulled down. Moving away from 'Murder Alley' was mainly a happy time, especially getting away from that spooky old house but sadly Mike lost contact with his childhood friends who had been his neighbours for all those years. It was to be many years later that Mike was to hear the news that his childhood friend was in prison for murdering his wife. He remembered them both fondly even though he had only met his friend's wife a few times and was therefore obviously stunned. You cannot help thinking that Mike may have left 'Murder Alley' to move on. But is 'Murder Alley' still haunting him?

Looking back over his life, he realises that there were many things which happened that terrified him. He now feels that if only I had been around then or someone like me that would have listened to him and believed the things he was saying without putting it down to his imagination, then: 'Maybe' just 'maybe' he would have believed in the existence of the Spirit World a lot sooner, which would have removed a lot of the fear from his childhood days growing up in 'murder alley. As it was, he grew up feeling very lonely and shy. Even in his work life through many different jobs, he felt as though he was not doing what he should be, but could not work out what he should be attempting to do. It took Mike nearly fifty years to work out what he should be doing and that was working with Spirit. I should imagine many people in our world could tell similar true stories of their knowledge of the so called dead. A knowledge which, created fear through lack of understanding by not only themselves but also those people who were around them.

We have grandchildren who have the ability to see and talk to those people on the Spirit side of life. I can assure you that they will be listened to and helped to understand that there is no need to be afraid. However, children should never be pushed. They should be brought up with excessive amounts of love and assured in the knowledge that it is alright to talk to their 'Imaginary friends'. because these unseen friends are only there to bring love and guidance for the child's happy future. Who knows, if encouraged, maybe they will be some of tomorrow's best Mediums, without having to struggle and be afraid like Mike did in his early days.

Mike unfortunately had to do it the hard way. He did experience the fear, loneliness and uncertainty about the Spirit World purely because there was no one to guide him and help him understand. However, he made it in the end and happily works with and alongside Spirit now without any fright whatsoever. This chapter was Mike's contribution to this book about a Spirit World that he now works with daily.

Chapter Seventeen.

Understanding Dream Communication From Spirit.

Dreaming and disturbed sleep are classic signs of psychic powers that are not being used to their full advantage. People, who are extremely aware of the after life, tend to have a history of sleepwalking.

From early childhood, I used to sleepwalk. Usually my parents would find me on the landing or half way down the stairs and gently tell me to go back to bed, which generally I did. If someone is walking in their sleep it is not safe to make them jump or awaken that person suddenly. Therefore, if occasioning upon someone who is asleep but out of bed, then it is important to speak quietly, whilst being loud enough for their brain to acknowledge that they are being spoken to. The person's name should always be used because they are at that time in a meditative state and as such need to be slightly nudged towards reality without being woken up. My family and I have many memories of my past episodes of sleep walking, but some stand out in our memories more than others.

When I was approximately ten years of age these episodes of sleepwalking excelled, so that I was walking off during my sleep several times a night. One night my father discovered me walking out of the front door in my nightclothes at two o'clock in the morning whilst asleep. He therefore decided that it was time that something was done to ensure my safety. He set about putting a lock on the top of our bedroom door on the outside. He did this thinking that if I could not get out of the bedroom then I would go back to bed. That night however, my parents were in bed when they heard someone rattling our bedroom door as if trying to get out of, or into the bedroom. Because their bedroom connected to ours, the noises were extremely audible. Therefore, even though my father's initial comment was not to worry because I could not leave the bedroom, my mum was very concerned. She insisted that she would not be able to sleep if he did not get up and check what the noise was, and also that us three girls were safe. My father was not too impressed by this but decided that he was not going to be allowed to get any sleep if he did not take notice of my mum's request. He consequently unlocked our bedroom door just in time to see me on the bedroom window ledge about to step out of the window into thin air which would have obviously caused me to fall to the ground below, probably either seriously injuring or even killing myself.

After this, I was taken to the doctors in the hope that they could help, however, apart from being told that it is not a good idea to lock the bedroom door unless they lock the windows too, the doctor could not help. This is because a sleepwalker does not recognise danger and if an exit is locked they will then go to the next exit, which in my case was the window. It is also highly likely that I would have just stepped off the ledge as if expecting to walk on thin air.

Spirit have informed me that when a person is asleep, they are on exactly the same vibration that a Medium has aspired to when they are able to communicate with those on the Spirit side of life. This is the reason why people who are very psychic, sleepwalk. Their brain becomes occupied with this communication and therefore, it becomes real to them. Causing them to recreate the actions they are seeing.

Walking is usually a safe pastime, but whilst asleep we are following a different set of rules. It is at these times that we see Spirit people walk through walls etc and because of a deep logic within our brain, we know that we cannot do this. On realisation that we are not going to follow them through the walls, Spirit walk out using the doors or windows. Not being aware of the fact that we will think that we can do the same, even whilst upstairs. This is because we know deep inside our brain that in life's experience these are natural exits that we can use safely. Spirit sometimes talk to us by example, using the knowledge already stored in our brain thereby not realising that we sometimes take them literally. This is especially so whilst we are asleep. A spirit visitor had obviously been talking to me that night whilst I was asleep and had shown me that they were outside. I had reacted by trying to go downstairs to join them outside. When I found the door locked, I thought that I could go through the window. I was therefore about to do just that when luckily my father came into the bedroom and stopped me.

It is an interesting fact that most of the people who are never aware of Spirit generally, will experience any little knowledge that they have of them existing whilst in the bedroom. This also extends to the fact that those who are already Mediumistic naturally receive more Spirit communication with ease whilst in the bedroom. My husband often jokes that our bedroom is always very active. He means with Spirit activity of course. The reason for this interesting fact of occurrence is simply because Spirit constantly try to communicate with people whilst they are in sleep state, purely because they are on the right vibration. Because people sleep more often in the bedroom, this constant link from those in the Spirit World builds up large amounts of psychic energy which in turn relaxes our body and mind to an extent that we automatically change our vibration and therefore, more Spirit activity is noticed in the bedroom and not because Spirits always haunt you whilst you are asleep which is a common belief.

Mike thinks that it is quite comical when people from Spirit come to converse with me about someone I love during the night when I am having trouble sleeping. I allow them to do just that, yet I am quite strict with them at other times. I actually think that some of my strongest evidence comes to me in bed at night. I therefore often wonder what a phenomenal service I could give if I held it in the bedroom. It definitely brings a new meaning to the phrase pillow talk, doesn't it?

Fortunately it is usually only the extremely psychic who have this kind of problem with either Spirit Communication keeping them awake or sleepwalking. Most people tend to receive a message from the Spirit World via a dream. These dreams are just like any other dreams accept for the fact that they are much clearer and as such are remembered clearly by the recipient of the dream when they wake up. Said like this, I am sure it sounds much easier for a person to be able to understand the message that their loved one is trying to portray. This being so, thinking that once you are awake and remember the clear dream, you know what they are saying and that it is Spirit, because you have a clear memory of it. However, I am afraid that like anything else to do with Spirit linking, it is not quite that simple.

During sleep state whilst we are dreaming, our brain picks up the images that make up the dream upside down. It then turns the picture around and forms it into a story that we can understand. As this process is taking place, the dream becomes a bit jumbled making it hard to understand. This is the reason why people cannot always understand what their dreams mean. Analysing a dream is usually a simple process, which is made difficult by people looking for something deeper than is actually required. Here are a few examples of dreams that were expressed by Spirit, how they were received and what they actually meant.

My husband Mike had a dream recently in which he was standing with a rope noose around his neck ready to be hung, and all the people that he knows were coming up to him and saying 'goodbye'. This understandably bothered him because he thought that it was a bad dream. But was it? Believe it or not, this was a futuristic dream which is trying to inform him of what his life is doing and what it will be like if he stands still and lets these things happen and get out of control. It is also informing him that he is thinking of taking the wrong steps, which will lead to no good. In other words he will lose all that is important to him if he carries on the way he is going and he will have in fact hung himself and cut off a life that he enjoys with people whom he loves. Therefore he is in control at the moment and is being given the chance to change direction before it is too late.

The factor that he is standing with a noose around his neck is telling him that he is allowing things that he is uncertain of from his past, hold him back from living his life the way it should be now, and this will end in sadness, loneliness and heartache if he lets it happen. All the people he knows saying goodbye to him means, that he will loose the love, company and respect of all those he loves most if he carries on the way he is going. He is standing up because he is not relaxed with the situation that he has found himself in emotionally. He is standing still instead of going forward, with a rope around his neck, which means he is tying himself to the wrong from the past that has led him into trouble before and given enough rope will hang him self.

The rope noose shows that he is aware that the end of a situation is near and he is uncertain of his future if new surroundings take place, he also knows that he really loves it where he is now, with the people whom surround him. Therefore, he is being shown himself on death row. Death, that is of a life that he is happy with. Everyone who he knows, are saying goodbye, to show him that he will be on his own and lonely if he carries on in the direction that he is heading So you see, it is not a bad dream but a prophetic one, which took place to advise him not to go on the way he is going or he will live to regret it.

In the dream, if you remember, he had not yet been hung; therefore he lived to see an end to a life he enjoyed, with people he loved. This was Spirit's way of advising him to be careful of the direction that he is being led, or he would in fact lose everything and everyone which would cause him great regret.

For my younger sister Hazel who is extremely psychic, dreams are frequently used to show her premonitions. One of these prophetic dreams was very clear in her memory from when she was a young child of about twelve years of age, living in our family home.

In my mum's house there are two rooms plus the kitchen and hall on the ground floor. At that time, in the back room there used to be a small kitchen table with four matching chairs and there was also a sofa up against the window. My sister remembers dreaming every night that as she looked up to the corner of the window in that back room, she could see a shiny white face pressed up against the pane looking straight at her. The face was approximately the size of a small ball. She said that they were told that whenever the face appeared, it meant that she and my brothers must get out whilst they still could, because if they did not get out then something bad would happen. However, on one occasion as they tried to get out, Ken got his leg caught down the side of the settee and could not get out.

Hazel said that this dream was so real that she was sure it was true. She remembered that I was still living at home at the time and that I moved out a few months later. This meant that Hazel was having these repetitive dreams just before my brother Kenneth died of kidney failure. Therefore, it is apparent that Spirit were informing her that something was going to happen to Ken and that he would be going to the Spirit side of life soon.

The white shiny face at the window was Spirit watching ready for Ken to go over. The fact that it was white and shiny was because the face was of a Spiritual appearance. She had the dream repetitively every night to indicate that he would be ill for a while before passing, which turned out to be the case. The fact that Kenneth was the one who was trapped by his leg getting caught down the side of the settee in the room where they had been told that if they did not get out when the face appeared something bad would happen, says that he would be the one to go to Spirit.

The same sister tells me that when she was sixteen years old she had a dream which she has always remembered. In this dream, herself and her friend were on their way to Sutton Coldfield Town Centre. It was during the evening, therefore it was dark at the time. In her dream they were walking down a steep road near to Sutton

Coldfield Town Centre, called Trinity Hill, and for some unknown reason her friend went to one of the houses. They walked down the front path, where they came to a little porch and there were lots of heads hanging from the top of this porch roof. In the dream the friend knocked the door and Hazel retorted: "No do not knock that door! There is a murderer inside the house." She knocked the door regardless of Hazel's warning, and a man came out brandishing a blade of some kind and he chased my sister down Trinity Hill. She remembers running for her life and being extremely frightened. At this point in the dream she woke up feeling panicky and it was so vivid that she still remembers it in detail to this day and she is forty years old now.

This dream had started off normally with Hazel and her friend going out together as they often did. With the added factor that it was dark yet in life they usually went to Sutton during daylight hours. That is the first message coming across from Spirit. It is indicating that there is a need to be more careful when you are surrounded in darkness, as you would be on a winter's evening. They walked down the front path of an unknown property without giving any thought to any dangers they could be walking into. Yet, as soon as Hazel, whose dream it was, saw the heads hanging up in the porch. She knew that they would be in imminent danger if her friend knocked the door. She was also aware that if there were all those people's heads hanging in the porch then there was most likely by process of elimination, a murderer inside the house. The friend did not take heed of this warning, knocking the door anyway. Yet it was Hazel whom was chased by the man with the blade in his hand.

My sister was being warned by Spirit, that she should always take notice of her own thoughts and feelings because they would always try to keep her out of danger and trouble. Whereas, if she listened to her friends instead of following her own instincts, which they could use to contact and guide her with, then they would not be able to help her. This would mean that she could find herself in danger. This dream was an informative dream combined with a warning. It took place in Trinity Hill because it was to be many years later that unfortunately a young lady was murdered in the Churchyard on Trinity Hill. It was therefore, also a dream that was in the form of a premonition. They do this for two reasons. One is to try to keep the recipient of the message 'or dream' safe, and the second is so that in the future, when the real murder took place, the dreamer would realise that she had an idea this may happen which in turn gave her the start of a belief in a Spirit World that could help and guide her through life. The hanging heads were telling her that she needed to keep her head at all times by using her common sense and not listening to other people like her friends when her instincts were telling her different.

Hazel recently dreamt that she was walking in a field with a colleague from work, when they heard a noise up above them. As they looked up an aeroplane crashed and broke up into pieces. Bits of the aircraft started to fall all around them so they both ran to shelter under a tree. However, pieces of debris were still falling around them. All at once fluid, which was pouring from the fuel tanks started to pour down to the ground and Hazel began to run. As she looked behind her she could see a line of this fuel chasing her and the faster she ran the quicker the flow of fuel seemed to follow in pursuit. Suddenly there was an explosion as a part of the aeroplane hit the ground on top of the flow of fuel, with which, flames began to lick at speed along the ground. Before she could do anything about it she was enveloped in flames, with the whole of her body totally alight. She became aware that she had died and a whooshing sound came over her. But she said that it was a really good feeling to be dead. After which she woke up feeling really happy.

I should explain to you before attempting to analyse this dream, that Hazel and her family were experiencing ghost activity around them in their home, because what is happening to us and around us at the time of the dream, has a bearing on what message Spirit are trying to convey to us at that time. I therefore, felt that it is important to mention this.

Hazel 'for her sins' worked as a traffic warden at that time and therefore would not generally be walking in a field with a colleague because cars are not usually illegally parked in a field, are they? Also it is appropriate to mention that aeroplanes are not the type of vehicle that she would normally be paying attention to either. Yet, here she was in a field with a colleague observing an aeroplane crash.

Once again we are in a situation that does not make sense to the dream recipient's normal routine. This is trying to explain to her that although life at the moment is not going in the straightforward way that she is used to, there is a reason for this. Watching the aircraft is indicating people above whom she is unsure of. (This is because she does not know who the people are, that are in the aeroplane) She is anxious and unsure at the moment about visitors from the Spirit World being around her home. People here tend to look on the Spirit World as being above because of an upbringing that tells them that heaven is up above the clouds. Therefore, it depicts unknown people above. She then sees lots of the aircraft pieces falling down as though raining on top of her which indicates that she feels burdened by what is happening around her that she does not understand. She feels inundated with unknown factors that appear to be pressurising her.

The line of fuel pouring from the aircraft and chasing Hazel is saying that she feels as though she is being followed constantly by unhappy or dangerous events. Yet, she knows deep within her heart that she is being watched over, even though these problems are around, which try as she might she cannot escape from because things always seem to go wrong.

In the dream she is enveloped in flames and died but felt really comfortable and at ease with her death and the situation that she found herself in. This is saying that Hazel need not be afraid because she is being looked after by those people who are in high places. It tells her that no matter how bad things appear to be, she will be alright and happy with the conclusion, and the situation that she finds herself in. This is made more certain by the fact that she woke up feeling really happy after this dream had taken place.

Another dream that she had fairly recently was that she and a colleague were on duty in Birmingham Town Centre when they walked down some steep steps and they saw a horse drawn black funeral carriage coming towards them. Her friend stood in front of it, placing her left hand up in front of her in an attempt to stop it. This was a little suspicious because the friend was right handed so would in life stop the carriage with that hand. In the dream the carriage however, took no notice and just drove forward chopping her left arm off as it went. As this occurred it threw her arm up into the air and sprayed blood everywhere as it did so. Hazel was covered in blood and feeling nauseous and her friend then died and she woke up feeling extremely shaky.

First of all I should explain that Hazel and her friend live and work in Derby, and not in Birmingham, which is where the dream took place.

Also, it is necessary to say that this dream was about twelve months ago. Whereas, horse drawn funeral carriages have only been used for funerals in the town where they work for the last six months. This means that when the dream took place, Hazel had never seen one or directed one through the traffic like she sometimes does now. This told her that the dream was talking about the future.

Being in a town where they did not in fact work was saying that some form of deception would take place. Coming down the steep steps to get to where the other traffic Warden was killed is say that she is sinking very low in her actions towards Hazel. It is this way round because as the dreamer she would have been the one to be killed if she had been the deceiver instead of the one to be deceived. Yet she came down the steps with the other person therefore, she would prove to be the target of the underhandedness and deception.

The fact that the colleague had her arm ripped off in the dream, is telling Hazel that she needs to watch this person as she will do the dirty on her and be the one to deceive her. This is indicated by the fact that she was showered with her colleague's blood which, remember also made her feel sick. The person who died had their left arm ripped off because they were using that arm when they were in fact right handed, which was also saying that this person was not to be trusted because things were not as they seemed? The colleague's death was the final action, which was making it clear that their friendship would be over, therefore, 'the colleague would be as good as dead,' because that person would no longer be intimately involved in Hazel's life.

Once again this was a warning dream combined with a premonition. The dream was warning my sister, that she should be careful otherwise this person would deceive her in the not too distant future. However, it was also a premonition, because it indicated something that would happen in the future and I must add that it did take place in the future.

Once these things were explained to her, my sister began to realise that she had in fact been having premonitions for some time. Hazel said that before she had become pregnant with her twins, who are now almost five years of age. One day she said to her partner: "I am pregnant." He looked shocked and answered: "What?" To, which she, repeated: "I am pregnant." Then later on my sister found out that she was pregnant. She had a scan, which was followed by a second scan a fortnight later. It was when this scan took place that they found out that they were having twins.

After this, Hazel had a dream in which she was also pregnant carrying twins, just as in real life. However, in the dream she saw one baby dressed in a pink romper suit and one in a blue romper suit. She therefore thought that she must be having a girl and a boy. On the strength of this her partner bought a pink romper suit and a blue romper suit, so when the twins were born both girls, one was dressed in the colour blue. In the dream the child dressed in blue had a poorly tummy button where its umbilical cord had been. And Melissa, one of the twins had problems with hers when she was born. She was put into the blue romper suit and her sister in the pink. Melissa is also stronger minded than her twin sister Amelia, who on the other hand is much quieter.

As soon as the twins were old enough to see, Amelia stared constantly at me wherever I happened to be in the room. She was obviously watching my Spirit Guides and other Spirits around me. This meant that it became really apparent from a very early age that she is extremely psychic. Therefore, she is very in touch with her feminine side. People who are very psychic from the word go tend to be overly sensitive, which is just how I am. The only problem with this fact is that as people, we tend to get hurt by others easily because we can be too forgiving, although, from a personal point of view, I would not want to be any other way.

Hazel's psychic abilities were trying their best to come to the fore and Spirit were informing her that they were around and able to help and guide her. She dreamt that her daughter Michaela was standing in the kitchen near to the washing machine when a big ray of light came in through the window. Michaela started to walk towards the light and Hazel shouted: "Micki, don't." As she called this out, Hazel started to pull her back. You need to bear in mind that my niece was only three at the time. My sister was pulling her back by holding onto her ankles and suddenly our father came into the picture. In the dream he took hold of Michaela and pulled her out of the light. He placed her into Hazel's arms and said: "Hold her tight. Do not let her go, no matter what." As he did so he stood in front of the ray of light and disappeared into it. On waking, she felt that her daughter would have died if she had gone into the light and our father had saved his granddaughter. Yet it was hard to understand.

Micki was a little unwell just after this dream and it was only a few weeks later that our father died after becoming ill with lung cancer. Hazel felt that he had taken her daughter's place and gone to the

Spirit World in her place. The dream definitely indicated this and once again Hazel's dream gave her a premonition of the future. They were trying very hard to communicate to her that she could talk to the 'dead'.

I myself had a dream recently where a close friend told me that she had just handed in her resignation at work, but had been advised to reconsider. She said to me in the dream: "For Gods sake, I am seventy five now and still stuck in this job. I will never get out if I do not go now." In the dream she looked old, overly thin, tired and worn out with bags beneath her eyes. This does not describe my friend in life at all. She is an extremely vibrant and attractive person. Her age is nearer fifty and although she is not overweight she is not too slim either. This dream came to me by way of advice for my friend but sometimes it is not easy to pass this kind of information on. Spirit however felt that they were not managing to reach her. Yet they knew that I had her best interests at heart and would help if I could. Therefore, I dreamt about it.

The dream was saying that she needed to take a risk and go for the new career being offered to her otherwise she would never escape the drudgery that she feels she is in at the moment. It was saying that we would still be friends and I would still be there to offer support and advice at that stage of her life regardless of any decisions that she should make now.

It also indicated that she would in fact change her career path. This is indicated by the fact that the dream was in the third person, in other words through me. She will obviously still be alive and well at the ripe old age of seventy five. Once again this dream appeared to be of a sad nature when in fact it was one that foretold prosperity and lifelong friendship, for both my friend and I. It also shows that she is right to feel that it is time to move on career wise and that she will not regret taking a slight risk by changing pathways. This is shown by the fact that the dream is indicating regret if she stays where she is, thereby the right action is for her to take a chance and change career path which she will not regret. I know that this particular friend had in fact dreamt of me on occasions, so you see her loved ones in the Spirit World made sure that they connected to us both through our dreams to ensure we would get the message.

My son, Dean, is extremely psychic even though he is very uncertain of the Spirit World. His dreams can therefore sometimes be of a very Spiritual nature. He was unfortunate enough some years ago to witness a close friend getting killed, which really knocked him about emotionally as it would anyone. I cannot imagine the horror of this happening and hopefully will never experience it personally. I feel that it is bad enough when a close friend decides to go their own separate way and out of your life, but at least you have the knowledge that they are alright.

People tend to look on grief as something you experience when someone you love goes out of your life because they die. This is indeed the form of grief that we hear about most of all. Yet when someone you love chooses to walk out of your life because they do not care about you as much as you do them, grief still comes into play.

In my experience this type of grief is harder to overcome because you know that, that person has decided that they want no more to do with you. Whereas, if someone dies they have no choice and anyway even to a non-believer in life after death, at these times people tend to feel there is a chance that maybe the loved one is still around close to them. However, watching a close friend die makes the person feel inadequate because they did not save that friend. They then feel as though they have let that friend down. Although this is not true, the grief extends throughout all parts of that person's life. The person who has died however, comes in exceptionally close during this time to try and reassure their loved one that they really are alright and it is not their fault.
This means that any dreams that person experiences at this time will take on an extremely Spiritual nature. Two of my son's clearest memories from during those really difficult months were as follows.

Dean is not certain whether he was asleep or awake at the beginning of this unusual experience. I say unusual, but that is to the average everyday person and not to someone like myself. At the time that it occurred he was in bed leaning back against his pillows and the bedroom wall, which was directly behind his headboard. He became aware of a really old Native American Indian, whose face appeared worn and weathered. He was at first standing with a hand on each hip and a frown on his face. Dean shot up in bed as suddenly a very young Native American Indian appeared and stepped forward. At that moment the older Indian took another step nearer again and placed the palm of his hand with arm outstretched onto the younger man's face and pushed him down onto the floor. At this point Dean fell backwards onto his pillow with his back against his bedroom wall once more. The older man then smiled at him gently and disappeared. My Son was then left wondering what it had all been about.

The older Indian had been trying to tell Dean that sometimes, younger men like Dean's friend who had just passed to Spirit, need the hand of experience behind them to go forward in life in the right way. He was saying that Dean too was young and therefore did not understand all that had happened. However, he would be there to protect them both from now on. This was indicated by the fact that my son saw the older Indian push the younger one with him, yet Dean had felt the pressure of the push and had been projected back onto his pillow.

He wanted him to realise that he could not join his friend because the time was not right for his passing although it had been for his friend. This was relayed to him by the change of the push from the young Spirit person across to the reality of himself feeling the projection. Meaning he had to stay with the living where he belonged for the time being and he inferred that he will look after both of them. The two he would look after being, Dean's friend over in the Spirit side of life and himself here in this side of life. He was also saying that he was strong and in charge and therefore Dean should step back and do as he was told.

On the second occasion, the same weathered old Indian appeared in front of him. This time, though he did not seem quite as aggressive as he had been the first time. I believe this was because he could see that Dean's anger at the situation had changed to a type of deep inner sadness, which needed addressing if my son was going to get through his time of grief safely.

Any person who is suffering from grief will always go through a stage where anger takes over. This is good because until this has happened the grieving person will not be able to move forward in their life. However, unfortunately a deeper depressive type state always follows. This is when the grieving person needs loved ones close around them to help. Dean was at this stage in his grieving process when the old Native American Indian put in his second appearance. This time the Indian squatted down in a crouching position in front of a fire, as if warming his hands. He was chanting quietly at first but then became louder as he stood and spread out his arm, palm of his hand facing upwards and turned as if to point out the river, which was now visible in the scene that Dean was being shown. He looked my son straight in the eye and spoke in a quiet calm voice: "My son, the bear looks aggressive and cruel when he with great speed dips his sharp dagger like claw into the water and scoops out a living fish to kill and eat." Dean could now see moving pictures of the bear actively scooping a writhing fish out of the riverbed. He watched and listened, motionless as the Indian went on: "But the bear needs to eat to live if he is going to live on the earth for the length of time that he is meant to. However, the fish only lives his earth life for a short period and he helps the bear to live a long and happy life by returning to Spirit early, thereby helping the Spirit of life?"

He was trying to ease Dean's pain by using a Spiritual analogy in an attempt to try to make him understand that although his friend had been run over and killed by a car and therefore snatched maliciously into death by the driver of the car, it was in fact always intended that he should go back to the Spirit World early so that he could help others to live on and have a happy and full life here on the earth.

The bear that plunged the fish to its death learnt a valuable lesson from this event taking place. He was able to acknowledge for certain that with speed and precision he would be able to eat that day. The driver of the car would have learnt an opposite lesson because he would know that maybe he could have stopped in time had he been driving more slowly at the time. Yet, in reality what took place in both cases was meant to be. Both, the fish who was killed by the bear and the young man whom was killed by the car had returned home to Spirit early in order to help others. The bear or the driver of the car, were not in reality wholly to blame for the soul going to Spirit early, this was meant to be.

The bear and the driver were, however, responsible for their actions and as such would pay for their deeds, which were carried out whilst still here on the earth. For instance, the car driver's actions had 'had a stone in a pond ripple effect' which had in turn caused heartache and distress to many people including his own close family and friends. This in turn had taught many people a valuable lesson, and also given the young man a feasible passage home to Spirit. In other words, the young man who died had not done so in vain because in fact many people had been helped by his somewhat untimely death.

We people who live on to grieve need to understand that no matter how untimely a death may seem, it is always necessary because someone, somewhere gains from that death due to that person's soul returning to the Spirit World where they can help others. I cannot tell you that Dean knew instantly what the Native American Indian had been trying to tell him, but I can definitely say with certainty that the whole Spiritual incident had taken him closer to Spirit. It had also made him reflect upon his grief and started to help him through those really tough times. It is also true to say that he still reflects upon this incident now and I am sure that he is a more Spiritual and understanding individual because of it.

My son moved forward Spiritually due to his friend's death, therefore that is at least one person whom has been helped and moved forward because of a death, which was thought to be untimely. The visit from the Native American Indian should prove to at least one person that the young man in question has arrived home safe in the Spirit World and that his death was already helping others within hours of his dying. That one person is my son Dean who was and is after all a close friend of the deceased and was the last person whom he spoke to before his soul departed his body for the Spirit World. So therefore, it makes sense that his first Spiritually connected message would come to that very person who was suffering because of his friend's gruesome departure.

Just because a person receives Spiritually channelled messages such as this one, where Dean is not entirely certain to this day whether he was asleep or awake, it does not mean that all his dreams will follow the same pattern. He is after all human with human failings, although I must add at this point that he is at least ninety percent sure that he was awake when these incidents started and one hundred percent certain that he was awake and totally alert towards the end of these Spirit messages.

I think that it is also appropriate to tell you at this point that on the day of Christmas Eve 2004, one of my best friends and I were visiting Streetly Crematorium to take some Christmas wreathes to put on the memorial stones of her father and aunt whom were in different parts of this very large crematorium and graveyard. Jason had died in April 1994. As we were entering the gates I explained to Chris that my son's friend, Jason, had been buried in that very graveyard but unfortunately we could not remember where. Dean would like to visit his grave, if only we could find it but this was a difficult task because the place was so big and contained so many graves and memorial stones.

As we disembarked from the car to approach her father's headstone I heard a voice whisper a name which I did not quite catch fully. Although Spirit kept repeating the name it was far too quietly for me to hear properly. Each time I heard it I enquired from Chris if a name sounding similar meant anything to her? She replied each time that it did not. After placing the flowers and cleaning up her father's headstone we headed back towards where the car was parked and Spirit kept whispering a name that sounded like Ryan or Ry something over and over again. Chris still could not understand it. We were both very puzzled by this. We clambered back into the car and headed across to the other side of the large graveyard where Chris' aunt's memorial stone had been placed.

Parking the car nearby, Chris was taking the flowers out of the boot when someone from Spirit placed a hand on my left shoulder. I also clearly heard "Look at those two gravestones there, the one at the end first." My eyes darted across to the gravestone on the end, which read nee Ryder after the Christian name, this sounded like the name I had been hearing whispered to me since first arriving at the crematorium. I could not believe my eyes and quickly looked at the gravestone next to it. There in front of my eyes was Jason's grave picture on the front and all. I was so shocked and excited that I screamed out to Chris and made her jump. We both agreed that this was amazing considering the hundreds of graves and memorial stones within the crematorium. So you see, when Spirit thinks that something is really important they can help to bring it about.

Recently Dean told me that he had been having a recurring dream where he would wake up from sleep and hear something moving by the side of the bed. He would look over the side to see his partner sneaking along bending over so as not to be seen. In this dream she was totally naked and there was a man with her. He always wakes up at this point in the dream. This is purely and simply showing the fact that he was feeling insecure at the moment. When you consider that he was recently made redundant from his job and he is worried about supporting his family. It becomes very clear where this insecurity is coming from and therefore, when the problem is sorted the dream will go away. However, we need to remember that Dean's Spirit Guides predicted his future would be alright before and that he would come through his grief which he did. Therefore, it becomes fairly obvious that his relationship may be in trouble and that his partner would be the one to walk away from the relationship, not Dean.

This dream was plain and simple. His brain was running through the problems that he was dealing with at that time and Spirit was informing him of the likely outcome in a way that he would understand. The dream would not show an exact picture of how events would be, but would depict the outcome which was his partner walking away. It was saying that he would loose her to someone else and the situation indicates that she would leave in such a way that would be a vulnerable situation for them both.

We have to remember that our brain works in opposites and the dream becomes jumbled as in this case. In the dream he felt that he could not take care of his partner, so someone was stealing her from him. In reality this is his fear about not being able to take care of her. He is worried that someone else will. This is not going to happen it is just his brain re-enacting his worries through his dreams. The other person in the dream does not have to be a sexual partner as it seems in the dream, it can be a family member but there would definitely be a certain amount of trickery involved which is why Spirit showed her sneaking off with someone. The other person could simply be a person who is encouraging the break up and helping it to happen in some way.

It is also worth mentioning that during the same time period his partner dreamt that there was a black cat sitting on the window ledge of their flat looking in at her. This dream is saying that good luck is watching over them and they would be alright so not to worry. A black cat always depicts good luck in a dream. The fact that it was looking into the flat from outside, but close up and looking directly at her means that she thinks the good luck is outside her life at that time and encouraging her to think that she would be better off elsewhere, because the cat was looking directly at her. Once again we need to take into consideration the circumstances around them at the moment. The breadwinner is unemployed and with two young children to support, they are both naturally worried. Their dreams both depict this fact, his enacts the worries he has and hers predicts her thoughts of being insecure too and wanting to escape. The conclusion, which tells them they are being watched over and not to worry because some good luck is on its way, indicates that although things will not go well for them as a couple they will be alright. As the black cat is outside, they will find their luck away from each other. Unfortunately the couple did split up which was a difficult time but it did work out for the best for my son, the luck on the outside of his then relationship definitely came true for him, and I sincerely hope that it did for her too.

A young man, whom is a friend of my son, told me that he had a recurring dream that had started approximately two years ago. Dreams that are clear and repeat themselves are in fact messages from Spirit that come to us in our sleep. Spirit is trying very hard to portray some information to the recipient of the dream, which they feel will help guide that person forward and help clear up any uncertainties.

In Kerry's dream he was in a room where he could see a large rocket shaped bomb being made. This bomb was huge and reaching for the sky. At that point he became aware that the police were on their way into the building. In the dream he quickly climbed up onto a shed, which had a corrugated roof. He could see a policeman standing below the shed and a wall on the other side of him. On the other side of the wall it was all clear so he decided to slide down the roof and off to the other side of the wall away from the policeman. As Kerry slid off the roof in the dream towards the wall, he suddenly found himself bouncing off the wall and floating up through the air. He then bumped into a window ledge and went through a window into a room where there were lots of old ladies sitting drinking cups of tea.

They turned to look at him and appeared to be frightened by his sudden appearance into their gathering. He quickly told these people that he did not want to hurt them but just wanted to get out. Across the room on the far wall there were several doors all in different colours. He anxiously tried them one at a time, rattling each one in turn as hard as he could to try to escape from the unwanted position that he had found himself in. Finally one of the doors opened and he ran out onto a stairwell, up the stairs where he found himself in a library that had thousands of books in it. As he looked around the room anxiously, he woke up.

In this dream, Kerry at first found himself in a position that appeared to be extremely dangerous. This was because a large bomb was being made in front of his eyes, a situation that must have appeared good in the first instance because it was reaching for the sky. Yet although he was not actually involved in making the bomb, if it had ignited then he would have been too close to escape danger. This part of his dream indicates that at that point in his life he had found himself in a position that he did not really want to be in. He also, felt out of control and unable to alter his predicament at that time.

The police closing in on him meant that there were people of authority making their presence known and he felt closed in as though he had no alternative or escape from his predicament. These authority figures were most likely parents of himself and his partner. Who were trying to make him take responsibility for his actions at that time. However, he was feeling closed in. When he was about to escape over the wall 'in the dream' and safely away from the policeman, he hit the wall and floated upwards. This indicated that the authority figure may appear worrying but in fact they are really a safety net in the situation where he has found himself. This is reinstated by the fact that he found himself in a room full of elderly ladies drinking tea, and the fact that these ladies appeared to be concerned by his presence. The dream was saying that the older people around him were simply concerned about him and the situation that he had got himself into, but were there to direct him in the right direction should he listen to them.

The only door that would open to allow him to escape the room where these authority people were, led him to the library. This was telling him that these older people had all sorts of information and help that they could offer him because between them their knowledge was vast and they knew a lot more than he did on his own because they had lived longer and experienced more. The dream indicated that he was safe with the advice of his elders, so therefore he should listen to their advice and everything would turn out well in the end. The police presence also indicated imminent danger for anyone who was either involved or appeared to be involved in the making of that bomb. This was telling him that purely by being present in that room with the bomb meant that he was in danger. His immediate thoughts were the need to escape the situation that he had found himself in, hence climbing up on the shed roof and trying to slide off and over the wall past where the policeman was standing and could catch him. This dream was meant to resolve the problems that Kerry had found himself in, by suggesting that he should not fight the advice of his parents etc because in this instance they probably knew best. Yet once again the recipient of the dream had misunderstood and got the message backwards and thought that it was something to be afraid of.

These next two dreams came about when two close friends of mine were the recipients of the dreams. Firstly, a friend dreamt this very vivid dream, which she found to be a bit scary at the time. In the dream itself there were three men whom were all dressed in yellow leather roundhead style top and breeches. These men were obviously from that time in our history. They were fighting in a field and one of them suddenly attacked somebody. My friend at that point intervened and kicked the attacker between the legs, after which the man walked off across the field. It was at this time during the dream that a man on a horse came riding towards the dreamer. As he did so a great shadow overcast her and everywhere turned dark. She instantly asked for protection because in life she believes in Spiritual matters and this had therefore been carried through into her dream. The horse rider then said his name and my friend woke up.

This dream may have been short but it had a very explicit meaning and was in fact quite straight forward to analyse to the trained eye. This dream went back in history but included my friend in modern day life. This indicated that she herself was allowing something from her past to affect her now. Herself watching someone getting attacked and going to their rescue by kicking the attacker in a vulnerable place, meant that something is about to take place in her life that is a bit delicate and should be handled as such. As the man walked off across the field, the horse appeared and the great shadow which turned everything dark. This meant that whatever trouble was causing my friend to worry was being overshadowed with protection from Spirit. She assumed that the darkness meant that there was evil surrounding her because she had kicked the attacker. Whereas it did in fact reflect that she should be careful and not turn the situation that she is in, to an attack on the other person because that person is protected by Spirit. It was in fact indicating that her past can only overshadow her life now if she allows it to. The man walking off across the field is telling her that the past should be put back where it belongs because things are being taken care of in the here and now. It also indicates that she herself is in charge of putting things right because she gave the action that made the man walk away.

This dream was in fact informative. It was relaying events that were already happening to reassure my friend to go forward in her life.

The second of these dreams that I will tell you about, was received by my close friend called Chris. In her dream, the thing that puzzled her most about it was the fact that the pictures were standing still with no movement whatsoever. It showed a clear, still picture of a man hanging, although she could not see the rope. His feet were off the ground and his head was to one side but no noose was visible. This dream although appearing to be confusing, is in

235

fact fairly straightforward to understand. It is pointing out to Chris that something out of the ordinary is about to take place, but that situation will not be as it seems therefore, she should not worry. The joint fact that the dream was in still pictures and no rope could be seen, tells her that the situation that she either is or will be involved in, is unusual. The missing rope also indicates that things are not as bad as they appear. This is because you cannot hang without the rope and there was no rope in this scene. Because the picture did not move, it is telling the dream recipient that the next stage of this scene has not yet happened and therefore the end has a variable meaning, that it can be changed to a favourable outcome. She was being informed that this was definitely a sleep received message because of its starkness.

Apart from this unusual dream Chris had a strange experience a few days later which totally puzzled her. She was walking through Walsall town centre going about her business, when an elderly lady approached her saying: "Excuse me love." Chris stopped to acknowledge the lady and was expecting her to ask for either the time, or directions. However, the lady asked: "Can you tell me, what take for granted means?" At this, Chris was totally taken aback. She answered the woman's question as best she could, then turned to see her walk off down the road. It is at times like this that it comes in handy to have a friend like myself whom can link to the Spirit World and find out all sorts of information that is not readily available to most people. Chris therefore, telephoned me that evening to enquire what I thought about this most unusual incident. Under normal circumstances in this life of ours, we come up against some unusual people because each one of us is after all, unique. The fact that this happened just after Chris had received the strange dream about the hanging man, emphasises the factor of something unusual about to happen. Chris for her part was not even sure whether this woman was real or not. Even though she knew that the incident had taken place. She was left feeling that maybe the lady was a Spirit because she and her question were so different to the norm. I assured her that the lady had been real as she put it (even Spirit people are real). Misunderstanding what I was telling her she commented that in one way she was a little disappointed at this because she had never seen Spirit and if this woman had been, then she had seen her clearly and she quite liked the idea of this. I do, however, know that given time and patience, Chris will see Spirit anyway but not like she did this time. The person she sees will be more obviously Spirit, because it will be someone whom she knows to be dead.

Those close to us on the Spirit side of life, often use solid things here to help convey their message. If they are doing this, then the incident that occurs is out of the ordinary compared to what else is taking place. They do this so that their point will be noticed even if it is not understood at the time it happens. This usually means that later on the person becomes aware what the incident was all about and at the same time accepts that they knew of the thing that happened before it took place. Unfortunately most people would not put the two incidents together, which is a shame because together they make more sense. In the dream the man was hanging in unusual circumstances because he was motionless and there was no rope.

When the lady spoke to Chris in the shopping centre, she was unusual because of the strange question that she chose to ask a stranger without any further explanation of her actions.
We need to now take into consideration, any words that were spoken. In the dream there were none, but the woman asked: "Excuse me love, can you tell me what take for granted means?"

Chris is therefore being told not to take things for granted, just because a situation looks bad it may not be because things are not always as they appear. The hanged man could not have been hanging without a rope or something else to hang him by. It is also true that just because the lady was a bit unusual this did not make her unreal. The stillness of the dream is also untrue because things happening in life 'or death' never stand still. She needs therefore, not to worry about any problematic incidents occurring around her because it will not be as it appears and will all turn out right in the end.

Sometimes dreams are not quite so easy to establish their reason for appearing when they do, or to understand why the person who had the dream, dreamt what they did at that time. My daughter telephoned me only the other day, because she was extremely upset by the dream she had been woken up by the previous night. In this dream, she was aware that all of the people close to her, including herself were in a room that she did not recognise at all. In that room there was a bed and she said that Mike, her stepfather, was in the bed and looked extremely poorly. He looked so ill that he was yellowish white in colour. She also noticed that all the people in the room looked very anxious and upset, especially me. At that moment in the dream, a doctor came into the room and said not to worry Mike was going to be alright. Everyone got really excited by this news but then, Mike suddenly dropped down dead into the pillows. With this, all of the people present started to cry and get very upset. This happening in the dream shocked Toni so much that she woke up. She then could not get it out of her mind and was worried in case the dream was prophetic, or in other words due to happen.

Once again, this was only a small dream which generally means that it is a prophetic dream. This however, is not always the case. This dream is a warning to us all not to take our own health and the health of those close to us for granted. When you add to this dream the recollection of the dream I first told you about with Mike standing with a noose around his neck, the reason becomes clearer. Mike's dream took place only days before Toni's, which indicates that Spirit are trying their best to get the message across to Mike. They knew that Toni would tell us about her dream because they knew that it would upset her and they also knew that she always told us when she was upset by anything.

As I explained earlier his dream when his neck was in a noose, was warning him about the end of a life he enjoyed with people he loved if he did not change his actions. In Toni's dream, at first he

238

was getting better then died. Therefore, they are reminding him that he has been given a chance to change things but if he does not, death of a situation and sadness brought about by the end of happy surroundings, are inevitable. They are also saying that he is not the only one who will be hurt by this, but many people who love him will be hurt too.

My son-in-law Ted came to visit the other day and he and my daughter Toni explained that she had woken up and had spent ten minutes sitting in bed to compose herself before rising because she was pregnant and the baby was due in three weeks time. After approximately ten minutes had gone by Ted suddenly shot up in bed and retorted that there was a large bumble bee in the bedroom.

Toni assured him that this was not true because she had been awake and sitting up for the last ten minutes so therefore would have seen and heard it if there was one. He insisted that he was not dreaming and said that he had seen a very large bumble bee about the size of a football sitting on his shoulder buzzing and looking at him. Toni laughed and tried once more to reassure him but he shot out of bed making Toni get out too so that he could strip the bed to look for it, after which he did the same to their young daughter Georgina's room. But there was no bee to be found.

Ted asked me why he would have this dream and I explained that if he remembered, a few months earlier when they visited the Safari Park Georgina had been stung badly by a bumble bee and the first aid nurse had sent them to see the doctor because she had a bad reaction. He assured me that he would never forget it and said that he had only been talking about it the day before. I then explained that he was preparing for the burden of being soul carer for his daughter whilst her mum was in hospital having their second baby. This was quite a weight of responsibility upon his shoulders.

They had also been told the day before that the babies head was engaged and Toni was in slow labour so to expect the baby any time. The memory of the bee sting had been awoken the day before when they discussed it and because he was worried the dream took place. It indicated that he had a great weight of worry on his shoulders as to whether he would cope with taking care of his daughter whilst Toni was in hospital, which is why the bumble bee was large in size. After all a normal sized bumble bee would not weigh very much would it?

It was a bee because he had been reminded of the previous worry with his daughter and a bee that caused her to need medical assistance and them to worry greatly. The bee was looking at him because he felt that he was in the face of danger. However, the good news is that because the bee did not move off his shoulder it was saying that he would cope because danger would not come.

So as you can see by this, Spirit orientated dreams tell a story, but usually it is the opposite of what it at first appears. You must take into account that they use whatever means are available to them to get their point across. There are many different types of dreams and I have only just touched the surface here, but know that the topic is one of extreme interest to many people so therefore I will endeavour to go deeper into it in my next book.

Chapter Eighteen.

Hairy Experiences.

Not everyone realises that we all have an Animal Guide in the Spirit World, who can be called upon to look after us. Although those of you who have read my previous book, 'Oblivious But True', not only know this but know that mine is a silver-backed gorilla.

This animal is there by our side for protection right through our life. Just like our Guardian Angel they usually represent a part of our character that is weak, and a part of our character that is strong. For instance, I as a person think that family and friends are very important and that we should surround them with love and understanding, being there for them through the good times and the bad, showing understanding and forgiveness whenever it is needed. Gorillas are very family orientated too and always look after, protect and support their own kind. They show an extensive amount of love to all those who are close to them. Secondly, I tend to be too soft at times and therefore need the strength and power that a gorilla has, to help me stand my ground when it is needed. The truth is that gorillas are one of the gentlest animals on earth, only becoming fierce to protect themselves or those close to them. This description is a good description of me.

My gorilla who I am told by Mr R is called Abundwi, usually comes very close and allows his presence to become obvious at times when I am unwell or upset, or about to be either. This can be worrying at times because if I become aware of him I know beyond a shadow of a doubt that trouble is looming. The problem is that I do not always know what the trouble is until it occurs. I choose not to ask Spirit in case I do not like the answer.

At the tender age of ten I was a happy go lucky type of child who was known for smiling a lot by most people who knew me. One of my earlier strong memories of my Guardian gorilla came when I was that age. Each Sunday morning my sister Chris and I and sometimes my brothers, Keith and Ken, would go to visit my mum's friend, to put some money on the tote for my parents and pay my mum's club money. This friend lived at the top of Carhampton Road, which is not far away from where we lived in Lingard Road, Sutton Coldfield. One Sunday, the four of us were on our way home and half way down the hill, which was Carhampton Road, when we stopped to climb the trees. This was something that Chris and I enjoyed as we both tended to be tomboys. We both climbed a tree as Keith and Ken, collected acorns below. Suddenly we heard a woman's voice shout: "Get down from that tree now." We glanced across to see a lady leaning out of one of the flats windows. Chris and I, looked across to each other, giggled and turned to jump. Unfortunately, as I went to leap down, I looked at the ground below and I noticed that my two brothers were sitting happily underneath me, at the foot of the tree collecting some acorns. I quickly changed the direction that I was about to spring and jumped to the opposite side. However, as I was about to let go of the branch I was holding onto, I saw my gorilla but at that moment the lady in the window shouted once more for us to get down the tree. So I jumped anyway.

As this jump took place, I felt something tear into the top of my leg and fell to the ground like a sack of potatoes. Sitting on the ground, I reached down to lift my leg upwards to enable me to see the back of my thigh where it was hurting like mad. I was crying and aware of the blood trickling down, but before I could see the injury the lady's voice from the flats echoed out once more, shouting: "See you have hurt yourself now. Serves you right, now clear off home." At this point I could see that my gorilla was looking very concerned, but even at that age I was a very proud, or some would say, stubborn person. Therefore, I struggled to my feet and limped off down the road so that she would not see how hurt I was. The gorilla was constantly making a snorting sound, which he often did whilst trying to catch my attention, indicating that there was a need for worry. So after hobbling far enough down the road to be out of sight of the flats, I took notice of this and told my sister that I would have to stop and look at my leg because it was really hurting, which it was. With the help of my sister I sat down on the driveway to the doctors' surgery, which was closed due to the fact that it was Sunday. However, I was aware of the gorilla darting back and forward from myself towards the door of the surgery and back again. I did not realise it at the time but he was trying to tell me that I needed medical attention.

Once again I lifted my leg upwards to take a look, and there staring back at me was a gaping hole, approximately two inches deep and at least two inches across in each direction. As the gorilla jumped up and down, I looked at the hole in my leg which looked like an open tin of dog meat, accept the gravy was red instead of brown because it was blood. I immediately started to cry again, because of the shock of what I was seeing and the gorilla, true to form stopped jumping up and down, and gently wiped a tear from my cheek with the index finger of his right hand. I did not mention him to my sister and brothers in case they thought that I had lost the plot, because in past experience, people acted strangely whenever I mentioned him. I therefore soon learned that it was wiser to keep his presence to myself. Instead, Chris helped me to my feet and with her help we went home as quickly as we could.

We entered the kitchen to the familiar smell of Sunday lunch cooking and Chris blurted out that I had hurt my leg. Keith and Ken were both trying to talk at the same time, due to mixed feelings of excitement and nerves about the days out of the ordinary adventure. My mum took one look at the wound on my leg and felt queasy. She asked Chris to bandage my leg until my dad returned home from the pub, when she would ask him to look at it. He was due home very soon and in fact arrived home a couple of minutes later. My dad entered the kitchen and mum said straight away: "Jean has cut her leg open will you have a look at it?" My dad was taking off his jacket as he answered: "I will take a look after dinner." My mum tried to object, but he was not taking much notice because he thought that she was exaggerating and that my wound would turn out to be just a scratch. Instead he asked how long dinner would be. She explained that the gravy had yet to be cooked and he showed irritation as he retorted: "Well, I may as well look at Bean's leg now then whilst I am waiting?"

He smiled at me as he crossed to the chair where I was sitting on one side of my body to keep the weight off the injured leg. I knew him well enough to know that his smile meant that he was a bit concerned and had decided not to wait. He chatted away to me as he unravelled the bandage that had been put on very professionally by my sister Chris. As he took off the last piece of padding under the bandage, and had his first view of the wound, I could not help but notice the shocked and worried expression on his face before he changed it just as quickly back to a smile. It was at this point the gorilla started to become anxious again. The two factors together started to make me feel very nervous and worried. My dad wrapped the wound back up and taking me up in his arms he carried me upstairs and placed me in his and mum's double bed, telling me that I should rest my leg and he would be back up in a few minutes to see me. He left the room leaving me alone and I became aware that Mr R, the nurse whom I had known for most of my life and the gorilla, were fussing around. A few minutes later the bedroom door opened and my sister came into the room retorting with gasps of breathlessness: "Dad has telephoned for an ambulance for you. He thinks that you may be kept in hospital because your leg is bad."

The sheer thought of this had me worried, my only experience of being in hospital was when I was four years old, and the thought of that was still with me in a scary sort of way. A couple of minutes later, my Dad came to tell me that he thought it might be a good idea if we went to hospital to have my leg looked at properly. He tried to reassure me and told me not to worry, as he would come in the ambulance to the hospital with me, but he added that it was possible they may have to keep me in for a night or two. I was afraid but smiled because I could see that he was already worried. My father was not too impressed with my sister for telling me about the ambulance, because he had expressly told them all not to tell me in case it made me afraid.

I was taken to the Cottage Hospital in Sutton Coldfield town centre, where they stitched up the wound, painted it with a red medicine that looked like war paint, gave me a lollipop and arranged an ambulance to take me home. I was given an appointment for a few days later, but was relieved to be going home just the same. To this day, I have a large V shaped scar on the back of the top of the thigh on my right leg. It does sink in a bit because in those days they did not pack deep wounds like they do today. It also hurts when the weather goes cold, and it reminds me of the first time that I realised for sure that the gorilla got upset whenever I was in trouble.

One night whilst Mike and I were asleep in bed, he was woken by the sensation of leathery fingers rubbing across his arm in a scratching motion. He sat up and looked over at me but could see that my arms were elsewhere. He sat upright in bed and the fingers, which belonged to my gorilla from the Spirit World, disappeared. The following morning I was quite poorly and told Mike that the gorilla was only trying to let him know that he should look after me. The gorilla's job in the Spirit World is to protect me and that is exactly what he was doing. That is why he was so gentle on Mike's arm, careful not to hurt him.

Unfortunately, I was very poorly at the beginning of the year 2003, and he was therefore around a lot. Although something happened with Spirit and my gorilla during that illness, that even served to surprise me, yet I have been aware of his existence for many years. Because I had been suffering with pleurisy and pneumonia, my breathing was very bad and one night I was lying awake struggling for breath at about two o'clock in the morning, when suddenly the room filled with members of my family and friends, who had passed to the Spirit World. At the beginning, my gorilla just stood by my bedside as he often did during these times. I am not at all afraid of Spirit, and feel that we have more to be afraid of with the living, than we have from the dead. Unfortunately this factor has been proved true to me on many occasions. I am therefore not usually bothered, no matter how many people from Spirit come to see me.

On this occasion however, I was a bit disconcerted by the fact that so many of the people close to me had come to visit at the same time. My reason for feeling uncertain was because I know that all of the people who are close to us in the Spirit World, come to meet us when it is time for us to cross over to the other side. Yet here they were, all gathering around me. Therefore, I became afraid, thinking that maybe my time had come. At that point my gorilla stretched up on his hind legs, standing up straight and started to pound his chest making a growling noise as he did so. This startled me and within seconds the room cleared of most of the Spirit visitors. Needless to say, I did not pass to the other side of life so my friends and relatives had not come to meet me in readiness for my crossing over, but were there to help and bring support at a time when things were really bad for me. For his part, my gorilla was not angry with myself or those in the Spirit World but had realised that I was afraid and needed to clear the room of what was scaring me. He did this in the only way he could, by beating his chest to protect me as he would any member of his family.

As I have already said Mr R informs me that my gorilla's name is Abundwi, and if I feel that I am in trouble or distress I should think his name and he will come to my aid. Although this is generally not necessary because he appears before I have the chance to call him. This is reassuring because I know that I am being watched over and taken care of, just as you are by your animal protector in the Spirit World. All you need to do is find out something about this animal. To do this just lie or sit in the quiet and send out your thoughts to your animal and in time it will show itself to you.

From a very young age my niece, Amelia, who is one of twins, could not take her eyes off me, as I explained earlier. She would just stare at me wherever I went. It later proved to be a fact that she was extremely psychic, and we decided that she had been more interested in my Spirit Guides than she was in me. However, when she became four years of age, she developed a great interest in gorillas. She even exclaimed that when she grew up she was going to marry a gorilla. She too has a gorilla as the animal to protect her and this makes you more aware of her great interest in me when she was a baby. She was obviously more interested in my gorilla than she was in me, but it also shows that we have a lot in common.

One Thursday evening as I lay in bed trying desperately to go to sleep, I was aware of my gorilla standing by the bed holding the cutest looking baby gorilla that I had ever seen. This was unusual because in all the years that I have known of my gorilla's existence, and that has been many, he has never had a baby with him. I was obviously surprised by this, but the following day my daughter, Toni, who was pregnant was taken into hospital after her waters had broken prematurely. Although she was pregnant, she was not quite twenty-nine weeks, which is fairly early for the baby to be trying to put in an appearance.

My gorilla was obviously making me aware that he was taking care of the baby. The only thing that I was not certain of was, would he be taking care of the baby by making sure that she was safe and born in good health, or was he saying that the baby would be going to Spirit, but he would look after her there. I considered asking Spirit for the answer to this question but decided that it was best to wait until the baby was born one way or the other. This was because I felt that I would find it difficult to hide it if the answer was a bad one. At times like this you have no choice but to wait for the results, however either way, I knew that the baby would be safe and well looked after. Because lets face it, my gorilla has not let me down so far has he?

Fortunately my granddaughter, Georgina, was born safe and sound six weeks prematurely after a very difficult few weeks as I have already indicated at the beginning of this book in chapter one. From the very beginning she seemed to be drawn to me and it was not until later on when she was quite poorly and taken into hospital that I realised that the baby gorilla had made an appearance with my gorilla because her animal in the Spirit World is also a gorilla. They therefore, depict this by showing a baby gorilla in the hopes that I will understand and feel safe in the knowledge that she is being taken care of. Georgina is two in September and she is fascinated by my statues of gorillas. I also have a huge cuddly toy gorilla that my friends bought me and you would think that a baby would be scared of it but she loved it even when she was only three months old. This is because she is used to seeing gorillas around her so is not frightened because it is normal to her. Equally, she is very obviously a Nanny's girl and cries when I hand her back to her parents even though she does not get to see me very often because I am too busy with my Spirit work at weekends when she is not at nursery. I believe that her fascination with me is because she sees Spirit around me and feels safe because she is used to the same things around her. I am very proud to have a silver backed gorilla by my side and hope that she carries on feeling that way too.

I should add that the reason why certain members of my family have a gorilla as there Spirit animal is because we are of a similar character, which is obviously passed down in the genes.

Chapter Nineteen.

Scary Happenings Away From Home.

To prove a point, that these situations are either bought about, or altered by the people present in that particular place at that time, I am including this chapter on some of the events, which have happened in a few of the places where I have been. As I have said before, in my experience we have more to fear from the living than we do from the dead. As a Medium, you are called out to either give sittings, or clear a ghost or ghosts in a place and with people whom you do not know. Here are a few of those occasions that served to give me reason for concern. I will leave you to judge for yourself whether the living or the dead caused the most fear on these occasions. However, I know what I think.

Before I met my husband Mike, who now works with me, or I make sure that I am chaperoned all of the time whilst at the homes of strangers, I was asked by a lady if I could visit her at her flat to give her a sitting. She said that she desperately needed to know that someone close to her from Spirit was definitely around in her home. I told her that whilst I could not promise that this person would come to see her, I would do my best to help and we made an appointment for me to visit her at home in her flat. It was a place that was out of the way and difficult to find, but after much frustration I found the estate that the flat was on. After stopping several times to ask directions I finally turned the corner into her street. As I clambered out of the car, the lady in question came across the lawn to meet me. She at once threw her arms around my neck, hugging me as if we were long lost friends and it was for all her life was worth.

She then pointed up the path towards a block of flats that looked dark and dingy from the outside. At that point I gave an involuntary shudder although, I was not really sure why. Noticing this, the lady asked if I was cold, but before I could answer she said not to worry because the heating was on in her flat. I just smiled because I was not sure myself what had bought about that shudder. To get into her flat, the lady in question, whom we shall call Anne, used three different chub keys and a Yale key. The chub locks were situated middle, top and bottom of the door. I at once asked her if the area had a high burglary rate, to which she smiled and answered: "You can never be too careful, especially when you do not want people to see things." I was now beginning to feel slightly uneasy, but felt that it was too late in the day to change my mind without giving a good reason. At that time I did not own a mobile telephone but began to wish that I did. As I went in through the front door, I asked Anne if I could use her toilet. She gestured down the hallway to the first door on the right. As I walked towards it, she was locking the front door, including putting a large padlock and chain on. I have to admit that I was so scared, that being in the bathroom came in handy, in more ways than one. I spoke to my Guide, who suggested that it would be a good idea to go along with anything that the lady said for safety reasons.

Anyone who knows me well will tell you that I am not a very geographical person at the best of times but the fact that I am linking to Spirit, and therefore my brain is occupied elsewhere, and on this occasion was very nervous, then it became even easier for me to loose direction. I came out of the bathroom and turned right. The next door along was open and was clearly the kitchen, but the door straight ahead and facing the front door was not only closed but there were chains and padlocks all the way down the door, which really puzzled me. At that moment Anne's voice called down to me from the other end of the hallway. This made me jump and I turned to see her coming out of a room to my right, up close to the front door. (The room was just before the bathroom and across the other side of the hall.) She was now laughing as I explained that I can be easily confused when about to start work. As abruptly as she had started to laugh, she suddenly stopped and spoke quite loudly: "I hope you do not mind, but we will have to do the sitting in my bedroom because the lounge has too many secrets that you should not see if you want to stay safe." I assured her that this was fine, and that I thought we should get on as I was expected at home at a set time and my family investigate if I am late, adding that my family are always told the address where I am. She half smiled as she led me into the bedroom. I was breathing quite heavily, partly due to apprehension and fear and partly because I knew that I had lied and my family did not have the address or even have a clue where I was, or might be.

Being human, and of course, my dad was right, having an over active imagination meant that I felt sure that I was going to be murdered or kept prisoner in that room with the padlocks. 'After all, the fact that there was a heavy smell of air-fresheners all over the flat, my logic was telling me, rightfully or wrongly, that if it was so heavily locked then that room could be full of dead bodies!!! Even after I realised that I would have picked the fact up through my psychic powers that Spirit were possibly in there, I still thought that maybe there were people who were alive but had been drugged and therefore sleeping in that room. Over active imagination or what!!!

The bedroom contained an old wardrobe, two single beds with a space between them, where there was a bedside cabinet full of clutter, and at the bottom of one of the beds was an old dressing table. The dressing table mirror was worn in several places, which tended to distort the view of the room and there was a silver dagger shaped letter opener placed almost ceremoniously on a cloth doily in the centre of the dressing table top in front of the mirror. She motioned for me to sit down on the end of one of the beds, apologising for the lack of chairs as she did so. I said that this did not matter and started to explain how I worked. She sat on the end of the second bed, picking up the letter opener as she did so. I watched her intently but carried on talking. At this point she interjected: "I only wanted a sitting for one reason, therefore I only want to speak to one person from Spirit."

I once again explained that whilst I would do my best I could not guarantee anything because we cannot and do not call up the dead, they have to decide to come to talk to us. Anne said that she understood but appeared to be getting agitated. She passed the letter opener to her left hand and started to score lines on the top of the dressing table as she spoke. "I know, but this is important. They are trying to say that I am mad because I say that a certain very famous singing star comes to visit and help me, because we are friends. I did not know her before she died but we are friends now. I am not mad."

She obviously named the star, but I felt that this was not important to the story. Before I could answer, Mr R stepped forward and reminded me of his advice, to go along with anything that she said for safety reasons. I then told Anne that the lady in question was there and that she was trying to help. She seemed to calm down instantly and placed the letter opener gently and precisely back in its original place, straightening the doily with the palms of her hands as she did so. After talking to her for a while, and satisfying her that she was not mad, it was time for me to leave and thankfully a very happy lady not only let me out of the flat but walked me to my car. That is the one and only time that I have ever told someone that I could see someone there from Spirit when I in fact could not. I do however, feel that the end justifies the means and whilst I will never know why that room was locked so tightly, I did leave the flat safely with Anne being reassured that Spirit are with her, which of course they are.

From that day on, I always made sure that someone at home would know where I would be and when to expect me home, just in case it became necessary for my family to look for me. It is of course possible that I was in no danger at all but when you consider all those locks, the letter-opener and of course the advice from Mr R, I am sure that you will agree that I had every reason to be concerned. Concerned, that is by the living and not the dead.

On another separate occasion, I went to a flat to give a sitting to a man who was a professional gentleman. A lady originally made the booking and said that the sitting was for her brother, and I made the mistake of assuming that she would be there for the sitting. The flat was on the third floor of a block of flats that were very well lit. Therefore, when I arrived I was not at all bothered by my surroundings. The flat itself was well furnished and clean and I thought that I could hear someone moving about in another room of the flat and assumed that it was the lady who had booked the sitting. I therefore, said yes to a cup of coffee before we started. Paul disappeared into the kitchen to make the drinks and I casually looked around me.

At this point I noticed two things that bothered me; first I spotted a Camcorder up on the bookshelf aimed right at the chair I was sitting on, with a red light flickering to indicate that it was recording. I instantly got up and moved to the sofa across the room and as I sat down, I noticed someone closing the door of a room across from me. I knew that it was a man because I saw half of his body as he realised that I had moved and that maybe now I would be able to see him. He pushed the door almost shut. I at this point, immediately reached out my senses to that room to discover whether that man was living or dead. He was definitely not the latter. I now knew therefore, that Paul was not the only man in the flat yet nobody else had been mentioned!! Paul returned with the coffees, saying: "You have moved?" I tried not to falter as I answered: "Yes, I feel more comfortable over this side of the room, which will make it easier to link with Spirit." As I said this, I hoped and prayed that he did not know that I was able to link anywhere. I could not help but notice the colour rise in his cheeks, as he half stuttered: "I am sorry Jean, but I wanted to record the sitting and the tape recorder will only pick your voice up if you sit in the chair next to it."

I was about to suggest that maybe someone could write it down for him when he went on: "I will not remember, it would have been alright if there had been anyone else here, but I am on my own tonight." Alarm bells were ringing in my mind and I was trying hard to think what to do for the best, when I jumped half out of my skin at the sound of his telephone ringing. After talking to the person on the other end of the receiver for a couple of minutes, Paul turned to me and said: "I do not believe this. That was work, I have to go in." I rose to my feet and told him not to worry, we could rebook the sitting for another time. He first of all suggested that I wait at the flat for his return because he would only be a short time but I told him that I was expected elsewhere and that they would come to find out why if I did not turn up on time. He then suggested that he paid me for my time but I told him not to worry. I did this because I did not want to be put in a position where I felt that I would have to return. Once in the car a giant sigh of relief left my body and needless to say the next time that Paul's sister telephoned me I was too busy to make another appointment. Once again, the living were creating the fear.

Chapter Twenty.

Ways For Spirit To Portray Evidence Of Life After Death.

As part of a large family I was always busy which also helped a great deal because Spirit can only communicate with us through love when we put our emotions to one side. Being one of a family with many siblings allowed me to do this, meaning that you spend a lot of your time distracted from your emotions because of an already busy lifestyle. This helps because there is a part of the brain that connects via a stem straight to our heart. We use this function in our attempts to link with the Spirit World. Emotions occupy the heart and therefore the brain because of the connection via this stem. Because of the connection that joins the two, it means that when we hear something that affects our emotions, it occupies both our heart and our brain at the same time making it impossible for Spirit to come through strongly. If we learn to release these emotions, the way becomes clear for our heart, brain and therefore, the Spirit World to connect.

I will give you an example. Recently Mike and I were on our way to Stirchley Spiritualist Church in Telford, a Spiritualist Church that we had been to many times before. Mike decided that we would travel a different route to the Church that night and we got lost. It was pouring with rain and we could not understand why we had gone wrong. Mike became very agitated and upset which in turn was getting me worked up. We found the Church with only two minutes to spare before the start of the demonstration. The president of the Church was so pleased to see us walk through those doors. She told me that they had decided to give us five more minutes then they were going to announce that the service was cancelled and the people could have their entrance fee returned. I decided that I was not going to let Mike's attitude get to me so cut myself off from any thoughts of the perilous journey, thinking only of the love and pleasant atmosphere that can be always found in this particular Church. The service that evening was a good one according to all that were present, and also gave a lot of evidence of survival of life after death. This was because I cleared my emotions and allowed my heart and brain to be free for Spirits' use. This is also the reason I shut myself off from listening if someone is trying to agitate me before a service.

Sometimes it can be a bit confusing when Spirit start to work with you in a different way than they have always worked previously. On that occasion when we were recently on the rostrum holding the demonstration after our perilous journey things started to get just a little confused. As I said, Mike and I went straight onto the rostrum and the service began. The service was going well but whilst I was giving communication from Spirit to a young lady in the congregation a second lady who had passed with cancer came through informing me that she wished to speak to her daughter. The lady in the congregation with whom I was conversing said that her mother had died from cancer. The lady in Spirit then indicated that she wanted to let them know that she was watching over her grandchild who was here on the earth and was called by a name that sounded similar to Rory but was not quite that. (I could not quite hear it clear enough to be certain what it was, but I was certain that it sounded like Rory). The lady said that she did not understand a name like Rory, but I was sure that there was a name like it.

Suddenly a lady just a few seats away from her on the same row called out. "Excuse me. My mum died of cancer, and she fits the description you gave and my daughter's name is Tory."

I thanked the lady and said that the message must be for her, but I could not understand why I had mixed the message up when the two ladies were not together. (Spirit will start to come through on the same link to several different people in the same group of people, but not usually to someone outside that group without me noticing the vibration change.)

The lady who I was speaking to in the beginning then said:

"I know that lady, we are friends does it make a difference?" That did explain things. Spirit counted the fact that they were friends, as meaning that they could come in on each others link. Later on after a few more pieces of information were given Spirit told me that someone related had found it necessary to squat, neither ladies understood this. I explained that they did not squat through lack of money, but because there were some repairs needed on their home and they squatted in a house a couple of streets away whilst the repairs were being done. I added that Spirit was clearly calling out Caroline Avenue as an address connected to this information and the name Geoff. One of the ladies said that she could understand about the squatter but not the name of the road they lived in. As time was going by and the end of the service near I asked her to remember Caroline Avenue and Geoff because there is definitely a connection to the people who squatted somewhere.

After the service had finished a young couple came up to speak to me who had been sitting the row behind Tory's mum. The young lady told me that her dad was Geoff and her mum and dad lived in Caroline Avenue and they had recently had to move out of their home and squat whilst repairs were done on their home because they had nowhere to stay. I asked if she knew the other two ladies and she said yes we are all friends who usually go to a different Spiritualist Church than this one. This explained a lot to me because it meant that the Spirit friends and relatives of these people were used to coming through at the same service and through the same Medium. This meant that as soon as a Medium spoke to one of them, the other Spirits would join in. The young lady could not wait to get home to tell her mum because she said that she would be amazed when she heard what her nan had said from Spirit. Her boyfriend told me that until that night, he had been a total sceptic because he had been going to the Spiritualist Church every week because it made his girlfriend happy and during that time they had seen many different Mediums, yet he felt that most of the information was general that anyone in the room could take. However, he felt that I had bought through some information for them only and he could not understand where I had got this information from, so therefore thought that maybe Spirit did exist after all.

What people need to understand and realise is that although a lot of information is general that could be taken by several people, there is always the more personal stuff which will be given if the reciprocate of the message allows the vibration energies to build up. This is because it then allows the Spirit visitor enough extra energy to speak to and show the Medium more detail.

As soon as we connect to someone in the Spirit World by sending out love and therefore raising our vibration this surge of love follows up this stem to our brain which allows the Spirit World to use our brain. This and the fact that Spirit step up close within our auric field which is magnetic, is the reason why our heartbeat speeds up whenever someone from the Spirit side of life comes near. It is also the reason why a lot of people in the Spirit World sometimes come through at the same time.

They are attracted by the light that is given out into the Medium's aura once this brain and heart capacity is being used in unison. Then the fact that our aura is magnetic gives that extra pull that is needed to make a complete psychic connection. Psychics use this magnetic pull to gain all sorts of information about the person here on the earth that they are linking with. They, however, can only gain information about the present and past via this means because we hold the present and past within our auric field. This information can then be extracted using a magnetic pull, which is our psychic ability. When linking to Spirit, however, this magnetic pull, although helpful, is of no use on its own. Love is the light of vibration eternity and we use the love within our heart to create a surge to our brain, which allows Spirit to connect their vibration with ours. Once our brain is being used in this way more love comes back and forward to fuel the link with the so called dead. This is also one of the reasons why the more energy there is the more a Spirit visitor can say. They use the combination of love that connects the heart and brain and the magnetic energy to vibrate the

Medium's voice box to make the sound necessary for them to talk so that the Medium can hear them.

Sometimes the hardest job for a Medium is to help the recipient of any messages from the Spirit World to understand why they are different to what that person has anticipated. There are many reasons for this, but the main ones are:

The fact that we as people expect the very thing that is top of our list of priorities, to be the most important thing on our loved one's mind. This unfortunately, is not always so. Because as human beings we are all in possession of a character all of our own, which is obviously going to mean that, we care about different things in totally separate ways to one another. This is so, even when the person in question is exceptionally close to us. Secondly, the Spirit World, require a lot of energy to portray their message to us in a way that they hope we will understand. This can be done in several different ways. However, they will choose the easiest way to do this, just as we would if trying to get a message to a loved one at the other side of the world. Here are just a few of the messages that have given some hope of proving survival of a loved one in the Spirit world to a person here.

These messages will also hopefully help to portray some of the reasons why it can become difficult for a Medium to bring through exact information at all times whilst portraying the messages given from the Spirit world. Names and gender may have been changed in certain instances during the telling of these true life messages in order to protect the identity of both, the people here and those in the Spirit World.

A gentleman came along for a sitting, after being given our name as a recommendation from a previous recipient of messages from the Spirit side of life, via us. As soon as he walked through the door, one look at him gave the information that this man most probably lived alone and took care of his own apparel. I did not need to be a Medium to gather this information. I just needed to observe the obvious fact that he felt uncomfortable about himself, as he apologised for his clothing.

I would at this point, like to break off for a moment to explain that one of the first pieces of advice that I would give to any would be Medium is, take no notice of what your physical eyes are telling you. In other words, just because the appearance of this man gives you this information, does not necessarily mean that this is a fact. Some people deliberately try to give a false impression to try and fool the Medium to test if they are genuine or not. This in turn makes the job of communicating more difficult for their loved ones in Spirit, because when the dead person gives the Medium information it contradicts what the Medium and giver of the message see with their own eyes, whilst looking at the recipient of this message. An un-experienced Medium could then decide to keep some of the information to his/her self, for fear of sounding ridiculous, when in fact his/her message is correct and would please both the recipient and the Spirit visitor, if given as received.

As an experienced Medium, I would never pay too much attention to how the person looked. This includes whether or not they are wearing a ring, are smiling or looking sad etc. It pays to remember that if those in the Spirit World are telling you something then they are saying it for a reason. They never get it wrong although on occasions, even an experienced Medium can mix up the message during deliverance of that communication to the recipient.

The gentleman in question told us that he did not really believe in the existence of the Spirit World, but it would help if he knew they existed. He had been to see another Medium, who unfortunately had done little or nothing to remedy his disbelief. We had then been recommended to him and here he was.

As soon as the man had taken his seat, I was aware of a lady standing in front of me, who said that she was the gentleman's wife. I proceeded to describe this lady, adding some information about how she had passed to Spirit and what type of character she had, whilst giving the fact that she had told me she was his wife. He immediately started to cry and I handed him a tissue. He apologised to which I answered that an apology was not necessary and asked if he wanted me to carry on. Nodding his head profusely, he said: "Yes please. I am alright." His wife went on to say that he was feeling guilty because he felt that he was not there for her when she died and did not do enough. He agreed that this was true as he blew his nose on the tissue. His wife told me to tell him that it was not his fault there was nothing he could do, as it was already too late. The gentleman inferred that he understood why she was saying this and that the information so far was correct.

His wife was now showing me a man's watch without a face and a question mark by it. The watch looked just like the watch that the gentleman having the sitting was wearing. I, for my part was really confused, because I knew by the sense that I was getting with this picture that it was the time that was questioned, not the watch itself. I decided to tell the man what his wife was showing me, whilst admitting that I did not understand what she was trying to tell me. This is sometimes the case when Spirit, just show you a picture and put everything else on your senses, which they were doing at that moment. You have a fact, which you know is correct but you are uncertain why. However, on hearing this information he looked surprised and immediately replied, crying once again as he did so: "I understand. I do not know what time my wife died." This then made sense to me. She at this point made me aware that she had had a fall in the garden shortly before her death, which he agreed to without hesitation. She once more, showed me the watch with the question mark and kept making me aware of the lounge in their home. She would not take these images away so I told him without delay what I was getting. Once again, he was crying. I handed him another tissue as he told me that his wife had died in the lounge. At this point Mike interjected, saying that the gentleman's wife kept making him aware of their dog, which she loved. He nodded his head in agreement, adding: "She did love our dog. I have still got it now." I resumed, by saying. "You were not home when she died because you were out walking the dog. She says, that is why you are not sure of the time of her death."

He in turn, admitted that this was true and she went on to say that he had not sent for the emergency services straight away on his return home because he thought that she was asleep. So now he thought that it was his fault that she had died, due to the fact that he did not get her help quick enough.

I explained that she was already dead when he arrived home as she had died whilst she heard her husband and their dog approaching the house, but it was already too late for anyone to save her. The gentleman explained that this fitted in with the approximate time that he had been told she had died. There were obviously a lot of other things talked about, which were of a more private nature, but it was in this information that the main things that the gentleman needed to hear at that time were found. After the sitting had finished, the gentleman said that he was feeling a lot better about things and he would definitely consider the possibility that the Spirit World were really there after all. I feel I should add that this was not the last time that he came to see us for a consultation, therefore a seed has been sewn towards his belief in the Spirit World and the fact that his wife is alright and needs him to get on with his life and be happy.

I would hope that those of you who are reading this book will begin to understand by this, why messages can sometimes become a little mixed up if the Medium is not prepared to admit that they are uncertain of why they are being given the information. I am sure that if I had guessed what this information had been all about, I would probably have got it wrong, thereby wasting the time of the Spirit visitor and that of the recipient of the message as well as myself. For instance, if I had made an attempt to guess what the watch and the question mark meant, I would probably have said that the watch was missing and I would have been totally wrong. Making me say once more, to any would be Mediums or indeed anyone who is trying to understand what Spirit are trying to tell them: "Do not think, whilst you link." Thinking will make you change the message out of recognition, thereby maybe losing a very important piece of information. This would be like filling in a crossword when the wrong answer had been filled in to one of the other clues, and changed the whole puzzle.

Sometimes Spirit, manage to really catch me by surprise. Just like the day I was giving a lady a sitting and she had recognised and accepted her grandmother was visiting from Spirit. Mike went on to say that the lady having the sitting was feeling unloved. After a moments thought, she agreed to this. At that point her grandmother said to me: "It is that partner of hers, Richard. He has made her feel that way, by messing her about." I at once turned to the recipient of the message and said: "You have got a partner haven't you?" She immediately without hesitation answered: "No" I was so shocked by this reply because I had clearly heard what her grandmother had said, and not got it on my senses, therefore I knew that I had got it right. I immediately retorted: "Who is Richard then?" She fell back in her chair gasping as she did so, covering her hand across her mouth with her eyes becoming wide as she expressed: "I do not believe it. How do you know about him?"

I told her what her grandmother had said, and she said that she had been dating Richard for eighteen months, but had told him three weeks ago that they should finish because he was having trouble committing. At that point I saw the word Australia written above her head, then the feeling that she should have gone. In the same moment I also heard: "She will go to Australia you know." I told the recipient about this, and once again she was shocked and told me that she and Richard should have been going to Australia so that she could meet his brother later that year. It was however, now all off or so she thought. She told me afterwards that she was totally: 'GOBSMACKED' with the information that had come through from Spirit. When you are certain you are right about the information you are receiving and the recipient is saying that it is wrong, it can really catch you out. However, it always turns out to be right in the end. You just need to find out why they are saying no and Spirit is saying yes. It is just necessary to nudge the recipient of the message's memory, because they have not remembered the information that you have already given and may remember other things if you ask Spirit to give you more.

Sometimes being a Medium can create very upsetting things to take place around you. One of those occasions usually takes place when a murder victim or a child comes through who has been abused and has consequently died from their injuries. At these times the Spirit of that person can come through very dramatically, which can be quite a shock to the Medium's system.

I was once giving a sitting to a lady, when her little boy who had died at the age of three came through to speak to his mum. He was a really cute young man and it was difficult to understand how anyone could justify hurting him. When these children first come through, they are always exceptionally dramatic in the beginning, which can be upsetting to the Medium. The way they have died goes against all my beliefs and it is difficult not to be biased in the child's direction thinking that the person receiving the message is in the wrong. It is sometimes hard not to state this opinion. However, this would not be right, because after all we are there to do a job and not there to judge.

This particular young man had been supposedly found lying unconscious on the kitchen floor one morning, whilst he was being taken care of by his mum's boyfriend, and had subsequently been taken to the Accident and Emergency Department of the local hospital. He was wearing only a pyjama jacket and was wrapped in a bath towel, when he was taken in to the hospital. Young Sam died from his injuries later that day. But it was also found that he had sustained a lot of previous injuries dating back over a few months. The boyfriend, who was the child minder, said that Sam frequently climbed onto the kitchen counter and was always falling off. He stated that on the day of the so called accident, he had left Sam colouring in the kitchen whilst he went to the bathroom, and had found Sam on the floor lying on his back with his eyes rolling backwards in his head when he had returned. Sam however, had a different story to tell, and was insistent that I tell his mummy that her boyfriend had pushed him off the kitchen counter because he had been talking too much. This is obviously a difficult thing to tell any mother, but Sam was worried that is mummy would stay with his murderer and his mum was expecting another baby within two months and he feared for the baby's safety which I explained as best I could to the mother and she told me that she had suspected it for a while, but without being sure she could not throw her boyfriend out because of the baby being his.

Young Sam was becoming quite distraught and I tried my best to make his point to her, but I am afraid it fell on deaf ears. Although I did tell her that her boyfriend would go to prison for Sam's death, which he eventually did. From that day on, Sam was a constant visitor at my home. He was desperately trying to sort things out and help his mum and future brother or sister. He could be quite noisy at times, because he needed to attract my attention, but unfortunately there was nothing that I could do. It was about three weeks later that I was woken up at about two thirty in the morning by the sound of a thudding noise and a child screaming. It took me a few minutes to realise that I was not dreaming and could actually hear a child crying. Getting out of bed, I went to investigate and found Sam was crying in my kitchen. He was afraid for his mum, but I could not get him to say why.

Three days later I received a telephone call from Sam's mum. On the night that Sam had woken me, she had been pushed down the stairs by her boyfriend and lost the baby that she had been carrying. She had telephoned to ask if I would give her another sitting and tell Sam that she was sorry. Of course my answer was yes, but really it was not necessary because Sam already knew, and now that his murderer would go to prison he could rest in peace. He turned towards me, touched my hand with his chubby little fingers and smiled before disappearing. I have never seen Sam since that day and I know that the reason for this is, that he is at last happy and in the company of his baby sister and other people who love him in the Spirit World.

On one occasion whilst over seas, I was asked to visit a lady's house where she was experiencing a lot of ghost activity. Mike was very new to anything to do with Spirit at the time, but I asked if he would like to join me if the lady did not mind. Both he and the lady in question agreed. We arrived at the lady's home, which was a beautiful bungalow. She explained to us that the worse problems seemed to come from the two bedrooms. One day she had been holding a large jar of face cream in her hand when suddenly the room went as cold as ice and the jar was snatched out of her hand. After a couple of minutes when all had returned to normal, she searched the room for the jar of face cream but to no avail. She never saw it again. There were also important papers which, had disappeared in the same way, the situation was therefore becoming critical. At first we went into the lady's bedroom, and as soon as we walked through the door, the cold, the smell, and the sheer fact that your head began to spin and your chest became tight told me that yes, there was ghost activity within this room.

Mike said that he could not stay because it was making him feel really ill, which frequently happens to people when standing in a space that is heavily haunted. I checked the next bedroom and part of that room was the same, but only about twelve inches into the room against the adjoining wall to the previous bedroom. At that point a lamp was thrown towards me, and I became aware of a man from Spirit who was wearing a raincoat. He then made me aware of being in bed and kept making me aware that he was not wearing any clothes. I, after a small amount of resistance and difficulty on his part, made sure that this man had gone home to the light (because he was earth bound and did not realise that he was dead). I then called Mike back into the room. At first he did not want to return but I assured him that it would be alright now. On his return he was amazed at how the room felt, not only normal but warm.

It turned out that the man in question, had been a flasher whilst he was here on the earth and had been arrested for it on several occasions. Before his death he had become ill and had been looked after whilst he was ill in bed by his cousin who owned the bungalow. Apparently he still kept flashing his bits whilst ill in bed, so the lady informed me. The lady had had her bedroom shortened to make a bigger spare bedroom so that she could use it for visitors to stay, but before the alterations had been made she used to sit with her friends in circle in that room. They sat in such a position that meant that the wall was now in between. The lamp had belonged to the man in Spirit with the raincoat, and they had used it whilst sitting for Spirit contact. They had in turn been given the energy to make their presence as Spirits known by the circle, which, of course he made full use of.

Sometimes Spirit brings information through in unusual ways. One evening after our granddaughter came out of school we took her mum, my daughter, Dawn, to meet her and took her to the pictures then MacDonald's. When we left the cinema it was dark and as we headed down Mucklows Hill, which is a steep Hill in Halesowen near to where they lived at that time, Leah suddenly tapped me on the shoulder saying: "Nanny, aren't those lights wonderful?" She was referring to all the house, street, and car lights that could be seen shining brightly at the bottom of the hill. I replied: "Yes sweetheart they are beautiful aren't they?" She went on to say: "They are just like all the lights that you see when you go to Heaven aren't they nanny?" I was surprised by this and answered: "Do you think that they are darling?" She was getting quite excited at this point as she said: "Yes they are, and there is so much love." She lowered her voice to a whisper: "But we are not allowed to tell everybody are we nanny, because if we did they would all kill each other so that they could go to heaven?" I simply smiled and answered softly: "Yes darling that is right." I was otherwise speechless because I was amazed by this statement from such an innocent child, as were my husband and daughter, and you have to admit that it is quite a philosophical statement for a five year old to make. Spirit does work in mysterious ways at times to perform their wonders, don't you think?

My friend Chris and I were in Birmingham town centre on Saturday, November 13th 2004 when Chris retorted "Beware of low flying wheelchairs." I was distracted by something in the shop window and was totally surprised by her comment. "What are you talking about?" I asked. She was shocked by my response and insisted that a young man, approximately in his thirties, had rushed by in his wheelchair really fast. I assured her that she was wrong and immediately took her back down to the corner where she had said that she saw him turn, to prove that there was not one there. She was even more shocked when she realised that I was right and that she had in fact seen a Spirit person go by in his wheelchair. This is all part of Spirits' help with her development.

On Saturday 14th May 2005, Chris her mum Ethel, and myself were travelling back from Blackpool when Chris who was driving at the time, suddenly waved up towards the overhead bridge that we were about to pass under. I instantly looked up and smiled as I asked her who she was waving at because there was no one there. This shocked her and she gave me a stunned look as she retorted are you having me on. There was someone there wasn't there?

I could not help but laugh because Mr R had already told me about the gentleman and the little boy, who were from the Spirit World and had waved at Chris from the bridge. She of course thought that they were living people because she is not trained enough at the moment to always know the difference. Sometimes in the early days of linking to Spirit we all make the mistake of assuming that the solid people whom we see are alive and in the here and now when they are in fact in the Spirit World.

The following day Chris asked me if I knew whether the man on the bridge was named Mike and the boy was named Joe and they called him Joey. I confirmed that she was right. This was the reason why I did not divulge any information about them to her the day before. Because I knew that Spirit would inform her and this would be more proof to her that her Mediumship is improving daily. Every trainee needs to find out for themselves that they can do it without help from their Spiritual teacher. I am very proud of Chris and how well her development is going and I hope that you will agree by the information that I have given you that she is improving leaps and bounds.

I was talking on the phone to my close friend Tess the other day when she asked me if I knew whether her father-in-law had been around. "Yes, he asked me a couple of days ago to ask you, what is, the matter with the skipping rope." I replied immediately. "Oh my God," she answered, "As we speak, Amy is outside playing with it. I can see her through the window, but last week she asked me if she could take Dennis' skipping rope to school because all her friends took theirs. I told her that she could as long as she looked after it because it used to belong to her granddad, because he used it to exercise his false legs. She promised that she would look after it and said that she would put it straight back into her school bag as soon as she had finished playing with it so that it would not get stolen. Anyway, yesterday when she came home she was a little upset." "Why?" I enquired. "I asked the little dude what was the matter and she looked at me a little uncertainly as she said, "I did look after it mum but a boy at school pulled it too hard and broke the handle a bit." I put my arm around her and asked her to show me the rope. The rope had come away from the handle a bit, although I did manage to push it back into place, I told her that she could not take it to school any more because it had belonged to her granddad and was of sentimental value and therefore important." She went on to explain that her father-in-law had used the skipping rope to build up his muscles to help him walk better on his prosthetic legs. I should explain, by the way, that Tess' daughter coincidentally shares the name of my young friend Amy in the Spirit World, although Tess also calls her 'my little dude'.

Chapter Twenty One.

Friends Both Here And In The Spirit World.

I felt that it was only right to make this final chapter a discussion about the end of life here on earth as we know it and our return home to the Spirit World where our life began, because I started the book with life at the beginning of life here on earth as we know it with the aid of Spirit.

My brother Ken passed away to go home to the Spirit World aged eleven and it appeared to be a long time before he started to visit his family and friends who are back home here and alive as we know it. He was at the age to learn and as such found some fascinating knowledge and learned some different skills in his new home. Because there was so much of interest to him with his already inquisitive mind, he chose not to practise his new found skills of getting himself noticed by a world full of people, who either doubted his lasting existence, or could not deal with the fact that he may be still around for one reason or another. However, he must have been practising these new found skills that are afforded to everyone (people and animals alike), on their return home to Spirit. I say this because he announced to me whilst we were away on a working holiday in America, that he was now going to be working as a Guide. He said that he had chosen to guide my close friend, Chris, in her development with Spirit linking. She and I were both delighted by this, although I did comment to Chris that although he is my brother and we were close before he passed to Spirit, I have only seen him on a few occasions over the many years that he has resided on the Spirit side of life since 1971, yet now she would get to see him regularly and probably daily. I have to admit though, that it is good to know that he is doing such important work and that he has chosen such a special person to do it with. It also means that I get to see him more now because I am training Chris. I can pass on long awaited messages to my family, God bless you Ken. We love you.

My father on the other hand called himself an atheist yet he was back to visit fairly quickly after his passing to the Spirit side of life. He has visited on numerous occasions and I hope that he will carry on doing so. He has some new friends in the Spirit world who are Chris' dad and Charles. They frequently visit together and seem to be having lots of fun in the Spirit world. My sister Chris accompanies them on many occasions too, and also visits on her own.

I was fortunate enough to become friends with a very special lady called Shirley as were many people because she was and is an exceptionally nice person. Unfortunately for us she is now also in the Spirit World after suffering from cancer.

Shirley has to be one of the bravest people I have ever had the privilege to meet. After being diagnosed with terminal cancer she set about writing a book all about her experiences involving her Spiritual progress whilst awaiting her final journey from this world to the Spirit side of life. She had been a Spiritualist for many years so therefore knew beyond doubt where she was going after her death. She had throughout those years however, constantly asked Spirit to show themselves to her, but her requests seemed to be in vain and fall on deaf ears. That is until she was made aware that her journey to depart this life and reside in the Spirit World had begun.

Shirley was then lucky enough to have several experiences which gave her personal proof that Spirit not only existed but were preparing for her arrival amongst them and home at last. I, recommend that you read Shirley's book, which will be out soon. It will be published by Trafford Publishing.

I know that Shirley's journey home was a safe one because I have seen her on several occasions. She wants her husband, son, relatives and friends to know that she is safe and happy. She imparted messages to her loved ones to let them be aware of this, which I was happy to pass on, as have many other Mediums. God bless you Shirley till we meet again.

271

I spend many hours of my time communicating with many different people from the Spirit side of life and consider myself extremely lucky and privileged that I have the gift to be able to do this. Sometimes I am linking to help the many people who need to be assured as I am already that there is no death, only everlasting life. At other times it is because I cannot sleep because of the pain that my health inflicts upon me. It is at these times when Spirit, tend to surprise me the most by bringing through some really surprising evidence that we do not die but live on into eternity pain free and happy.

Jeans first book is: 'Oblivious But True.' It is still available for purchase through Jean's web site and various shops.

If you wish to contact Jean personally you can do so on:

info@kelfords.co.uk

where sittings are available if required, although there is a waiting list. All e-mails will be answered in due course, or if you would like to see Jean at work then look on her web site:

www.kelfords.co.uk

Please look out for Jean's third book, which should be out in a few months time.

ISBN 1-41205519-9

9 781412 055192